P9-CAB-428

30018000184462

DATE DUE

NOV 0 8

APR 2 4 2002

300180000009943.

# THE

# 1960s

# THE
# 1960s

## Other books in this series:

# THE
# 1960s

William Dudley, *Book Editor*

David L. Bender, *Publisher*
Bruno Leone, *Executive Editor*
Bonnie Szumski, *Series Editor*

Greenhaven Press, Inc., San Diego, California

Gregory Middle School
2621 Springdale Circle
Naperville, Illinois 60565

# AMERICA'S DECADES

Every effort has been made to trace the owners of copyrighted material. The articles in this volume may have been edited for content, length, and/or reading level. The titles have been changed to enhance the editorial purpose.

No part of this book may be reproduced or used in any form or by any means, electrical, mechanical, or otherwise, including, but not limited to, photocopy, recording, or any information storage and retrieval system, without prior written permission from the publisher.

Library of Congress Cataloging-in-Publication Data

The 1960s / William Dudley, book editor.
    p.    cm. — (America's decades)
    Includes bibliographical references and index.
    ISBN 0-7377-0306-7 (lib. bdg. : alk. paper) —
    ISBN 0-7377-0305-9 (pbk. : alk. paper)
    1. United States—Civilization—1945– . 2. Nineteen sixties. I. Dudley, William, 1964–    . II. Series.

E169.12 .A167  2000
973.92—dc21

99-087776
CIP

Cover photos: (top) Archive Photos,
(bottom) Popperfoto/Archive Photos
Library of Congress, 40, 146
NASA, 86

©2000 by Greenhaven Press, Inc.
P.O. Box 289009, San Diego, CA 92198-9009

Printed in the U.S.A.

# Contents

Russia was installing nuclear missiles in Cuba almost led to war between the superpowers.

## Chapter 3: The Vietnam War

North Vietnamese and Vietcong forces in South Vietnam, more Americans became convinced that the war effort was futile. In response, President Lyndon B. Johnson reversed his policy of gradually escalating American involvement in Vietnam.

## Chapter 4: The Civil Rights Movement and Minority Protest

## Chapter 5: Youth Protest and the Counterculture

tural change. White working class "middle Americans" felt threatened by economic vulnerability, ethnic competition, and a sense that cherished American values were under attack.

## Chapter 6: Gender and Sex Revolutions

# Foreword

In his book *The American Century*, historian Harold Evans maintains that the history of the twentieth century has been dominated by the rise of the United States as a global power: "The British dominated the nineteenth century, and the Chinese may cast a long shadow on the twenty-first, but the twentieth century belongs to the United States." In a 1998 interview he summarized his sweeping hypothesis this way: "At the beginning of the century the number of free democratic nations in the world was very limited. Now, at the end of the century, democracy is ascendant around the globe, and America has played the major part in making that happen."

As the new century dawns, historians are eager to appraise the past one hundred years. Evans's book is just one of many attempts to assess the historical impact that the United States has had in the past century. Although not all historians agree with Evans's characterization of the twentieth century as "America's century," no one disputes his basic observation that "in only the second century of its existence the United Sates became the world's leading economic, military and cultural power." For most of the twentieth century the United States has played an increasingly larger role in shaping world events. The Greenhaven Press America's Decades series is designed to help readers develop a better understanding of America and Americans during this important time.

Each volume in the ten-volume series provides an in-depth examination of the time period. In compiling each volume, editors have striven to cover not only the defining events of the decade—in both the domestic and international arenas—but also the cultural, intellectual, and technological trends that affected people's everyday lives.

Essays in the America's Decades series have been chosen for their concise, accessible, and engaging presentation of the facts. Each selection is preceded by a summary of the article's content. A comprehensive index and an annotated table of contents also aid readers in quickly locating material of interest. Each volume begins with an introductory essay that presents the broader themes of each decade. Several research aids are also present, including a glossary of terms, an extensive bibliography, and a timeline that provides an at-a-glance overview of each decade.

Each volume in the Greenhaven Press America's Decades series serves as an informative introduction to a specific period in U.S. history. Together, the volumes comprise a detailed overview of twentieth century American history and serve as a valuable resource for students conducting research on this fascinating time period.

# Introduction

Few periods of American history have retained the fascination and controversy of the 1960s. The tumultuous events of the decade—which include the Vietnam War and the antiwar movement, the civil rights struggle, the sexual revolution, the space program, turbulence on college campuses, the expansion of social welfare programs, and the assassination of one president and the political rise and fall of another—transformed the American society; their legacies are disputed to this day. "For conservatives, the sixties represent the bogeyman, the source of nearly all current social ills, the time when America got off track," writes historian Peter B. Levy. "For leftists and old-fashioned liberals, the sixties stand as an emblem of idealism and reform and as an inventory of unfinished agendas."[1]

A balanced examination of the 1960s as a watershed period in American history must not only take into account liberal/conservative political and cultural divisions but also explain the origination of the decade's notable legacies from two sources: political leadership and grass roots. Historians of the period strongly emphasize the actions of Presidents John F. Kennedy and Lyndon B. Johnson. From this perspective the 1960s was a period of liberal political ascendancy in which the nation's political and economic elite sought to expand the federal government to solve social problems and to increase America's influence in the world, with mixed results. But to focus on the programs and aspirations of Kennedy and Johnson would be to tell only part of the story of the 1960s. An arguably more significant source of change is what became known as "the Movement," a term used loosely to describe the many people who engaged in political, social, and cultural protest during the decade. For many people the 1960s is synonymous with black civil rights marchers, Vietnam draft protesters, hippies, radical feminists, and others who criticized or rejected aspects of mainstream American society, including the liberal reforms of Kennedy and Johnson.

# The Presidential Race of 1960

Many historians use the presidential election of 1960 as a convenient starting point for analyzing the decade. Republican candidate Richard M. Nixon was familiar to Americans as the two-term vice president under President Dwight Eisenhower, so the election was in some respects a public referendum on the leadership and direction of the 1950s.

Eisenhower, elected president in 1952, had presided over a time of peace and prosperity in the United States, a prosperity all the more welcome after the economic disruptions of the Great Depression and World War II. America's gross national product (GNP) grew at an annual rate of 3.2 percent between 1950 and 1960. Millions of Americans successfully attained middle-class status, complete with home ownership and suburban lifestyles. By 1960 half of American homes had television sets, and more than three-fourths of American families owned automobiles. Economic power was shared by large corporations that dominated American commerce and effective labor unions that secured rising wages for workers. It was a time, historian William E. Leuchtenburg writes, when "Americans turned away from public issues to take up more personal matters—fitting together the pieces of marriages sundered by war, nest-building, nurturing the psyche, enjoying the fruits of prosperity after the grinding years of the Depression."[2]

However, America's rising prosperity was not shared equally by all Americans, nor did it by itself solve social problems and inequities. Inner cities suffered as people moved to the suburbs. Poverty remained a problem among the elderly, in certain rural regions, and among minority populations; in his 1962 book *The Other America*, author Michael Harrington estimated that one-fourth of Americans lived in poverty. America was also divided by race as blacks and other minorities were barred from the new suburbs and racial segregation remained the norm in the American South. By the end of the 1950s many observers were debating America's "national purpose" and criticizing what they perceived to be a lack of direction in American leadership. Some argued that American consumer culture was characterized by a focus on private pursuits at the expense of the public welfare. Adlai Stevenson, who lost to Eisenhower in both the 1952 and 1956 presidential elections, stated that the United States suffered from a "paralysis of will" because Americans were committed only to "pleasure and profit" and the "pursuit of ease."[3]

Many who were dissatisfied with the state of the nation under Eisenhower supported Democrat John F. Kennedy for president in 1960. Young and charismatic, the Massachusetts senator repeatedly vowed to "get the country moving again" after the implied stagnancy of the Eisenhower/Nixon administration. Kennedy was one of the first politicians to effectively exploit the new medium of television. His televised debates with Nixon are widely considered pivotal to his success in the close election. However, British historian Iwan W. Morgan notes, "Kennedy's narrow victory by 0.2 percent of the popular vote, the smallest winning margin since 1888, showed that the desire for change was not dominant and that satisfaction and complacency were still strong."[4]

## The New Frontier

In his 1961 inaugural address, Kennedy asserted that "the torch has been passed to a new generation," and indeed Kennedy's presidential administration contrasted strongly with that of his predecessor in image and style. Eisenhower had relied on Establishment businessmen for his staff and advisers; Kennedy packed his cabinet, White House staff, and diplomatic corps with highly educated academics, labor leaders, and others of his generation (his younger brother, Robert, was named attorney general). Eisenhower had generally left legislative initiatives to Congress; Kennedy sent a record number of messages (twenty-five) to Congress in his first year in office, calling for a "New Frontier" of national undertakings including bolstering military spending, providing health care for the aged, and conserving natural resources. Eisenhower opposed "prestige schemes"[5] such as sending a rocket to the moon as a waste of government money; Kennedy called on Congress to spend billions of dollars to send astronauts to the moon by the end of the decade.

However, many liberal supporters of Kennedy were disappointed in his domestic accomplishments. For all of Kennedy's speeches, relatively few of his initiatives were passed by Congress. Kennedy's sketchy domestic record was in part a result of his caution in pursuing significant change in light of the close 1960 election and in part due to his focus on foreign policy crises and concerns. But undoubtedly a major reason for the limited domestic record of the Kennedy presidency was its premature end due to an assassin's bullet. Kennedy's death on November 22, 1963, in Dallas, Texas, and the events surrounding the tragedy, stunned the nation.[6] "Few events in what would be an extraordinarily catastrophic decade so shocked the American people," writes historian Irwin Unger. "The assassination in Dallas had not only killed an American president but it had also struck down a young hero whose career had come to symbolize all that was best and most worthy in American life. To the young, especially, his death seemed a bitter tragedy."[7]

## The Great Society

It is one of the ironies of history that Kennedy's death not only did not stop liberal reforms in government, but perhaps accelerated them. The period of most intense liberal government activism was that of his successor, Lyndon B. Johnson. An accomplished and ambitious political leader in the U.S. Senate before becoming Kennedy's vice president, Johnson rallied sympathies following his predecessor's death to press for Kennedy's incomplete legislative agenda. With Johnson's prodding, Congress passed several significant bills introduced by Kennedy. These included sweeping income tax cuts that have been credited with stimulating rapid economic growth through most of the 1960s and historic civil rights legislation banning racial discrimination. Johnson also declared a "war on poverty" and called for expanded government programs to help the nation's poor.

In the 1964 election Johnson scored an overwhelming victory over Republican Barry Goldwater. The Arizona senator was a strong conservative who, unlike Eisenhower and other moderate Republicans, argued for the dismantling of New Deal programs such as Social Security. Johnson was thus able to present himself as a moderate centrist and attract support from virtually all sectors in American society, including business and labor. In 1965, calling for America to achieve the "Great Society," Johnson obtained more significant domestic legislation from Congress than any president since Franklin Roosevelt in 1935, during the Great Depression. Congress enacted Medicare health insurance for the elderly, federal aid to education, the creation of the federal Department of Housing and Urban Development, consumer protection laws, and a voting rights act that removed barriers to black voting registration.

The ultimate impact of Johnson's Great Society remains a matter of controversy and an important part of the general debate over the 1960s. Many programs fell short of their lofty goals and have drawn criticism: Medicare for failing to contain health care costs, the war on poverty for unclear strategies and insufficient resources, and civil right laws for failing to address the socioeconomic problems of blacks and other minorities. Conservatives criticized government poverty programs for rewarding lazy welfare recipients; radicals argued that the government did not do enough to redistribute income or equalize wealth in America. Perhaps the most telling criticism was that Johnson's Great Society rhetoric raised expectations that were not fulfilled. By 1967 the pace of domestic reform legislation on the federal level had slowed considerably.

## The Cold War and Vietnam

Both Kennedy and Johnson grappled with foreign policy as well as domestic issues during their presidencies. During Kennedy's administration, the issues that drew the most public attention were related to the cold war with the Soviet Union. Johnson's foreign policy and related American public discourse was eventually consumed with one specific aspect of the cold war: the war in Vietnam.

When Kennedy took office in 1961, the cold war had been a central part of American life for almost fifteen years. The conflict had its origins in the falling-out between the United States and the Soviet Union over the fate of Europe after World War II; it evolved into a contest for global supremacy between the two ideologically opposed superpowers. U.S. policymakers, fearing the expansion of Soviet influence and believing that its Communist government was incompatible with American political and economic ideals, embarked on a policy of "containment" of Soviet power. Within a few years both superpowers had developed and possessed nuclear weapons capable of destroying each other in an actual war, resulting in a tense "balance of terror." Unwilling to risk war, the two sides competed with each other in obtaining alliances and influence in Africa, Asia, and Latin America. They also engaged in a race for technological supremacy in such areas as nuclear missiles and space satellites.

The cold war also had important ramifications for American domestic life. American Communists, never influential in American politics, were viewed as a serious threat to national security. People suspected of communist leanings—ranging from actual Communist Party members to those who expressed political dissent or agitated for civil rights—were barred from government employment and often fired from private-sector jobs as well. "Political conservatives took advantage of the [Communist] party's association with a wide range of social reforms to mount an attack on the entire Left and the legacy of the New Deal," writes historian Ellen W. Schrecker. By the late 1950s, she argues, "political dissent had almost disappeared—an ironic result at a time when the United States was combating communism throughout the world in the name of freedom and democracy."[8]

The few critics of the cold war in 1960 were marginalized as "un-American" radicals. The 1960 presidential election shows the extent to which a cold war consensus dominated American political and intellectual life. Both candidates shared major assumptions about the superiority of American economic and political institutions whose antithesis was seen to be communism, presumably a monolithic force headquartered in Moscow. Kennedy campaigned by accusing Eisenhower of allowing America to fall behind the Soviet Union in missile and space technology. As president, he boosted military spending and led the United States in some tense confrontations with the Soviet Union over Cuba and Berlin. Kennedy also helped negotiate a treaty banning the atmospheric and underwater testing of nuclear weapons, however, reducing to some extent tensions between the superpowers.

After communists took control of China in 1949, a central preoccupation of American policy makers was not to "lose" any more countries to communism. In the 1960s this concern became focused on South Vietnam. Following the French withdrawal from Vietnam in 1954, President Eisenhower had pledged American support to the South Vietnamese regime in its struggle with communist-led North Vietnam. From 1961 to 1963, Kennedy increased the number of U.S. military advisers in South Vietnam from seven hundred to sixteen thousand. Johnson inherited this commitment and steadily increased it, authorizing bombing missions, U.S. combat operations, and escalating troop deployments. He did not officially declare war on North Vietnam, partly because he did not want to risk a direct military confrontation with North Vietnam's ally China, and also because he did not want the conflict to siphon resources from or otherwise jeopardize his domestic Great Society programs. However, Johnson's limited war in Vietnam failed to establish an independent and strong non-communist South Vietnam. Its main effect was to create a "credibility gap" over government pronouncements about the war and bitter divisions in America as growing numbers of people questioned why America was in Vietnam. The Vietnam War led to the creation of the largest antiwar movement in American history and to the end of the cold war consensus among America's policy-making elite.

## The Other Side of the Sixties

The movement against the war in Vietnam was one of three developments that highlight the "other" side of the 1960s: the large numbers of people engaged on social and political protest and activism. Vietnam stands as the central foreign policy issue of the era, the "engine of the sixties" that "defined and shaped the decade,"[9] according to historian Terry H. Anderson. The central domestic issue was the civil rights movement. African Americans and their supporters waged a political and legal struggle for equality under the law in the United States that not only succeeded in passing important civil rights legislation, but made the direct defiance of laws and social customs thinkable, even acceptable and heroic, for many people. Both Vietnam and civil rights led many people to question—and reject—previously sacrosanct assumptions about American ideals, the meaning of patriotism, and the place of dissent within society. A third development was not a particular issue but rather a demographic phenomenon—the "baby boom" generation. During the 1960s the first wave of the large number of Americans born in the years following World War II entered young adulthood. Many attended college, leading to exploding growth of the nation's universities. Their numbers energized and shaped the Movement, helped to define popular culture, and indelibly altered the course of the decade.

## Protesting the Vietnam War

As late as 1965, the public generally supported American involvement in Vietnam. Voluntary military enlistment soared as *Time* magazine editorialized that the war was "the crucial test of American policy and will" and proclaimed it "The Right War at the Right Time."[10] Beginning that year, however, antiwar dissent became a significant phenomenon. In April 1965 student organizers were surprised when twenty-five thousand people turned up at an antiwar rally in Washington, D.C. Two years later, in October 1967, an antiwar demonstration in Washington drew a quarter of a million people. In October and November 1969 several million Americans participated in protest activities. Military conscription gave the war issue a special urgency to young men of draft age. Those who received induction notices were forced to choose whether to go to Vietnam, try to gain student or medical deferments, apply for conscientious objector status, or actively defy their draft orders. Many openly resisted the draft and were arrested or fled to Canada.

The antiwar movement was not a coherent organization under central leadership, but instead consisted of ad hoc arrangements of different groups who often differed on philosophy and tactics. As it evolved over the decade a general schism developed between liberal and radical elements within the movement. Liberals argued that the war was harmful to the United States and its ideals and used peaceful and legal means of registering protest to the war, such as campaigning for Senator Eugene McCarthy for president in the 1968 presidential primaries.[11] Radicals saw the conflict as emblematic of a fundamentally unjust and imperialist "Amerika" that deserved radical restructuring; they called for massive draft resistance and confrontations with authority. As the war persisted with no apparent end in sight, it became increasingly unpopular among a majority of Americans, although few embraced the radical critique of U.S. society.

## The Civil Rights Movement

Until it was supplanted by the Vietnam War in the second half of the 1960s, the civil rights movement was the dominant social issue of the decade. The movement began in the 1950s within America's black community and its struggles against racial discrimination and segregation in the American South. Throughout the region, an intricate system of legalized segregation (Jim Crow) confined blacks to separate and inferior schools, public facilities, and neighborhoods. Black voting, economic advancement, and interracial socialization was forbidden; those who questioned the state of affairs were often intimidated or even killed. Black organizations at first simply turned to the federal government as an ally to enforce equal citizenship rights where states and communities had curtailed them. In 1954 the U.S. Supreme Court outlawed racial segregation in public schools. The following year blacks in Montgomery, Alabama, successfully waged a boycott of the city's bus service. Their leader, the young minister Martin Luther King Jr., became recognized as the nation's foremost civil rights spokesperson.

President Kennedy's election in 1960 raised hopes among many that he would be more active than his predecessor in promoting civil rights. At first civil rights activists were disappointed. Historian George Moss writes that Kennedy

> delayed introducing civil rights legislation fearing that it would fail and also alienate southern Democrats, whose votes he needed on other measures. . . . President Kennedy believed that the best civil rights policy would be a gradual achievement of integration over the years without disruption and violence. Dr. [Martin Luther] King pointedly observed: "If tokenism were our goal, this Administration has moved adroitly towards its accomplishment."[12]

Grass-roots activism eventually compelled Kennedy and the rest of the nation to take a more forceful stand on civil rights. Students in the South in 1960 openly defied segregation in "sit-ins" in restaurants, libraries, and other public and private facilities. Small interracial groups of "freedom riders" rode together on interstate buses in the South in an effort to test the effectiveness of a 1960 Supreme Court decision outlawing racially segregated buses and bus terminals; their efforts drew national attention when white mobs set fire to buses and assaulted the riders. Nonviolent protesters in Birmingham, Alabama, led by Martin Luther King, were met with clubs, fire hoses, and police dogs in

Gregory Middle School
2621 Springdale Circle
Naperville, Illinois 60565

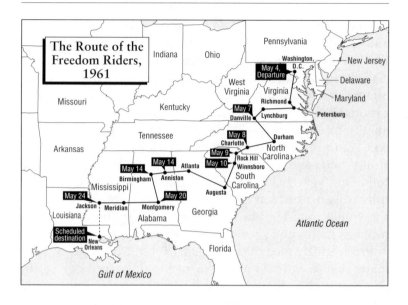

The Route of the Freedom Riders, 1961

Indiana

Ohio

Pennsylvania

New Jersey

Washington, D.C.
May 4, Departure

Delaware

West Virginia

Virginia

Maryland

Missouri

Kentucky

Richmond

Petersburg

May 7
Danville

Lynchburg

Tennessee

May 8
Charlotte

Durham

Arkansas

North Carolina

May 9
Rock Hill

May 14
Atlanta

May 14
Birmingham

Anniston

May 10
Winnsboro

South Carolina

Mississippi

Augusta

May 20

May 24

Jackson

Meridian

Montgomery

Alabama

Georgia

Atlantic Ocean

Louisiana

Scheduled destination

New Orleans

Florida

Gulf of Mexico

the summer of 1963. That same year, on August 28, the March on Washington drew 250,000 people marching for federal civil rights legislation. Young organizers led voter registration drives in the face of intense resistance in the states of Georgia, Alabama, and Mississippi.

All these actions and the nationwide media attention they attracted helped to impel Congress to pass historic civil rights legislation. The 1964 Civil Rights Act outlawed segregation in public facilities and racial discrimination in education and employment. The 1965 Voting Rights Act authorized federal officials to prevent racial discrimination in voting registration. The mid-decade triumphs of the civil rights movement led other Americans—including Puerto Ricans, Native Americans, Hispanics, women, and gays and lesbians, among others—to question their place in American society and to agitate to improve their political and social standing. Feminists, for example, founded the National Organization for Women in 1966.

However, as more groups were embarking on their own civil rights struggle, the movement among blacks was in growing disarray. The civil rights tactics that were so effective against Southern Jim Crow laws proved less so in dealing with poverty and socioeconomic inequality blacks faced throughout America. The commitment to nonviolence preached by King was questioned by many young black activists as an insufficient response to the injustice and hatred they perceived in American society. Some rejected cooperation with the white political establishment and called for "black power," a slogan of defiance that meant different things to different people. Beginning in 1965 a series of urban riots in predominantly black sections of American cities further polarized the nation along racial lines. "From 1966 onward," writes one historian, "opinion polls revealed a growing conviction among whites that blacks were asking for too much and that liberal politicians were undermining law and order through their willingness to reward rioters with federal largesse."[13] The assassination of King in 1968 removed from the scene the nation's most influential advocate of nonviolence and racial reconciliation, further weakening the movement.

## The Baby Boomers and Youth Culture

Both the civil rights and antiwar movements were heavily populated by young people born after World War II, and were part of that generation's broader questioning of American society. The sheer size of the baby boom generation—by 1965, 41 percent of all Americans were under the age of twenty—ensured that their beliefs and actions would have a disproportionately significant impact on the 1960s.

The antipathy that many, but not all, young people felt toward U.S. society went beyond Vietnam and race to call into question fundamental traditional values regarding work, sex, dress, and lifestyle. American society was found wanting not because it was unjust, but because it was sterile, repressive, and boring. In the 1960s a visible counterculture was embraced to varying degrees by many, especially among those who had been raised in comfortable middle-class circumstances in the 1950s. Social historian Leuchtenburg writes:

Upper middle class white youth, and some of their elders, advanced ideas and behaved in ways that ran "counter" to much that was cherished not only by Eisenhower's America but by Kennedy-Johnson liberalism—affluence, economic growth, technology, and the institutions and value systems associated with the Protestant ethic of self-denial and sexual repression and the more modern premises of the consumer culture."[14]

College students resentfully perceived themselves as cogs in huge and bureaucratic universities. Men resisted parental and social assumptions of devoting their lives to working up the corporate career ladder, while women questioned the assumption that they should forsake careers in order to marry and rear children. Such acts as growing one's hair long, openly cohabitating and experimenting with sex, communal living arrangements, listening to rock music, exploring Eastern religions, and taking marijuana and other illicit drugs became an essential part of many young people's desire for self-fulfillment and community—and a way of rebelling against one's parents and American society. The most extreme participants in the counterculture became known as hippies.

Mass popular culture, including movies and television, eventually absorbed numerous aspects of the counterculture, making it hard to discern where rebellion ended and consumerist conformity began. The counterculture's various fads, including hairstyles, clothes, music, even drug use, were ultimately amenable with American consumer culture. *Rolling Stone*, an "underground" magazine founded in 1967 to cover rock music and other aspects of the counterculture, soon took out advertisements in the *New York Times* touting its ability to connect the "youth market" to corporate America. "Before long," writes historian William H. Chafe,

> the dominant culture learned how to make a profit by catering to the new tastes of the young, from blue jeans and counterculture jewelry, to more sophisticated recording and

sound systems. . . . In its own way, therefore, the counter-culture simply became an additional market for corporate America, its own fierce conformity providing a ready outlet for new, up-to-date variants of the old affluent society.[15]

## A Decade of Disillusionment?

"The 1960s have gone down in American history as a decade of disillusionment," writes British historian Iwan W. Morgan. This disillusionment can be seen both in the liberal reforms of Kennedy and Johnson and in the aspirations and accomplishments of the Movement. The two presidents had promised much in their domestic reforms and foreign policy ventures. Kennedy had called on America to "bear any burden" for liberty at home and abroad, while Johnson had talked of creating the Great Society and of defending liberty in Vietnam. Their accomplishments, Morgan argues, did not live up to the raised expectations of Americans.[16]

In Johnson's case, public dissatisfaction with Great Society welfare programs perceived to favor minorities over other white working-class Americans, a sense that America's social order was breaking down, and above all public discontent over Vietnam led to his surprising withdrawal from the 1968 presidential election. The victor in that race was John F. Kennedy's 1960 opponent, Richard M. Nixon, who had capitalized on the Vietnam issue and on conservative backlash against the various movements of the 1960s. Historian Robert Kelley writes: "Rocked by massive disorders and frightened at the swiftly rising crime rate—for which black America was everywhere blamed—the white majority turned toward the law-and-order appeals of the Republicans."[17] Nixon made overt appeals to the so-called silent majority of Americans who he argued were sick and tired of antiwar protests, hippies, and urban disorder. His election can be interpreted as a closing point for the decade.

Just as Kennedy and Johnson had voiced lofty expectations about their programs, many youthful participants in the various movements of the decade entertained high opinions of their own abilities to change the world. Typical is the recollection of history teacher Terence Zeck:

> It was as if anything and everything was possible. We could join the Peace Corps to make a visible difference, or demonstrate with others, marching for civil rights. Those of us who were coming of age in the 60s all believed that we could do what no generation could ever have done; we were going to be the ones to set the world on its ear.[18]

Such exuberant optimism would be severely tested in the 1960s. The movement against the Vietnam War did not end America's involvement, as Richard Nixon would continue to involve America in the conflict until 1973. The leading radical student organization of the 1960s, Students for a Democratic Society (SDS), had begun the decade calling for America to become more fully democratic and embarking on antipoverty and antiwar campaigns. By the end of the decade it had splintered into several extremist factions, some of whom engaged in bombings and other terrorist actions. The civil rights movement lost influence as peaceful demonstrations gave way to urban riots. Illicit drug use led to addiction for many users and growing violence within the drug trade. The sexual revolution left many people dissatisfied. Rock festivals, with the famous exception of Woodstock, often degenerated into squalid exhibitions of drug abuse and violence. Countercultural communes dedicated to living in peace and harmony fell apart over ideological differences as well as more mundane concerns over cleaning up and paying the bills.

But to simply call the 1960s a "decade of disillusionment" does not do the complex era justice. The 1960s also stands as a time when America was generally prosperous, when the government expanded its role in caring for its citizens, when historic civil rights legislation was passed, when many legal and cultural barriers to free expression were lifted, and when America scored numerous triumphs in science and technology, including the sending of astronauts to the moon. Historian David DeLeon identifies two lasting legacies of the decade: a "pervasive questioning of American life" that asked to what extent America lived up to its egalitarian ideals; and the "common expectation" that ordinary people could change America for the better. The 1960s, he writes, was a time when "average people began to fight against racial injustice, sexual discrimination, and the arrogance of generals, politicians, and official experts."[19] The exhortations, dreams, aspirations, and actions of Americans ranging from presidents to "average people" are all explored in the essays in this volume.

1. Peter B. Levy, ed., *America in the Sixties: Right, Left, and Center: A Documentary History.* Westport, CT: Praeger, 1998, p. 1.

2. William E. Leuchtenburg, *A Troubled Feast: American Society Since 1945.* Boston: Little, Brown, 1983, p. 10.

3. Quoted in George Moss, *America in the Twentieth Century.* Englewood Cliffs, NJ: Prentice-Hall, 1989, p. 304.

4. Iwan W. Morgan, *America's Century: Perspectives on U.S. History Since 1900.* New York: Holmes & Meier, 1993, p. 159.

5. William B. Breuer, *Race to the Moon: America's Duel with the Soviets.* Westport, CT: Praeger, 1993, p. 154.

6. Lee Harvey Oswald, the man arrested and charged with Kennedy's assassination, was himself shot and killed two days later by nightclub owner Jack Ruby. An official investigation led by Supreme Court Chief Justice Earl Warren concluded that Oswald, a self-styled Marxist who had resided for some time in the Soviet Union, had acted alone in killing Kennedy. However, the investigation failed to quiet doubts and rumors that the Kennedy killing was the product of a broader conspiracy conceivably involving Cuba, organized crime, and/or right-wing elements within the federal government.

7. Irwin Unger, *The United States: The Questions of Our Past.* 4th ed. Englewood Cliffs, NJ: Prentice-Hall, 1989, p. 805.

8. Ellen W. Schrecker, *Reader's Companion to American History.* Boston: Houghton Mifflin, 1991, pp. 38–39.

9. Terry H. Anderson, *The Movement and the Sixties.* New York: Oxford University Press, p. 135.

10. Quoted in Anderson, *The Movement and the Sixties*, p. 137.

11. Although an intraparty challenge to a sitting president was generally unheard-of and considered a daunting proposition, antiwar activists who wished to work within the American political process had little choice. Members of the opposition Republican Party generally voiced support of the Vietnam war effort and the cold war reasoning behind it; their criticism generally focused on how America should *increase* its efforts to "win" the conflict in Vietnam.

12. Moss, *America in the Twentieth Century*, pp. 329–30.

13. Morgan, *America's Century*, p. 171.

14. Leuchtenburg, *A Troubled Feast,* p. 179.

15. William H. Chafe, *The Unfinished Journey: America Since World War II*. 4th ed. New York: Oxford University Press, 1999, p. 411.

16. Morgan, *America's Century,* pp. 180–81.

17. Robert Kelley, *The Shaping of the American Past*. 5th ed. Englewood Cliffs, NJ: Prentice-Hall, 1990, p. 760.

18. Quoted in Gail B. Stewart, *The 70s: A Cultural History of the United States Through the Decades*. San Diego: Lucent Books, 1999, p. 6.

19. David DeLeon, *Leaders from the 1960s*. Westport, CT: Greenwood, 1994, pp. xvii–xviii.

# CHAPTER 1

# Camelot and the Great Society

AMERICA'S DECADES

# Assessing President John F. Kennedy: Image and Reality

James N. Giglio

The 1960s in American politics began with a very close presidential election between President Dwight D. Eisenhower's vice president, Richard Nixon, and John F. Kennedy, a forty-three-year-old senator from Massachusetts whose father had groomed him for higher office. Promising to "get this country moving again" after what he criticized as the inactivity of the Eisenhower presidency, Kennedy was able to overcome concerns about his youth and inexperience to win the election. However, his presidency lasted only until November 22, 1963, when he was shot and killed in Dallas, Texas. The tragic event stunned a nation that had been captivated by the charm of the president and his family. Kennedy remained popular after his death among many Americans who recall his presidency as a golden age of "Camelot," a period seemingly unaffected by the social disruptions of the later 1960s. In the following excerpt from his book *The Presidency of John F. Kennedy*, historian James N. Giglio assesses Kennedy's accomplishments and examines the reasons for his lasting popularity. Giglio argues that the public's fascination with Kennedy is due in part to the tragic nature and timing of his death, but the esteem he gathered is also attributable to his cultivated image as an idealistic, dynamic, and likeable

Excerpted from *The Presidency of John F. Kennedy*, by James N. Giglio. Copyright ©1991 by the University Press of Kansas. Reprinted by permission of the University Press of Kansas.

figure. Giglio concludes that Kennedy's public image hid some personal flaws, and though his concrete accomplishments were considerable in some areas, especially in foreign policy, Kennedy's feats do not totally measure up to the shining Camelot image.

---

November 22, 1963, will forever be a day of national mourning. At approximately 1:00 P.M., John Fitzgerald Kennedy, 46 years old, 6 feet tall, 165 pounds, handsome, vibrant, maturing significantly as the thirty-fifth president, died of gunshot wounds in Dallas. He had visited Texas to mend a political squabble that had weakened the state Democratic party for the coming election year. Kennedy remains the only twentieth-century president to be assassinated since McKinley. In many respects how Kennedy died is as important as how he lived.

His tragic death has colored our perception of Kennedy and his presidency. To many Americans he is a martyred, gallant Sir Lancelot who enabled us briefly to embrace the legend of Camelot. All manner of good would have occurred had he lived. To others scorning such hagiography, he has become a cold warrior who created unnecessary crises and enmeshed us in Vietnam. These critics remind us of his faint-hearted response to the civil rights movement and of his inability to push New Frontier programs through Congress. They have also exposed him as a playboy willing to risk national security for sexual pleasure.

Further complicating the assessment is the enormous impact of the Kennedy style. No president in the twentieth century combined his rhetoric, wit, charm, youth, and Hollywood appearance. He inspired young Americans to choose politics and government service as honored professions; he motivated them to serve as Peace Corps volunteers in Africa and as Green Beret advisers in South Vietnam. He also affected us in lesser ways: His refusal to wear hats inadvertently influenced males to discard theirs, just as his longer hair style made crew cuts unfashionable.

Moreover, Kennedy's presidency has challenged historians because he served a mere thousand days in office. While some of his key legislative proposals such as civil rights and the tax cut showed promise of success by fall 1963, would an almost certain second term have resulted in the passage of medicare and other promised programs? At the time of his death, Kennedy had also negotiated the Nuclear Test Ban Treaty and fashioned a détente with the Soviet Union. Could he have avoided the debacle in Vietnam? In short, to evaluate Kennedy after less than three years in office is like assessing Truman's presidency before the Marshall Plan and the successes of the Truman Doctrine. Yet much can still be written about the Kennedy presidency and its legacy. . . .

## Kennedy's Lasting Popularity

Kennedy's sudden and tragic death contributed immensely to the romantic way in which Americans would remember his presidency, especially since it preceded violent social conflict, disillusionment, and the assassinations of Malcolm X, Martin Luther King, Jr., and Robert Kennedy. To many Americans, John Kennedy's death ended an age of excellence, innocence, hope, and optimism. . . .

[But] it is erroneous to attribute President Kennedy's elevation solely to the circumstances of his death. After all, he exhibited considerable popularity during his presidency, with an approval rating that never fell below 59 percent in the Gallup Polls. He will always be remembered for his style. His youthful and handsome appearance stood out among a generation of aging leaders such as Truman, Eisenhower, Adenauer, de Gaulle, Macmillan, Nehru, and Khrushchev. Yet more than this, he projected an almost indescribable aura that affected practically everyone who came in contact with him either personally or through television. Much of that appeal can be attributed to his good manners, vitality, wit, self-deprecating humor, and disarming casualness, which journalist Mary McGrory insisted made him the "most attractive man of his generation." Kennedy gave the impression of liking and caring about people, and they in turn felt that way about him. The Byrds, a musical group of the late sixties and seventies, expressed a common sentiment when they sang, "Though I never met him, I knew him just the same. He was a friend of mine."

Kennedy also succeeded in articulating a sense of hope and purpose that made a profound impression, particularly on the young and disadvantaged, causing them to connect with government in a way that they have not done again since then. He conveyed a lofty standard of excellence that became the perfect antidote to the mass conformity and mediocrity that seemed to characterize the society of the fifties. He stirred people the most through his moving speeches. As [historian] Daniel Boorstin writes, "a short life, unfulfilled in action, is commonly and disproportionally judged by the eloquent utterance." Programs such as the Peace Corps and the Alliance for Progress further embodied that same idealistic spirit, making Kennedy an appealing leader even in the remotest areas of the Third World. In Guinea, for example, Sékou Touré exclaimed at the time of Kennedy's death, "I have lost my only true friend in the outside world." At home many others expressed similar feelings.

Yet the Kennedy image also contains a lesser-known, unflattering side. Despite his promotion of the arts, ballet and opera bored him, and he knew little about painting; his tastes were more mundane. Less known until the 1970s were his frequent sexual indiscretions. Kennedy's obsession with image also caused a preoccupation with the press's treatment of him and his administration. At times he acted vindictively toward unfriendly journalists. There existed as well a certain underlying pettiness, which Kennedy displayed toward those whom he disliked. [Democratic party leader and United Nations ambassador] Adlai Stevenson fell victim to the Kennedy treatment following the Cuban missile crisis, when the president needlessly leaked unflattering information about him to the press. More than most politicians, Kennedy also masked an enormous ego and vanity. Yet, everything considered, this complex man will rightly always be remembered more for his attributes.

## Young Activists Disillusioned About Kennedy

*Historian Terry H. Anderson writes that although many people have fond recollections of the Kennedy presidency, young activists at the time were already expressing concerns about the president and his politics.*

Without a doubt, most baby boomers think back on the Kennedy years as a thousand days of idealism and vigor, an era of Camelot. American youth were infatuated with the handsome and dashing leader, and thousands of students realized those feelings by volunteering for community projects or joining the Peace Corps. A small minority of young activists, however, especially outspoken ones associated with SDS [Students for a Democratic Society] or SNCC [Student Nonviolent Coordinating Committee] who felt part of an emerging movement, became increasingly disillusioned. To them, Kennedy's liberalism meant an unprecedented peacetime spending binge on weapons, cutting taxes for corporations, and continuing cold war rhetoric: "Let every nation know, whether it wishes us well or ill," the president declared in his inauguration speech, "that we shall pay any price, bear any burden, meet any hardship, support any friend, oppose any foes, in order to assure the survival and success of liberty. This much we pledge—and more." Some students became concerned as the president decided to make South Vietnam, a country thousands of miles away with no history of representative government, the "testing ground" for democracy in Southeast Asia, increasing the number of American military advisers to that country.

Terry H. Anderson, *The Movement and the Sixties*. New York: Oxford University Press, 1995.

In the final analysis, as Kennedy himself believed, presidential success should be gauged primarily by concrete achievement. Such an evaluation must take into account Kennedy's untimely death, which curtailed his attainment as much as it enhanced his popular image and his pending programs. With this in mind, one might assess his presidency by addressing two questions: First, did he leave the country in better shape as a result of his tenure? Second, to what extent did he achieve his stated goals?

## Challenges Kennedy Faced

Kennedy had come into office with the future of West Berlin hanging in the balance. In Laos a Communist-based insurgency successfully waged war against an unpopular United States–backed regime. In South Vietnam the Vietcong had the autocratic [Ngo Dinh] Diem on the defensive. Civil war engulfed the newly independent Congo, where the Soviets hoped to capitalize, and a Communist regime in Cuba reportedly threatened to export its revolution into neighboring countries. Third World nations in general viewed the United States with suspicion if not contempt. Moreover, United States military and technological strength had seemingly diminished—causing Americans to believe that they were losing the cold war. At the same time, the Eisenhower presidency had made no progress in easing tensions or in obtaining a nuclear arms agreement with the Soviet Union.

Domestically, the challenges were nearly as formidable. The national government seemed almost oblivious to a budding civil rights movement. After several years of prosperity, the economy had stagnated, as the growth rate fell to a modest 2.5 percent and a balance-of-payments deficit drained gold reserves. Blight plagued the cities. Poverty remained an ignored problem, especially afflicting the elderly, blacks, Hispanics, and rural Americans. In spite of huge subsidies to major commercial farmers, agriculture had come out of the 1950s in the worst shape since the Great Depression. Federal efforts to bolster public education had been disappointing.

To turn the tide, Kennedy promised Americans a dynamic presidency—one that would formulate and fight for legislative enactments, provide moral and political leadership, and respond to the immense problems of war and peace. Probably no major-party presidential nominee had ever committed himself to doing as much—not even Roosevelt in 1932. Kennedy pledged to restore American military strength by increasing conventional forces and accelerating the missile program. At the same time, he intended to seek improved relations with the Communist world. No goal seemed more essential than an agreement for nuclear arms control with the Soviets. He promised to reassess United States policy on China, defend Berlin, rebuild NATO, increase economic assistance to the Third World, reconstruct relations with Latin America through an Alliance for Progress, encourage the newly developed nations of Africa, strengthen the UN—"our last best hope," rectify the payment imbalance, elevate the United States to the "uncharted areas of science and space," and honor all American commitments abroad. Notably, he promised to develop a "coherent and purposeful national strategy."

## Foreign Policy Goals

In the area of foreign policy, Kennedy accomplished several significant goals. He strengthened the United States militarily, which enabled him to deal effectively with [Soviet leader Nikita] Khrushchev in West Berlin and Cuba. Indeed by 1963 Berlin no longer seemed a major problem. Kennedy's substantial increase of ICBMS and other missiles, however, forced the Soviet Union into an extensive buildup, leading to parity in the 1970s and subsequent arms races. Not surprisingly, Kennedy's efforts to achieve nuclear arms control proved disappointing, despite the atmospheric test ban treaty of 1963. How much more was possible in light of a developing détente with the Soviets is uncertain. While Kennedy and Khrushchev had drawn closer, much suspicion still existed between their two countries. Kennedy probably would have accomplished no more than Johnson did in securing a nuclear nonproliferation treaty in 1967.

Moreover, Kennedy's success in increasing conventional forces and emphasizing counterinsurgency had a down side. The philosophy of flexible containment served to sink the United States more deeply into Vietnam, Kennedy's Achilles heel. Just as disturbing was the way in which Kennedy responded to an inherited Cuban vexation. Like Vietnam, Cuba—in spite of Kennedy's reputed missile-crisis triumph—became more of a problem as a result of his presidency. [Cuban leader Fidel] Castro afterward viewed the United States more suspiciously and found himself more dependent on the Soviet Union. Neither did American relations improve with Communist China, for Kennedy adhered to the stringent policy of the past. Efforts to improve economic relations with Eastern European countries such as Poland and Yugoslavia also failed, and Kennedy was unable to strengthen NATO. [French President Charles] De Gaulle and [German Chancellor Konrad] Adenauer instead became increasingly independent, partly in reaction to United States policy. In fact, Kennedy never did develop a coherent and purposeful strategy and oscillated between hardline and conciliatory approaches with little apparent rationale.

Still, of the major foreign policy crises facing Kennedy in early 1961 (Laos, Berlin, the Congo, and Vietnam), only Vietnam remained virulent at Kennedy's death. Except for Cuba, no new crisis had emerged. Kennedy performed well as a crisis manager, even though he did less well in preventing them. Furthermore, he did much to improve the image of the United States in the newly emerging nations of Africa and Asia. The Peace Corps, Food for Peace, and AID programs helped to reduce the mistrust of new governments, who retained their neutrality in spite of Soviet efforts to win their allegiance. In the Congo, Kennedy wisely exercised restraint in working through the UN. Indeed no president backed that organization more. In Latin America Kennedy's lofty Alliance for Progress improved conditions only marginally, but Latinos continued to hope that Kennedy would make that endeavor work. Kennedy also emerged as the father of the space program as the United States launched its first man into orbit and made significant strides toward placing a man on the moon. Soviet technology no longer seemed as imposing, and by 1963 Americans felt justifiably proud that the tide was turning in America's favor.

*John F. Kennedy's sense of hope and optimism appealed to many Americans.*

## Domestic Accomplishments

Kennedy had also sought to revitalize a floundering domestic America. In the tradition of his Democratic predecessors, he pledged to alleviate economic stagnation, rising unemployment, wide-scale poverty, and urban squalor. He proposed expanded coverages and increases in Social Security benefits and the minimum wage, a housing program under a new Housing and Urban Affairs Department, urban renewal, tax incentives, federal aid to education, health care for the aged, and action against organized and juvenile crime. He also promised to end racial discrimination, combat the farm problem, and preserve America's natural resources. All of this he acknowledged would not be finished in the "first one thousand days" nor "in the life of this administration."

Kennedy indeed fell far short of accomplishing his domestic objectives. Even when considering the relative conservatism of the times, one is hard pressed to give Kennedy high marks in the legislative arena, as programs for civil rights, medical assistance for the aged; education, and poverty failed to materialize. While the tax-cut and civil rights bills probably would have passed Congress in 1964 had he lived, his other major proposals remained in limbo. More disconcerting was Kennedy's wavering leadership in advancing civil rights, following his encouragement of it in 1960. In response to intense pressure from black activists, however, he did morally commit the presidency to the movement by 1963—resulting in the unavoidable Democratic party demise in the South in the years afterward.

To his credit Kennedy promoted economic growth in spite of his fiscal conservatism. The Kennedy years for most Americans were a good time to live—inflation and interest rates were low, unemployment was reduced, wages were rising, and taxes were about to descend. Additionally, the balance-of-payment problem showed modest improvement. Kennedy provided job-training programs, updated traditional New Deal commitments such as Social Security and the minimum wage, and reduced job discrimination against

41

women. Moreover, despite failing to obtain comprehensive agricultural legislation, he eased farm problems and extended rural assistance. He responded to the problems and needs of juvenile delinquency and mental retardation, implemented the first significant housing program since 1949, began urban renewal, and addressed the problem of organized crime. Even though several major domestic objectives remained unfulfilled, Kennedy left the country better off than he had found it in 1961. Too, partly because of Kennedy's efforts, the national mood seemed more receptive to change by 1963.

Kennedy's presidency was also remarkably free of notable scandal and incompetence. Not since the New Deal was the national government uniformly served so well. Kennedy had appointed an exceptional group of public servants—many of them attracted by his perceived idealism and style. . . .

In the 1982 Murray-Blessing presidential evaluation poll, some one thousand scholars have rated Kennedy as an above-average president in the ranking—ironically slightly below Eisenhower. Of the nine presidents who served less than one full term, Kennedy alone is ranked higher than average. To many historians at least, the Kennedy glitter and promise and the tragedy of assassination have given way to the realities of Vietnam, excessive presidential activism, and the perceived limitations of liberalism at home—all of which were rooted in the Kennedy presidency. In any case, above average is where he belongs. And for those of us who reached adulthood in the early 1960s, John Fitzgerald Kennedy will always be remembered as a remarkable person, if not as a great president.

# The Triumph of Liberalism: Lyndon B. Johnson and the Great Society

Frederick F. Siegel

Lyndon B. Johnson rose from poverty in Texas to become Majority Leader of the Senate in 1955 and John F. Kennedy's running mate in 1960. He became president of the United States in November 1963 following Kennedy's assassination and served until 1969. Historian Frederick F. Siegel describes the domestic achievements of the Johnson administration, a time of significant government growth and reform. Calling on the nation to honor Kennedy's memory, Johnson was able to help pass much of the slain president's stalled legislative proposals through Congress, including a sweeping civil rights act. Johnson subsequently sought to place his own stamp on the presidency by declaring a "War on Poverty" and proposing a variety of liberal reforms and domestic programs as part of what he termed the "Great Society." He successfully implemented many of these reforms following his landslide 1964 electoral victory over Barry Goldwater, an Arizona senator viewed by many Americans as a conservative extremist. These new programs included federal aid to education, Medicare and Medicaid programs providing health care to the elderly and the poor, and comprehensive air and water

Excerpted from *Troubled Journey: From Pearl Harbor to Ronald Reagan*, by Frederick F. Siegel. Copyright ©1984 by Frederick F. Siegel. Reprinted by permission of Hill and Wang, a division of Farrar, Straus, and Giroux, LLC.

pollution laws. According to Siegel, Johnson's Great Society was primarily an attempt to make American society more equitable and to bring the poor and blacks into the mainstream of American life.

---

To prove he was worthy of the office and not just another parochial Southerner, Johnson moved quickly to push Kennedy's civil rights legislation, long blocked by his fellow Dixie politicians. As Johnson explained it: "If I didn't get out in front on this issue" the liberals "would get me . . . I had to produce a civil rights bill that was even stronger than the one they'd have gotten if Kennedy had lived." And produce he did. Defying all the writers, politicians, and analysts who spoke of the "deadlock of democracy," Johnson used his unparalleled skills to break the Southern filibuster. He pushed through Congress the most sweeping civil rights legislation since the end of the First Reconstruction. The 1964 Civil Rights Act, described by Supreme Court Justice Arthur Goldberg as "the vindication of human dignity," became the cornerstone of civil rights law. It provided legal and financial support for cities desegregating their schools, banned discrimination by businesses and unions, created an Equal Opportunities Commission to enforce that ban, and outlawed discrimination in places of public accommodation.

## The War on Poverty

With the Civil Rights Act passed and his own legitimacy established, Johnson turned to putting his own stamp on the presidency. Declaring, "We are not helpless before the iron law of [traditional] economics," Johnson called for a "War on Poverty" as Kennedy had called for a war on Communism.

The "War," wrote *Time* magazine, reflected the "uniquely American belief" that "evangelism, money and organization can lick just about anything." Americans generally believed that "a rising tide lifts all boats," but a spate of books on poverty, particularly Michael Harrington's powerful *The Other America,* showed that a substantial number of Americans, black and white, silently suffered from such serious deprivation that they would be unaided by the general prosperity. The very poor, argued anthropologist Oscar Lewis, were trapped in a culture of poverty, a culture which, in the words of Harrington, meant that "the poor are not like us. . . . They are a different kind of people."

Social science promised a way to reach the culturally distant world of severe poverty. On assuming the presidency Johnson inherited an economic growth rate that had more than doubled from 2.1 percent to 4.5 percent since 1960 and which, with mild inflation, was pouring extraordinary amounts of money into federal coffers. This "social surplus," the excess of revenues over expenditures, provided nearly four billion dollars a year for new public spending. The flow of money was so great that Governor Earl Long of Louisiana whimsically suggested massive spending for two highway systems, one reserved for drunks. Johnson's economic advisers assured him that the unprecedented surpluses would continue indefinitely. Pointing to the great success of the 1964 tax cut, which seemed to demonstrate their ability to put their theories into practice, the "new" economists claimed that, through Keynesian "demand management," they had discovered the secret of constant noninflationary growth. In short, the continuing surplus created by "demand management" meant that poverty could be abolished without undue sacrifice from the rest of the population. There would be a "maximum of reform with a minimum of social disruption."

While the economists were guiding the fiscal ship of state, their fellow experts, the sociologists, devised programs to provide the poor with nutritional aid, health and schooling benefits, job training, and even dignity and respect. The programs were institutionalized as part of Johnson's Economic Opportunity Act of 1964. The act appropriated nearly a billion dollars for projects such as the

Head Start program to assist disadvantaged preschoolers, the Job Corps for high school dropouts, a domestic Peace Corps—Volunteers in Service to America (VISTA)—a Neighborhood Youth Corps, and a Community Action Program designed for the "maximum feasible participation" by the poor it was meant to aid.

## The Great Society

Flushed by his legislative successes, LBJ headed into the 1964 presidential campaign by asking for even broader social measures as part of what he called "The Great Society." Like Kennedy's New Frontier, the Great Society was a presidential answer to the quest for national and thus in many cases individual purpose in an increasingly secular age. It was to be the fulfillment of the American creed of equal opportunity—a grand mobilization of expertise, this time to fight poverty and disease, as depression, fascism, and Communism had been fought previously. In LBJ's own inspiring words: "This nation . . . has man's first chance to create a Great Society: a society of success without squalor, beauty without barrenness, of genius without the wretchedness of poverty. We can open the doors of learning. We can open the doors of opportunity and closed community—not just to the privileged few, but, thank God, we can open doors to everyone." Rhetoric (glorious though it was) aside, Johnson's proposals for a Great Society hinged on passing a twenty-five-year backlog of liberal Democratic legislation on health, education, racial discrimination, and conservation that had been sitting on the rear burner ever since the New Deal flame was snuffed out by the Republican/Dixiecrat coalition in 1937.

The Great Society program, which vested vast new powers in the federal government, promised to rearrange the relationship between Washington and the rest of the nation. For American liberals the growth of federal power meant the chance to complete the racial reforms begun by Reconstruction and the economic reforms begun by the New Deal without a fundamental restructuring of American society.

But for many others, those who "understood the American creed, not as a common set of national values, but as a justification for their particular set of local values," the Great Society proved to be deeply unsettling. Their fears, however, were never fully aired, nor was Johnson given the chance to build a national consensus for the Great Society, because Barry Goldwater, his opponent in 1964, gave LBJ the enormous advantage of running as a social reformer while still seeming to be the less radical of the two.

Johnson's Republican opposition came from a group of youth activists deeply opposed to American policies in Vietnam and bitterly hostile to what they called the "Establishment," symbolized by Nelson Rockefeller. Their movement was directed by Stephen Shadeg, who had been heavily influenced by the thought and tactics of Chairman Mao. Their candidate, described by conservative William Buckley as one of "the few genuine radicals in American life," was Barry Morris Goldwater, junior senator from Arizona.

## The Goldwater Movement

The Goldwater movement was built on the strength of the old Taftite right, the "veterans of the thirty years' war with the New Deal." Like [Senator Robert] Taft, Goldwater would say, "Yes, I fear Washington, more than I fear Moscow." But most of all Goldwater feared what he saw as Moscow's influence in Washington, so that as a first-term senator he was one of the diehards who opposed the censure of [Senator Joseph] McCarthy after almost the entire Senate had turned against the demagogue from Wisconsin. The old right had been repeatedly defeated, in its struggle to control the Republican Party, by what it called the Eastern establishment, otherwise known as the "two-bit New Dealers" or "me-too Republicans." But in 1964 the Goldwater movement defeated the Rockefeller Republicans by mobilizing two new political elements: nouveau riche anti-union oilmen and aerospace men of the Southwest, and ideologically charged conservative youth.

Like their left-wing counterparts, these young conservatives disdained the soft society of welfarism with all its compromises and government paternalism. They complained of a "sickness in our society and the lack of a common purpose" that might "restore inner meaning to every man's life in a time too often rushed, too often obsessed with petty needs and material greeds." Contemptuous of businessmen who placed profit before free market ethics, they dreamed of a world made whole by the heroic deeds of rugged individuals untrammeled by the heavy hand of the state. Their allies, the Texas oilmen and aerospace entrepreneurs, however, were beneficiaries of vast government subsidies such as the oil-depletion allowance. But both were united in their hostility to the Rockefeller wing of the Republican Party. And both subscribed to the notion that only a laissez-faire economy could create the disciplined individuals with the character and fortitude necessary to sustain democracy. Politics for the activists was not so much a matter of pursuing material interests as a national screen on which to project their deepest cultural fears. They were part of a mood, a mood of deluxe puritanism, as much as an ideology, and in the words of Richard Whalen, "Barry Goldwater was the favorite son of their state of mind."

But even with his activists and oilmen, Goldwater, like Taft before him, might have lost the nomination if it hadn't been for the first nationwide stirrings of a white backlash against the civil rights movement. Interest in Goldwater was flagging when Alabama's Governor George Wallace, a flaming segregationist, made a surprising showing in liberal Wisconsin's Democratic primary. The Wallace showing revived interest in Goldwater, who was seen as the Republican most opposed to federal intervention on behalf of Afro-Americans. When Goldwater was nominated, Wallace's candidacy collapsed, suggesting a considerable overlap in the two men's donors and constituencies. Tall, trim, and handsome, the altogether affable Goldwater was not personally a bigot. A member of the NAACP, Goldwater was the kind of terribly sincere fellow everyone likes to have for a neighbor or fraternity brother. He came to popular attention by spearheading congressional criticism of Walter Reuther and by his outspoken calls for a holy crusade against Communism in general and [Cuban leader Fidel] Castro in particular. But as Goldwater told reporter Joseph Alsop: "You know, I haven't really got a first-class brain." And it showed. His combination of bland and outrageous statements alienated all but the right wing of the Republican Party from his candidacy. He could in the same speech assert that "where fraternities are not allowed, Communism flourishes" and then, warming to his message, suggest that nuclear weapons be used against Cuba, China, and North Vietnam if they refused to accede to American demands. Goldwater was unafraid of voicing unpopular views. He called for the abolition of the TVA, an end to the graduated income tax, and the elimination of Social Security, while campaigning forthrightly for the elimination of the union shop. "My aim," he said, "is not to pass laws but to repeal them." Here, in the words of Phyllis Schlafly, was "a choice and not an echo."

There was really no need for Johnson to criticize Goldwater's campaign for being too radical. Goldwater did it for him, proclaiming on national TV that "extremism in the defense of liberty is no vice." When the Goldwaterites adopted the slogan "In your hearts you know he's right," Democrats responded with "In your guts you know he's nuts." Johnson replied to Goldwater's "no substitute for victory" rhetoric on Vietnam with a proclamation of restraint. "We are not," LBJ told the American people, "about to send American boys nine or ten thousand miles from home to do what Asian boys ought to be doing for themselves." It is a virtual replay of the Truman-MacArthur struggle, with the same outcome.

## The 1964 Election

With the successful focusing of the campaign on Goldwater's artless "shoot from the lip" pronouncements—"The child has no right to an education; in most cases he will get along very well without it"—Johnson's own measures at home and abroad went undebated. It was a curious consequence of the 1964 campaign that the fundamental issues raised by both Johnson's social innovations and Goldwater's ideological thrust went almost unnoticed, producing a curiously empty campaign which ironically denied Johnson the opportunity to build support for the Great Society. The consensus that emerged instead was that Barry Goldwater was unfit for office. The reaction to Goldwater was so broadly negative that the party which once denounced "economic royalists" now found Wall Street and big business flocking to its banner. Johnson attracted the nation's corporate elite in creating what Oscar Gass has called a Grossblock, a coalition of upper-middle-class professionals and lower-middle-class blue-collar workers, big business and labor, Catholics and Protestants, blacks and whites outside the Deep South, in a national replication of the Texas Democratic Party's "one big tent."

LBJ swept to victory with 61 percent of the vote, only 5 points short of doubling Goldwater's total. The Democrats gained 2 seats in the Senate and 37 in the House, creating enormous Democratic majorities.

LBJ's victory was so overwhelming that commentators openly speculated about the impending death of both conservatism and the Republican Party. We are left, said one observer, with a "one and a half party system." But an analysis of local voting patterns revealed something very different. On a host of social issues, ranging from prayer in the public schools to calls for cutting federal expenditures and reducing welfare spending, the electorate was far closer to Goldwater than to Johnson. Goldwater the candidate was repudiated, but on a local level conservatism was intact and even thriving. In California, for instance, areas which went strongly for LBJ also voted to repeal the state's anti-discriminatory fair housing laws by a better than two-to-one margin. Similarly, in Maryland, areas which had supported George Wallace when he made his strong showing in the Democratic primary there went overwhelmingly for LBJ in the general election. These Maryland voters were in favor of the civil rights bill even as they feared black militancy.

Goldwater's defeat was of such proportion that ironically it served to break the hold conservative Democrats held over their own party. So many Northern liberals triumphed in congressional races against Republicans "dragged down by Barry" that for the first time the Democrats had clear majorities in both houses without having to rely on their Dixiecrat allies. On the other hand, Goldwater, by piggy-backing his right-to-work rhetoric on George Wallace's states' rights racism, had carried the Deep South, breaking the Democrats' century-long hold over that region. And while the Goldwater campaign rhetoric was most noted for its fire-eating foreign policy, it was Goldwater's appeal to the white backlash against black militancy that had garnered most of his votes North and South.

## The Push for Legislation

Lyndon Johnson was keenly aware that the American political system's balance of powers had been designed for stalemate. As a young congressman, he had seen FDR, at the height of his power, humbled when he tried to pack the Supreme Court. Johnson realized that unless he moved quickly to take advantage of his landslide victory, the naturally parochial tendencies of the Congress would block his Great Society initiatives. Johnson moved rapidly to circumvent the established interests in Congress. Instead of asking congressmen for legislative proposals, he organized task forces composed of administration aides and social reform academics to draw up legislation which would then be presented to the sachems as a fait accompli. Or as LBJ put it to his aides, "I want to see a whole bunch of coon-skins on the wall."

The programs Johnson deemed most important were Medicare to protect the elderly from catastrophic losses and aid to elementary education to upgrade the schooling for both black and white poor. Legislation for Medicare and aid to elementary education had been proposed by Democrats ever since the mid-1940s but had always met fierce opposition from the American Medical Association and proponents of states' rights. Johnson knew that if he won on these two issues, "the momentum," as historian Jim Heath has put it, "would carry over, making it relatively easy to enact the rest of his legislative program." As before, the powerful AMA put up a tenacious fight against any form of federally guaranteed health insurance for the elderly, portraying it as a step on the road to socialized medicine. But Johnson, aided by the wily Wilbur Mills, of the House Ways and Means Committee, not only got Medicare passed; in a little-noticed maneuver, Medicaid, health care for the indigent, was tacked on. LBJ flew to Independence, Missouri, to sign the bill in front of a smiling Harry S. Truman. On January 12, 1965, only five days after the Medicare legislation was approved, LBJ sent the politically explosive aid to elementary education bill to the Congress. Part and parcel of the War on Poverty, the bill was opposed by Protestant fundamentalists who wanted to deny federal money to the Catholic schools and by segregationists who saw Washington's money as the beginning of federal control over local schools. Here Johnson, aided by Senator Wayne Morse, achieved what the senator called a "back-door victory," by overtly ignoring racial and religious questions in order to target money regionally on the basis of population below the poverty level in a given area.

With Medicare and aid to education passed, Johnson moved quickly to complete what critics called his "revolution from above." If the word "revolution" was overblown, the critics were right to see that LBJ made unprecedented use of the federal budget. "No previous budget had ever been so contrived to do something for every major economic interest in the nation." But LBJ offered something for almost all his supporters: tax cuts for big business; billions of dollars for Appalachian social and economic development; the first major additions to our national parks and the first comprehensive air and water pollution standards for environmentalists; truth in packaging legislation for consumers; federal aid for mass transit for city dwellers; a subsidy boost for farmers; a National Arts and Humanities Foundation for academics; and, in LBJ's own words, "the goddamnedest toughest voting rights act" and Model Cities, low-cost housing, job-training programs, and slum clearance for blacks. At the end of this spate of legislation, the Democratic leadership on the Hill spoke jubilantly of the "fabulous 89th" Congress as "the Congress of fulfillment," "the Congress of accomplished hopes," "the Congress of realized dreams."

In the words of liberal policy analyst Sar Levitan, a great deal of LBJ's agenda involved "unabashedly class legislation . . . designating a special group in the population as eligible to receive the benefits of American law." Class legislation was nothing new in American politics—federal insurance for overseas corporate investments and the mortgage tax deduction for homeowners are examples. What was different about the Great Society was that it extended such special benefits to those who were least well off. Johnson's left-wing critics complained that in order to aid the poor, his legislation provided a windfall for a multitude of contractors and middlemen who ultimately were the greatest beneficiaries. There is a good deal of truth to this charge. The doctors who fought Medicaid so bitterly were to number among its prime beneficiaries. Building contractors often became wealthy through Model Cities renewal efforts. This said, however, it is unlikely that any of the legislation directed at alleviating poverty could have passed a Congress composed of men representing American business and middle-class interests unless they too were cut in on federal largess.

Johnson, the adventurous conservative, was denounced as a "Red" by fiscal conservatives and simply a pork-barrel New Dealer by leftists, but both charges were wide of the mark. The New Deal was designed to aid widows, orphans, and the indigent; in short, it represented help for those worst off without addressing the underlying issues of social fairness. The Great Society, without being socialist, tried to partially redefine the structure of opportunity in America. Its aim was not simply to provide handouts to the poor; rather, it attempted to make the competitive race of life a bit fairer. The Great Society had a dramatic effect in relieving poverty. From 1964 to 1968 more than 14 million Americans moved out of poverty as the proportion of the impoverished was halved from 22 to 11 percent of the nation. Just as FDR's New Deal had incorporated working-class immigrants and organized them into the mainstream of American life, LBJ's Great Society tried to do the same for blacks and the poverty-stricken.

# Earl Warren Leads an Activist Supreme Court

David Chalmers

The 1960s marked an era of activist reform not only for legislative and executive branches of government, but for the judicial branch as well. The following passage by David Chalmers briefly describes some of the reforms made by the Supreme Court under Earl Warren, its chief justice from 1953 to 1969. In 1954, Warren, a former governor of California who was appointed to the Supreme Court by President Dwight D. Eisenhower, was instrumental in marshaling a unanimous ruling outlawing racial segregation in public schools in the famous case of *Brown v. Board of Education*. In the 1960s, aided by Kennedy and Johnson appointees, Warren led an activist liberal majority in the Supreme Court in making other controversial landmark decisions. The Supreme Court strengthened the rights of criminal defendants, broadened the free speech and press protections of the First Amendment, and outlawed school prayer as a violation of the principle of the separation of church and state. Chalmers, professor emeritus of history at the University of Florida, argues that the "Warren revolution" was part of a trend of shifting power away from state and local governments to the national level.

Excerpted from David Chalmers, *And the Crooked Places Made Straight*, pp. 49–51. Copyright ©1991, 1996 by The Johns Hopkins University Press. Reprinted with permission from The Johns Hopkins University Press.

In the history of the American Republic, the impact of the "Warren Court" has been matched only by [former chief justice] John Marshall's nationalism, the late nineteenth-century judicial advancement of corporate capitalism, and the later New Deal acceptance of the liberal regulatory state. None did as much to set the pattern of individual freedoms or created greater controversy.

In summing up his contributions to the law of the land, Warren singled out school desegregation (*Brown*), reapportionment (*Baker v. Carr* [1962]), and the right to counsel (*Gideon v. Wainwright* [1963]). The most important, he believed, was reapportionment. With its "one man, one vote" standard, *Baker v. Carr* went into an area hitherto considered "too political" for the courts and became the precedent for establishing equal election districts at all levels of government. Particularly in the South, where small groups of rural legislators dominated state legislatures, reapportionment meant accelerating the modernization of the whole region.

*Gideon,* along with *Miranda v. Arizona* (1966), which required the reading of rights at the time of arrest, and other Warren Court decisions, changed basic criminal procedure in the states. Their effect was to apply most of the national Bill of Rights as a limitation on state law. The "due process" clause of the Fourteenth Amendment was used to extend constitutional protection against self-incrimination and to guarantee legal counsel and jury trials. Illegally seized evidence, including the results of wiretapping, could not be used in court.

## Extending the First Amendment

Even this was not all of the "Warren revolution." In a series of libertarian decisions, the Court broadened the reach of the First Amendment. In overturning many of the cold war restrictions of the 1950s and the "age of McCarthyism," the Court drew a line between advocacy of doctrine and advocacy of action, freeing the former from prosecution. The recognition of a congressional monopoly overturned state sedition laws, and protection against self-incrimination nullified Communist-registration laws. Concern about fair procedure, and vagueness of legislative purpose, severely limited Congressional loyalty investigations and headline hunting.

In a case rising out of the civil rights struggle in Alabama, *New York Times v. Sullivan* (1964), the Court broadened the press's protection from libel actions by public officials. If the standards of "actual malice" or "reckless disregard" of the truth were less than definitive, they were clear by comparison with the Court's effort to define obscenity. The justices assumed jurisdiction from the states but were not able to decide what actually was impermissible, and thus they greatly increased the permissiveness of the law. In the areas of First Amendment rights, as with race relations and criminal procedure, the Warren Court was shifting power away from local communities and the states. This underlying nationalization of standards and power was the revolution within the revolution. In handling its cases, the Court broadened its "preferred-freedoms" standard to include race, voting, and fair criminal procedure as areas in which state action was subject to a more severe federal court scrutiny and justification. In the 1980s, legislation touching on women's rights would receive closer examination, although it was not fully added to this "suspect classification."

For all the controversy these changes produced, a more intense and lasting furor arose over religion and abortion. In a series of decisions centering on *Engel v. Vitale* (1962) and *School District of Abington Township v. Schempp* (1963), the Court found prayer and Bible reading in public schools to be in violation of the separation of church and state. In overturning state opposition to the distribution of birth control information and devices (*Griswold v. Connecticut* [1965]), the Court established the right of privacy as a constitutional principle. In 1973, the Burger Court applied it in *Roe v. Wade* and *Doe v. Bolton* to strike down state prohibition of abortion, at least in the first trimester. For decades after, as the segregationists' "Impeach Earl

Warren" billboards were a fading memory in the South, angry political and religious conservatives were still rallying in front of women's health clinics and on the steps of the Supreme Court Building as the abortion issue heated up in the 1980s.

In a time when the Supreme Court's docket was dominated by civil rights questions, the crucial measure for Earl Warren was not precedent but "fairness." "Yes, yes," he would say to the lawyers before him, "but were you fair?" Although the 1953–68 era will bear his name in history, Warren did not dominate the Court as John Marshall had done at its beginnings, and he did not match Marshall as a judicial thinker or draftsman. Despite the other justices' personal respect for him, the unity of the *Brown* school case was not typical outside of desegregation issues. What was decisive was the existence of an activist liberal majority among the justices of the Court, whose concern with equality and the rights of the individual continued to pervade the Court after Warren's retirement. In a period of economic growth and general well-being, the Supreme Court took the lead in making social and political adjustments, contradicting Alexander Hamilton's prediction in the *Federalist Papers* that the judiciary would be "the weakest" and the "least dangerous" branch of the federal government. Although it drew great public criticism, the direction taken by the Warren Court was in keeping with the emerging pattern of national history, whose consciousness and structure it helped shape.

# CHAPTER 2

# Aspects of the Cold War

# The Bay of Pigs and the Cuban Missile Crisis

George Moss

In 1959 leftist rebel Fidel Castro ousted Fulgencio Batista, a longtime dictator of Cuba who had supported America's dominant economic interests in that country. U.S.-Cuban relations quickly deteriorated; by 1961 Castro had led the island nation ninety miles from Florida into an open alliance with the Soviet Union. Cuba was at the center of two of the most serious cold war crises faced by President John F. Kennedy, both of which are recounted here by historian George Moss. In 1961 a small force of Cuban exiles trained by the Central Intelligence Agency (CIA) attempted to invade Cuba's Bay of Pigs and spark a popular uprising against Castro. The operation, conceived while Dwight Eisenhower was still president but approved by Kennedy and his advisers, was an utter failure that marred the beginning of Kennedy's presidency. In October 1962 an even more serious crisis was precipitated by the discovery that the Soviet Union was secretly trying to install nuclear missiles in Cuba. Moss describes how that finding almost resulted in a nuclear war between the United States and Russia before the Soviet leader Nikita Khrushchev agreed to withdraw the missiles.

Excerpted from *America in the Twentieth Century*, by George Moss. Copyright ©1988 by Prentice-Hall, Inc. Reprinted by permission of Prentice-Hall, Inc., Upper Saddle River, N.J.

The new Administration encountered its first Cold War crisis in Cuba. Kennedy no more than his predecessor could tolerate the existence of a Communist state in the Caribbean that expropriated American property and developed close ties with the Soviet Union. The CIA project to overthrow Castro, begun by Eisenhower six months earlier, readied for action. Anti-Castro Cuban exiles, many of them former liberal supporters of the Cuban dictator, had been trained for an amphibious assault on Cuba at a secret camp set up in the Guatemalan mountains. CIA officials believed that an invasion of Cuba would activate a general uprising within Cuba that would overthrow Castro. Kennedy, after consultations with senior advisers, gave the operation the green light. The invasion would be risky, but Kennedy and his New Frontiersmen were eager to strike the Communists.

About 1,400 invaders, debarking from a Nicaraguan port in ships provided by the CIA, landed before dawn at the Bay of Pigs, a remote area on the southern Cuba coast. Castro quickly deployed his forces to meet them. The invaders, lacking adequate artillery support and air cover, were pinned on the beach and overwhelmed. All but about 100 of them were killed or captured within two days. The invaders never made contact with Cuban underground elements and the expected anti-Castro uprising never occurred.

The Bay of Pigs disaster humiliated the Kennedy administration. The United States' European allies sharply criticized its actions and Third World spokesmen took turns condemning the United States at the United Nations. Within the United States, liberals attacked Kennedy for undertaking the invasion, and conservatives scolded him for failing to overthrow Castro.

America stood exposed as both imperialistic and inept, a pathetic combination of wickedness and weakness. The U.S.-backed invasion had violated the Organization of American States (OAS) charter that prohibited any Western Hemispheric nation from intervening in another's affairs. Latin American nations, resenting the thinly disguised American reversion to gunboat diplomacy, refused the United States request to quarantine Cuba from inter-American affairs. Castro and Khrushchev enjoyed a propaganda harvest. Castro emerged from the affair stronger than ever. Both Soviet aid to Cuba and the pace of Cuban socialization accelerated in the aftermath of the failed invasion.

The invasion project had been ill-conceived and mismanaged from the start. The CIA victimized itself with faulty intelligence data and wishful thinking. It underestimated Castro's military strength and exaggerated the extent of anti-Castro sentiment in Cuba. Kennedy insured the mission's failure when he curtailed CIA air strikes preceding the landings and then refused all requests for naval air support that might have salvaged the failing operation. Kennedy had concluded that the invasion had failed and that air cover could not save it, so he decided to cut his losses. He also did not want a war with Cuba, and he tried to preserve the fiction that the invasion was a Cuban affair.

Kennedy got a rough baptism of fire and the first serious criticism of his new presidency. He assumed full responsibility for the fiasco, but afterwards, ordered an investigation of the CIA. He forced its aged director, Allen Dulles, into retirement and replaced him with John McCone, a conservative California oil executive. He remained determined to get rid of Castro. According to the findings of a special Senate investigating committee that examined CIA covert operations, Kennedy ordered the CIA to eliminate Castro following the failure of the Bay of Pigs invasion. Robert Kennedy took charge of Operation Mongoose that included efforts to disrupt the Cuban economy and to support anti-Castro elements. CIA operatives plotted with organized crime leaders to assassinate Castro. There is also a direct connection between the failed invasion and the dangerous missile crisis that occurred eighteen months later. . . .

## The Missile Crisis

Following the Bay of Pigs, the Russians sent Soviet technicians and weapons to Cuba to protect the Communist satellite from American hostility. Castro also supported guerrilla actions and subversion in other Latin American countries. Republicans, looking for election year issues, attacked the Kennedy administration for allowing the Soviet arms buildup in Cuba. Kennedy opposed attacking or invading Cuba as long as the Soviets placed only defensive weapons in Cuba that posed no threat to the United States or any other hemispheric nation. But Khrushchev and Castro decided on a daring move to deter any further U.S. action against Cuba and to score a Cold War coup. Russia secretly tried to install medium-range and intermediate-range nuclear missiles and bombers in Cuba. These missiles and bombers were offensive weapons capable of carrying nuclear payloads to American cities and military installations.

On October 14, 1962, a U-2 reconnaissance plane photographed missile launching sites nearing completion in western Cuba. Kennedy immediately determined that the missiles and bombers must be removed from the island. His sense of strategic and political reality told him that they had to go. But how to get the missiles out of Cuba? How without triggering a nuclear war? The most dangerous Cold War crisis ever had begun.

Kennedy convened a special executive committee of thirteen senior advisers to find a way to remove the missiles and planes. For three days the committee debated several options. Some members wanted surprise air strikes that were likely to kill both Russian technicians and Cuban soldiers. Robert Kennedy, who proved to be the most influential member of the executive committee, rejected that idea saying he wanted "no Pearl Harbors on his brother's record." The Joint Chiefs proposed an invasion to get rid of both the offensive weapons and the Castro regime. The President rejected this suggestion as too risky; it could involve a prolonged war with Cuba, provoke a Russian attack on West Berlin, or even bring nuclear war. Secretary of Defense [Robert] McNamara proposed a naval blockade to prevent further shipments of weapons to Cuba. The blockade would allow both sides some freedom of maneuver.

The United States could decide to attack or negotiate later, depending on the Russian response to the blockade. The President accepted the blockade tactic.

President Kennedy attended few committee sessions. With the 1962 midterm elections only three weeks away, he was on the campaign trail, acting as if everything were normal. He campaigned mostly about domestic issues, trying to build support for his New Frontier reform programs that were stalled in Congress. Neither the media nor the public had any inkling of the serious crisis that was building. The Russians did not know that the missile sites had been detected, nor that Kennedy was planning his response.

## On the Brink

On the evening of October 22, Kennedy went on television to inform the nation and the Russians about the missile crisis. He bluntly told his audience around the world: "unmistakable evidence has established the fact that a series of offensive missile sites is now in preparation on that imprisoned island." He spoke of the naval blockade, which he called a "quarantine," that would soon be placed around Cuba. He demanded that the Russians dismantle and remove all missile bases and bombers from Cuba immediately, and he stated that the quarantine would remain in place until all offensive weapons had been removed. Then a grim leader spoke these chilling words:

> It shall be the policy of this nation to regard any nuclear missile launched from Cuba against any nation in the Western Hemisphere as an attack by the Soviet Union on the United States, requiring a full retaliatory response upon the Soviet Union.

Kennedy confronted Khrushchev with the risk of nuclear war if he did not remove the missiles. For the next five days the world hovered at the brink of catastrophe. Khrushchev denounced the United States and denied that he was installing offensive weapons in Cuba. Meanwhile, work on the missile sites continued. The first sites would be operational in a few days. The Air Force prepared strikes to take them out before they could fire missiles at targets in the United States. Russian merchant ships hauling more weapons continued to steam toward Cuba. The U.S. Navy positioned its blockade fleet to intercept them. U.S. invasion forces gathered in Florida. B-52 strategic bombers took to the air with nuclear bombs on board. U.S. strategic missiles went to maximum alert. The moment of supreme danger would come if a Russian ship tried to run the blockade, for American ship commanders had orders to stop them.

The first break came on October 24. Soviet ships hauling offensive weapons turned back. Two other Russian freighters, hauling no offensive weapons, submitted to searches and were permitted to steam on to Cuba. Two days later, Khrushchev sent a letter to President Kennedy offering to remove all offensive weapons from Cuba in exchange for an American pledge not to invade Cuba. Kennedy accepted the offer, but before he could send his reply, the Russian premier sent a second letter raising the stakes: America would have to give a no-invasion of Cuba pledge plus remove its medium-range Jupiter missiles that were stationed in Turkey, which were targeted at the Soviet Union. Kennedy refused to bargain. It was his view that Khrushchev's reckless initiative had threatened world peace, and it was the Russian leader's responsibility to remove the missiles from Cuba quickly.

As the point of no return neared, Kennedy, heeding the advice of his brother, made one last try to avoid the looming cataclysm. The president sent a cable to Khrushchev accepting the offer in the first letter and ignoring the second letter. The next night, October 27, Robert Kennedy met with the Soviet ambassador to the United States, Anatoly Dobrynin, to warn him that the United States had to have "a commitment by tomorrow that those bases would be removed." He told Dobrynin this was the Soviets' last chance to avoid war: If the Soviets "did not remove those bases, we would remove them." He also indicated to Dobrynin that the American missiles in Turkey, although not part of any quid pro quo, would be removed soon after the Cuban missiles were removed.

The next morning Khrushchev agreed to remove the missiles and bombers in return for the President's promise not to invade Cuba. He claimed that he had achieved his goal of protecting Cuba from American attacks. The United States suspended its blockade. The United Nations supervised the dismantling and removal of the Cuban bases. American missiles were removed from Turkey a few weeks later. The missile crisis had been resolved without war. Kennedy received high praise for his actions. The Democrats gained in the fall elections. Kennedy's standing in the polls soared to new heights. It was the young hero's finest hour. Americans who had been on the defensive in the Cold War for years, were elated. National pride soared along with Kennedy's popularity. America had stood up to the Russians and forced them to back down.

Although Kennedy was showered with praise for his handling of the missile crisis, it proved humiliating to Khrushchev. The Russian leader fell from power within a year, and his actions during the crisis contributed to his demise. The Russians had been exposed as strategic inferiors to the Americans. A Russian official told his American counterpart, "Never will we be caught like this again." The Soviets embarked on a crash program to expand their navy and to bring their missile forces up to parity with the United States. Within five years they achieved their goals.

## Serious Questions

Analysts have raised serious questions about the missile crisis. Why had Khrushchev tried to put the missiles in Cuba? There are several possible factors. He wanted to strengthen Cuban defenses against possible U.S. attacks, but he miscalculated, a dangerous thing for a superpower leader to do in the nuclear age. He did not expect Kennedy's strong response, having sized him up as weak under pressure. Kennedy's behavior in previous crises had fed Khrushchev's suspicions that he lacked courage. During the Bay of Pigs invasion, Kennedy had backed off from a war with Cuba, let the invasion fail, and allowed Castro to consolidate a Communist revolution right in America's backyard. He had let the Berlin Wall stand. These acts of restraint sent the wrong signals to the adventurous Soviet ideologue. Khrushchev was not looking for a confrontation with the United States over Cuba, and he certainly did not want a war. Khrushchev may also have been trying to appease Kremlin hawks and to silence Chinese criticisms that Soviet foreign policy was not protecting Third World countries from American imperialism.

Kennedy has been accused of manufacturing the missile crisis to silence Republican critics and to promote his party's chances in the fall elections. Even if the Soviet Cuban missile caper appeared to give the Russians an advantage, the President knew that the presence of Soviet missiles in Cuba did not appreciably alter the strategic balance of power. The United States had over four times as many missiles as the Russians, and the Cuban missiles would have given the Soviets only forty-four more. Did President Kennedy unnecessarily take the world to the nuclear brink for the sake of appearances and domestic politics?

## The Test Ban Treaty

The missile crisis forced both sides to tone down their Cold War rivalry. Khrushchev shifted back to emphasizing peaceful coexistence. Kennedy stressed the need for arms reductions. Direct phone communications, a "hot line," were established between Moscow and Washington so that the two leaders could talk to each other in time of crisis to reduce the chances of miscalculation and war. A mutual desire to control nuclear testing gave the two leaders an opportunity to improve relations.

President Kennedy, hoping to move arms negotiations forward, gave one of his finest speeches on June 10, 1963 at American University. He called upon all Americans to reexamine their attitudes toward the Soviet Union and the

Cold War. He called peace between the superpowers "the necessary end of rational men." He spoke of "making the world safe for diversity," conceding that every world problem did not require an American solution. Following the speech he sent Undersecretary of State Averell Harriman to Moscow to negotiate an agreement. The Russians proved eager to conclude a treaty. The agreement, signed July 25, banned all atmospheric and underwater testing of nuclear weapons. The Senate promptly ratified the treaty. The Nuclear Test Ban treaty was the first agreement that imposed a measure of control on the nuclear arms race. Soon after signing the treaty, the United States and the Soviet Union concluded an agreement for Russian purchases of American wheat. A year after the showdown in Cuba, Americans and Russians enjoyed relations friendlier than any time since World War II.

# Fighting Communism with the Green Berets and the Peace Corps

David Burner

David Burner, a political historian at the State University of New York, Stony Brook, writes that two seemingly disparate initiatives of John F. Kennedy—the Green Berets and the Peace Corps—were both designed as ways of waging the cold war. Kennedy and his advisers sought to counter Communist "national liberation movements" in Vietnam and other Third World nations without risking direct confrontation with China or Russia. The Green Berets were an elite force of the U.S. Army trained in counterinsurgency whose numbers and operations increased greatly when Kennedy was president. The Peace Corps program, begun in the Kennedy administration, enlisted American volunteers to live in developing nations and participate in education, agriculture, and health care projects. Burner argues that the Peace Corps held a special attraction to the young who responded to Kennedy's call for sacrifice and service.

The Peace Corps and the Green Berets, a new version of the special military unit of the 1950s, had a number of things in common. Both were intended as instruments of the war against communism. Each was, at least according to its original intellectual architects, to convert that war as far as

Excerpted from David Burner, *Making Peace with the 60s.* Copyright ©1996 by Princeton University Press. Reprinted by permission of Princeton University Press.

possible into a project for social reform and technocratic economic progress. The Special Forces warriors and the Peace Corps volunteers must be elites of purpose, intelligence, and technical sophistication.

## The Green Berets

The Green Berets, whose official title was the Special Forces, were in the same tradition of a mobile, autonomous elite to which the PT-boat officers of World War II had belonged. Kennedy, along with Secretary of Defense Robert McNamara, included them in the administration's design for the renovation of the country's arms. The Secretary had an appetite for efficiency and a reliance on modern methods of gathering information. Our need, the administration reasoned, was for a more versatile and flexible defense than the existing city-killing nuclear weapons, for if an emergency should arise, they would limit us to choosing between doing nothing and incinerating the globe. Kennedy and McNamara developed a system that targeted Soviet missile sites rather than cities. Troops of the Special Forces as the administration imagined them looked something like a human equivalent of this projected missile force. They were supposed to be independent, skilled in individual combat, sensitive and knowledgeable in working with civilians. Any Special Forces personnel parachuted into Hungary, it was suggested, ought to be familiar with the major Hungarian poets.

## Origins of the Peace Corps

The idea for a Peace Corps had in fact been around for some years before Kennedy's presidency. The notion, which Kennedy took up in the 1960 campaign, stood in counterpoint to an unflattering image that many Americans had come to have of their compatriots abroad—an image to which a novel published in 1958 by William J. Lederer and Eugene Burdick had notably contributed.

The figure from whom their book *The Ugly American* takes its name is physically ugly, a sign of plain moral character, and he is committed in a blunt earnest way to service and good work. He is an engineer whose ideas of appropriate technology, shaped to the needs and resources of traditional impoverished communities, have no appeal for the American, French, and Asian officials he encounters. Living simply in an Asian village, he demonstrates how bicycles can be used for water pumps. His wife, observing the bent backs endemic among the elderly women of the village, shows them that by using long-handled brooms they can liberate themselves from an affliction brought on by constant stooping. Standing in sharp contrast to the protagonist and his wife are the pleasure-seeking, the time-serving, and the merely incompetent Americans who live luxuriously in Third-World cities as pampered representatives of their country and its policies. The point of the novel, of course, is that the United States needs fewer of their kind in the rest of the world, and more Ugly Americans bringing unvarnished honest skills and knowledge to people who need them. In conformity to their times, the authors were concerned above all about the fortunes of the war against communism, which they believed American blundering was losing in the Third World.

The title, though not the argument, of the novel was quickly misconstrued. "Ugly American" soon came in common parlance to designate Americans who were the opposite of the novel's virtuously homely figure: Americans who flaunted their money, made loud demands for American standards of comfort, disdained knowledge of the language and culture of the country they were invading, and in general insulted their host population and embarrassed their homeland. The point of the Peace Corps was to field American teachers, agronomists, road surveyors, and the like who would be rewarded only by pride and commitment to the work: "Ugly Americans" in the original meaning of the book title.

## An Appeal to Young Idealists

No program advanced during Kennedy's presidency so perfectly fitted his call as did the Peace Corps to "ask what you can do for your country." During the presidential election campaign on October 14, 1960, he questioned extemporaneously a huge crowd of University of Michigan students about how many of them would be willing to spend years in Asia, Africa, or Latin America. His call to sacrifice stirred the audience. In San Francisco on November 2 he further developed the theme, observing in an address that people "without compassion" had been sent to represent the United States in countries suffering from poverty, disease, and illiteracy.

Once in office, Kennedy put his brother-in-law, R. Sargent Shriver, in charge of the Peace Corps. Installed before Vietnam and the dynamic of the civil rights movement radicalized much of the nation's politically articulate youth, the Corps attracted volunteers who could accept the government as a vehicle for social change. Peace Corps volunteers became the pride of their home communities. The program was, to be sure, meant to be an arm of the battle against communist infiltration of the Third World, and participants had to take a loyalty oath. But the designers of the Peace Corps sincerely intended the lessening of illiteracy and poverty as goods in themselves and perceived economic and social justice as integral to democratic pluralism. The condensed training was rigorous; Americans were actually required to learn to speak foreign languages; volunteers prepared to serve in the outlands, far distant from any access to exported American luxuries. The liberals of Kennedy's time shared in the continuing American preoccupation with the nation's character and ethos.

The Peace Corps was designed to target specific pockets of need in impoverished regions. In this it spoke more directly to the problem of deprivation and injustice than does the most militant of ideologies, Marxist or other, in which there is an intrusive element of love for the internal architecture of the ideology itself. The enlistment of idealists was superior to revolutionary philosophies that can define no way of relating individuals to one another save by some sort of exterior historical or social logic.

The Peace Corps has not limited itself to any age group, but it was intended to appeal especially to the young. Kennedy's identification with youth, which was an element in the ambience of his presidency, began in a simple and direct fact: he was young. And like the celebrants of youth during the later sixties, his admirers made much of it. But events had not yet moved to the near self-worship of youth. The Peace Corps' hundred thousand volunteers [as of 1996] with a median age of twenty-four are the most lasting of Kennedy's legacies to a responsible idea of youth. By respecting the cultures of their host nations, those members of the Corps who were not seduced by the American golden ghettos abroad built a good will whose face is as unsusceptible to measurement as is President Kennedy's effect upon them.

# The Race to the Moon

William B. Breuer

On May 25, 1961, President John F. Kennedy called on America to commit to a manned expedition to the moon. In the following excerpts from his book *Race to the Moon: America's Duel with the Soviets*, writer William B. Breuer examines the context of Kennedy's proposal, arguing that the president was motivated by a desire to best the Soviet Union in a cold war–inspired "space race." Breuer goes on to describe the Apollo space program and the triumphal flight that sent American astronauts Neil Armstrong and Edwin "Buzz" Aldrin to the moon's surface in July 1969.

Sending an American to land on the lunar surface was an urgent crusade for idealistic, energetic Jack Kennedy. Like most Americans, the president was chagrined and frustrated over a series of Russian space spectaculars. Only recently, he had reached a decision: the United States would not give up on the manned "space race," even though the Soviets had a commanding lead that many American scientists were convinced could not be overcome.

America's global prestige, Kennedy concluded, could not endure a second-place finish in man's quest for the moon. He was convinced that the Dwight Eisenhower administration and Americans as a whole had not and did not fully grasp the worldwide political and psychological impact of the space race with the Soviets. Since the conclusion of

Excerpted from *Race to the Moon: America's Duel with the Soviets*, by William B. Breuer. Copyright ©1993 by William B. Breuer. Reproduced with permission from Greenwood Publishing Group, Inc., Westport, Conn.

World War II in 1945, the United States and the Soviet Union had been competing vigorously to convince the world, especially the new and undecided Third World nations, which way to turn, which was the wave of the future—a free enterprise system like American capitalism or a regimented structure like Soviet communism. . . .

During his heated 1960 presidential campaign against Republican Richard M. Nixon, Kennedy had hit hard and repeatedly at the "space gap" he said that the Eisenhower-Nixon administration had "allowed." Kennedy told audiences across the land that the space gap symbolized the nation's lack of initiative, ingenuity, and vitality under Republican rule. Privately, Kennedy made no bones of the fact that he considered 70-year-old Eisenhower, who was completing his second term, to be both "tired" and "shallow" and lacking in the creation of innovative goals. . . .

On November 8, 1960, Kennedy defeated Nixon by a razor-thin margin—34,227,096 votes to 34,107,646. While the tally was hardly a mandate from the American people, Kennedy eagerly set into motion plans for implementing his New Frontier ideas. One of his first acts after being sworn into office, in January 1961, was to establish a blue-ribbon task force headed by his scientific advisor, Jerome B. Wiesner. Much to Kennedy's dismay, Wiesner and his panel threw cold water on the new president's space goal, concluding that the United States could not win the race with the Soviet Union to put a man on the moon. Russia was simply too far ahead in rocket thrust and other technological know-how.

There was no shortage of space-flight scoffers in the scientific community, at home and abroad. One of these was Vannevar Bush, chairman of the Board of Governors of the prestigious Massachusetts Institute of Technology, who had headed the Office of Scientific Research and Development in World War II. Testifying before the House Committee on Science and Technology in Washington on April 6, 1961, the 70-year-old Bush had sharp criticism. "There is too much hullabaloo over the propaganda aspects of the space program," the noted scientist declared. "Soviet space achievements have merely hurt our pride. . . . Putting a man on the moon is a stunt. Man can do no more than an instrument, in fact can do less. The days when men will be in space for long periods and for varied purposes are so far off that we need not hurry." Bush said that some of the futuristic proposals for space projects were "simply unadulterated absurdity."

## Soviets Send Man into Orbit

Across the Atlantic, the Astronomer Royal of England, Richard van de Riet Wooley, publicly declared that the idea of space travel was "utter bilge." When a Soviet Army major named Yuri Alekseyevitch Gagarin was launched into space on April 12, 1961, and orbited the earth for four and a half days, members of the British Interplanetary Society gleefully reported that Gagarin had penetrated "utter bilge."

Gagarin's stunning feat—the first human in space—electrified the world and provided the Soviet Union with an enormous propaganda tool with which to trumpet the superiority of the Communist system over America's free enterprise system. In a jab at the United States, Nikita Khrushchev loudly proclaimed Major Gagarin to be "the new Christopher Columbus."

President Kennedy was among the millions of Americans who were crestfallen. "It'll take some time to catch up to the Soviets," a somber Kennedy told the media. "We are, I hope, going to go in other areas where we can be first, and which will bring perhaps long-range benefits to mankind. But we are behind."

Kennedy fired off a message of congratulations to Premier Khrushchev, then began a frantic series of conferences with Jerome Wiesner and other space advisors. Everyone agreed that something had to be done—fast. American know-how was being ridiculed around the world for not being able to launch a man into space. Jack Kennedy was more determined than ever to put an American on the moon, ahead of the Russians. . . .

## Kennedy's Challenge

On May 25, 1961, President Kennedy was standing before a joint session of Congress to deliver his dramatic challenge to Americans. Speaking in his crisp New England accent and jabbing the air with his forefinger for emphasis, Kennedy declared:

> I believe that this nation should commit itself to achieving the goal, before this decade is out, of landing a man on the moon and returning him safely to earth. No single space project in this period will be more impressive to mankind, or more important for the long-range exploration of space; and none will be so difficult or expensive to accomplish. . . .
>
> In a very real sense, it will not be one man going to the moon . . . it will be an entire nation. For all of us must work to put him there. . . .
>
> No one can predict with certainty what the ultimate meaning will be of mastery of space.
>
> I believe we should go to the moon.

Seated at the side of the rostrum, Theodore C. Sorensen, Kennedy's close friend and confidant, thought the president looked strained in his effort to win over the legislators. Sorensen noticed that the president suddenly departed from his prepared text—the only time he had ever done so in addressing Congress—to declare: "Unless we are prepared to do the work and bear the burdens to make it successful, there is no sense in going ahead." Sorensen reflected that Kennedy's voice, while urgent, sounded a little uncertain.

At the conclusion of Kennedy's 47-minute message, which was televised "live" by the CBS, NBC, and ABC networks, there was only routine applause. As they left the crowded House floor after the president departed, members of Congress were split over his proposal to spend $40 billion in the decade ahead in an all-out crusade to beat the Russians to the moon.

What the Republicans and the conservative Southern Democrats derided as Kennedy's "huge spending schemes," the Democrat liberals described as "necessary sacrifices."

Fears were expressed that the huge outlay of funds might divert money from social programs such as aid to the elderly. But one fact was certain: President Kennedy had lobbed the ball into Congress' side of the court.

Riding back to the White House, Kennedy remarked to Ted Sorensen that the applause that greeted his proposal to go to the moon was "hardly enthusiastic." Despite the president's gloomy reading of the mood on Capitol Hill, he proved to be a consummate salesman. Congress bought his pitch for "this great American enterprise" and hiked the space budget by 50 percent for that year. The next year the space budget would be more than the combined funding for space exploration in all the years prior to mid-1961.

Landing a man on the moon first was a symbol of the continuing struggle for the minds of men between the United States and the Soviet Union, but no one could be certain that ultimate success would prevail. President Kennedy had committed the United States to a mighty endeavor with all possible speed and colossal expenditure of money and human resources. . . .

## The Saturn 5 Rocket

Aerospace scientists in mid-1967 agreed: the race to land a man on the moon between Uncle Sam and Ivan the Bear was nearing the home stretch, and the competitors were running neck and neck. Whether Uncle Sam would cross the finish line first depended in a large measure on the development of Saturn 5, by far the largest rocket ever built.

Everything about the Saturn 5 was gigantic. Weighing nearly 6 million pounds when fully fueled, the rocket was . . . four times more powerful than any American or Soviet rocket ever launched.

When topped with the Apollo spacecraft, the Saturn 5 stood 363 feet tall, six stories higher than the Statue of Liberty in New York harbor. It was designed to have the capability of boosting a spacecraft weighing nearly 50 tons to the moon or to place a 150-ton payload into orbit around the earth.

The Saturn 5, which had been in development since five months after President Kennedy issued his call for a moon trip back in 1961, had three stages. Its first stage contained five engines, which together generated 7 million pounds of thrust at sea level. This first stage was the biggest aluminum cylinder ever machined. Its valves were as big as beer barrels; its fuel pumps (for feeding engines at the rate of 700 tons of fuel a minute) were larger than refrigerators. Its pipes were big enough for a man to crawl through, and its engines were the size of trucks.

The first stage would boost the upper two stages and the spacecraft on the nose of the third stage to earth-orbital height (nearly 120 miles) and to near-orbital speed of more than 15,000 miles per hour. Finally, the third stage would inject the spacecraft into orbit around the moon.

There had been a mad scramble within the entire aerospace industry to gain the Saturn 5 contract. "But to give the entire financial and technological plum to a single contractor would have made all the others unhappy," Wernher von Braun [director of Marshall Space Flight Center of NASA] once recalled. "More important, Saturn 5 needed the very best engineering and management talent the aerospace industry could muster, so by breaking up the parcel into several pieces, more top people could be brought to bear on the project."

Consequently, the Boeing Company was awarded the contract on the first stage, North American Aviation won the second stage, and McDonnell Aircraft fell heir to the third stage. Systems engineering and overall responsibility for the rocket's development was placed in the hands of von Braun's team at the Marshall Space Flight Center. . . .

## The Apollo Spacecraft

The Apollo spacecraft had three basic components: the command module (CM), the service module (SM), and the lunar module (LM). Built by North American Aviation, the CM was the control center and the three-man crew's basic working and living area. The SM provided propulsions, power, and storage room for consumables, while the LM would ferry two of the three astronauts from the orbiting CM to the moon.

One of history's most complicated contraptions, the lunar module, although only a part of the Apollo spacecraft, was a huge vehicle in its own right. It was 12 feet in height, 14 feet in circumference, and almost 17 tons in weight. . . .

There were two stages to the LM: descent and ascent. With its four bent landing legs, each containing aluminum shock absorbers to lessen the impact, and the other protrusions, the LM had the appearance of a gigantic insect that Hollywood might have depicted as being alien life from some distant galaxy. . . .

## Flight Around the Moon

In November 1968, the Soviets barged back into the lead in the space race by sending the unmanned capsule *Zond* into orbit around the moon. Apollo leaders were jolted by the feat and Radio Moscow trumpeted: "This is the trailblazer for a manned moon landing."

Five weeks later, Uncle Sam surged out in front in the moon sweepstakes when *Apollo 8*, with Lieutenant Colonel Frank Borman, Colonel William Anders, and Navy Captain James Lovell aboard, orbited the moon ten times on Christmas Eve and Christmas.

A half-billion people saw on television what man had never seen before: the moon, close up. "The vast loneliness is awe inspiring," they heard Jim Lovell exclaim. On Christmas Eve, Bill Anders commented: "For all the people on earth, the crew of *Apollo 8* has a message we would like to send you." Pausing for a moment, he began reading: "In the beginning God created the Heaven and the Earth." After four verses of Genesis, Jim Lovell took up the reading: "And God called the light Day, and the darkness he called Night." At the end of the eighth verse Frank Borman picked up the words: "And God said, let the waters under the Heavens be gathered."

It was a time of rare emotion—in the orbiting *Apollo 8*,

in Huntsville, in Houston, in Washington, at Cape Kennedy, and throughout much of the world. The mixture of the Christmas season, the immortal words, the ancient and inscrutable moon, and the dazzling new technology combined to create a scenario never known before by humankind. . . .

## The Moon Mission

Before dawn [on July 17, 1969], astronauts Neil Armstrong, Edwin "Buzz" Aldrin and Michael Collins were awakened in their quarters at the Operations and Checkout Building in the Kennedy Space Center. After breakfast and a last-minute physical examination by doctors, the trailblazers donned spacesuits and, burdened by their heavy gear, waddled toward the transfer van that would carry them to launchpad 39-A.

There stood the awesome Saturn 5 rocket, the early morning rays of a bright sun glistening on its smooth surface. . . .

Many years later, Neil Armstrong recalled his thoughts as the moon pioneers headed for the Apollo spacecraft:

> Although confident, we were certainly not overconfident. In research and exploration, the unexpected is always expected. We would not have been surprised if a malfunction or an unforeseen occurrence prevented a successful moon landing.
>
> We knew that hundreds of thousands of Americans had given their best. Now it was time for us to give our best. . . .

Since being inched from the Vehicle Assembly Building to launchpad 39-A 57 days earlier, Saturn 5 had been undergoing the most exhaustive checkout that ingenious scientific minds could conceive. Them were some 500 engineers and technicians, working 12- or 13-hour days in the pre-lift-off operation.

Rocco Petrone, . . . director of launching operations, recalled the tension-racked period leading up to the lift-off:

> The pressure on our people was pretty severe. At a launch, a person just sat there glued to his console, watching the needles for any sudden changes, knowing that he would be

committing this big vehicle, with men aboard. The entire world was watching.

I walked through the console panel area right up to about the last 45 minutes before lift-off. I'd be checking on alertness, especially among men who had been working long hours. Were they fatigued? Were they concentrating on the dials? Was there any unnecessary chit-chat going on? . . . The team had to be as well rehearsed as any ballet, or any football team.

Now the historic flight of *Apollo 11* was ready to begin. At 9:32 A.M. (Eastern Standard Time), the astronauts were perched atop a pillar of fire as the first-stage engines of the Saturn 5 ignited for launch. Soon, the entire rocket-spacecraft assembly roared skyward, at first ponderously, then with greater and greater velocity. Thrown left and right against their straps in fitful jerks, the three astronauts felt as though they were riding a wild beast and hoped the animal knew where it was going.

Twelve minutes after blasting off, *Apollo 11* was in orbit around the earth. As it made one and a half revolutions, the astronauts, along with Mission Control in Houston, checked all systems. Ground stations in the global network tracked the spacecraft to determine if it were following the proper trajectory. Until this point, Mission Control could have altered the flight plan, causing the vehicle to remain in earth orbit or preparing it for an emergency landing.

Two hours and 42 minutes after leaving earth, Houston gave the green light, and the vehicle broke from the earth's gravitational pull (by increasing velocity to in excess of 25,000 miles per hour) and began the 238,857-mile, 73-hour trip to the moon.

On the fourth day of the flight, with the pockmarked moon as a spectacular backdrop, the three crewmen began the critical maneuver of inserting the spacecraft into orbit around the moon. All were aware that the honeymoon was over. As Michael Collins would express it: "We were about to lay our little pink bodies on the line."

Lunar orbit was achieved by slowing the spacecraft's velocity enough to allow it to be captured by the pull of the moon's gravity. After circling the planet ten times, the three men were awakened at 7:00 A.M. on the fifth day. Struggling into bulky spacesuits in the cramped *Columbia*, Neil Armstrong and Buzz Aldrin transferred to the lunar module, which they had christened *Eagle*. This was the moment of truth in America's decade-long endeavor to put men on the moon.

Seven months earlier, in *Apollo 10*, Colonel Thomas P. Stafford, Commander Eugene Cernan, and Commander John Young had performed a dress rehearsal of the mission by orbiting the moon, but no one had descended to the lunar surface in the weird-looking ferry. . . .

At 3:08 P.M., when *Eagle* was behind the moon and out of touch with Houston, Armstrong and Aldrin made ready for the final, precarious run to the lunar surface. Tension built at Mission Control until 3:46 P.M., when radio contact was reestablished with Collins in the orbiting *Columbia*. Collins reported to Houston: "Things are going just swimmingly, just beautiful!". . .

Armstrong and Aldrin continued their descent to an altitude of 3,000 feet and saw that the computer guidance system was taking *Eagle* toward a crater filled with boulders that could wreck the vehicle—and strand them on the moon with no hope of rescue. In this latest crisis, Armstrong took over manual control of the steering. Moments later, a red warning light came on: there were only 115 seconds of fuel remaining.

The *Eagle* touched down on a level plain near the southwestern shore of the arid Sea of Tranquility. Buzz Aldrin felt goose bumps over the strange sensation of actually being on the moon. It had been a close-run thing: only 45 seconds of fuel was in the tank.

At 4:18 P.M.—102 hours, 45 minutes, and 39 seconds after leaving earth—Neil Armstrong radioed to Mission Control: "The *Eagle* Has Landed!"

"You can be sure there are smiles on faces here!" Mission Control told the first moon men. . . .

For the next six and one-half hours, Armstrong and Aldrin remained aboard the *Eagle* and kept busy making the adjustments necessary to prepare for ascent back to the circling *Columbia* in an emergency. Perhaps they silently pondered what fate awaited them once they climbed out of

## Reactions to Apollo 11

*Social historian William E. Leuchtenburg describes how America reacted to the landing of two astronauts on the moon in July 1969. While some criticized spending so much money on the Apollo program, many viewed it as an affirmation of traditional American values that were being questioned in the later 1960s. President Richard Nixon, Leuchtenburg writes, sought to use the moon landing to enhance his political position.*

Not everyone joined in the applause for the great odyssey. The Nobel laureate Harold Urey asserted that the endeavor was not a scientific undertaking but pyramid-building. Critics pointed out that the astronauts were returning to an earth plagued by festering social ills, and argued that the vast sums Apollo 11 cost would have been better spent in solving terrestrial problems. Some doubted that twentieth-century civilization ought to be exported to other parts of the universe. "If there are people up there," said one teenage girl, "I hope they can stand us." Still others saw the lunar landing not as a triumph for "all mankind" but as a delayed consequence of the cold war, beginning with President Kennedy's resolve to out-race the Russians and ending with the flagstaff of the Stars and Stripes planted on the resistant surface of the moon.

Even the fantastic achievement of televising live color pictures of the moon walk to one billion viewers 240,000 miles away found nay-sayers. Admirers marveled both at the advanced technology and at the openness of a society that was willing to per-the craft and onto the moon. A few experts, prior to the flight, predicted that a good bit of difficulty would be encountered by humans due to the strange atmospheric and gravitational characteristics of the moon.

Their preparations completed, the astronauts opened the *Eagle*'s hatch and Armstrong began backing his way down

---

mit the world to witness an experiment in which the possibility of tragic failure was highly conceivable. But the telecast, it was said, added to the public relations nature of the proceedings. . . .

Many, perhaps most, in Nixon's America had few such doubts, for the voyage to the moon offered reassurance that the institutions and the beliefs the counter culture had mocked were essential to worthy achievements. Apollo 11, said Eric Hoffer, marked the "triumph of the squares.". . . *Time* concluded:

> The astronauts themselves were paragons of Middle American aspiration. Redolent of charcoal cookouts, their vocabularies an engaging mix of space jargon and "gee whiz," the space explorers gave back to Middle America a victory of its own values. It was little noted, except in Middle America where such things still matter, that among Neil Armstrong's extraterrestrial baggage was a special badge of his college fraternity, Phi Delta Theta.

For Nixon, the successful moon expedition provided otherworldly assistance to his strategy of offering himself as the exponent of middle-class ideals. He had shared in the glory through his trans-spatial phone call, and when the returning astronauts were plucked out of the Pacific and set down aboard the *Hornet,* Richard Nixon was on the deck of the carrier waiting to greet them. Even though he had contributed nothing to the exploit, the trip to the moon made more credible his claims for a stable social order that rewarded men of energy and perseverance. Like the astronauts, he would guide the ship of state through the perils of a dangerous universe to a safe destination on a sea of tranquility.

William E. Leuchtenburg, *A Troubled Feast: American Society Since 1945*. Updated ed. Boston: Little, Brown, 1983.

the ladder. At 1:56 A.M., the first human footprint was planted on the moon.

Armstrong's movements were televised to an estimated one billion awestricken earthlings by means of a small camera attached to the *Eagle*. They heard him say: "That's one small step for man, one giant leap for mankind!"

*Astronaut Edwin "Buzz" Aldrin poses beside the U.S. flag during the* Apollo 11 *lunar landing. The photograph was taken by Neil Armstrong.*

Fourteen minutes later, Buzz Aldrin came down the ladder. Like any typical moon tourist, Neil Armstrong had his camera ready to photograph his companion's arrival.

Armstrong and Aldrin were in high spirits, hopping about like bunny rabbits to display the ease of movement possible in lunar gravity. With his big backpack and heavy spacesuit, each astronaut weighed about 360 pounds on earth and only 60 pounds on the moon.

There was much serious business to do and little time in which to do it. While the two astronauts set up a seismometer (an instrument that records ground vibrations), collected 45 pounds of rock and soil to take back to earth for analysis, and conducted experiments in maneuverability, Houston came on the air to announce that President Nixon wanted to talk to them. In typical low-key fashion, as though a president talks to men on the moon every day, Armstrong replied: "That would be an honor.". . .

One fifth of the earth's peoples watched the dramatic and emotional flourish to man's conquest of the moon by way of television. In a similar scenario 437 years earlier, a brash young explorer named Christopher Columbus, who had sailed into the unknown from Europe, reached the uncharted New World and implanted the banner of Spain on a small island in the Bahamas. In contrast to the 1 billion people who watched Armstrong and Aldrin, Columbus had an "audience" of three or four bewildered natives.

Now the two moon men climbed into the ascent stage of the *Eagle* to return to *Columbia*. . . .

## Return to Earth

This was a crucial moment in the *Apollo 11* mission. Should the ascent stage engine fail to function, Armstrong and Aldrin would be doomed—marooned on a bleak and inhospitable planet 240,000 miles from their home base, earth.

Tension in the cabin and in Mission Control was thick enough to cut with a knife. Many millions of television viewers were also gripped by jangled nerves, although few realized the full consequence should the engine fail to start.

Suddenly, the ascent-stage engine began to fire. Then the vehicle lifted off the surface, ending the astronauts' stay of 22 hours and 17 minutes. It was 1:55 P.M. About four hours later, the ascent stage and the orbiting *Columbia* docked. Aldrin and Armstrong, one after the other, crawled into the *Columbia,* where a beaming Michael Collins grabbed each man by the hand and pumped it vigorously. Elated like mischievous schoolboys who had just pulled off a unique prank, the three astronauts broke out with a severe case of the giggles.

Now began the 64-hour journey back to earth. At 12:51 P.M. on July 24, 1969, the three Americans splashed down in the Pacific Ocean 950 miles southwest of Hawaii. A helicopter-borne recovery team plucked them from the water and the chopper headed for the aircraft carrier USS *Hornet.*

On the flight deck awaiting the moon men's arrival was President Nixon, who had winged nearly 7,000 miles from Washington on the first leg of a world trip in order personally to greet America's newest legends. Because the command module was named *Columbia,* the president requested the Navy band to play *Columbia, the Gem of the Ocean* when the astronauts stepped onto the deck.

Beaming broadly and freshly shaven, Neil Armstrong, Buzz Aldrin, and Michael Collins, emerged from the chopper; the band broke into the designated tune; and a few thousand sailors stirred up waves with rousing cheers. The tumultuous reception was short-lived: the three astronauts, on the slight chance that they might carry moon germs, were hustled into a mobile quarantine van. "We learned how monkeys in a cage feel," Collins would quip. . . .

The quarantine van holding Neil Armstrong, Buzz Aldrin, and Michael Collins was unloaded from the *Hornet* at Pearl Harbor, Hawaii, and then flown to the Manned Spacecraft Center in Houston. There the astronauts and their precious cargo of moon rocks and soil were transferred into an 83,000-square-foot lunar receiving laboratory.

After 18 days "in custody" (as Michael Collins described it), the three moon men were given conquering heroes' parades in New York City, Chicago, and Los Angeles. Then, flying in the presidential jet, *Air Force One*, they went on a 45-day, 24-nation goodwill tour that focused the world spotlight on America's superiority in science and technology. In the Cold War that was raging globally, it was a victory march.

# CHAPTER 3

# The Vietnam War

# The Kennedy Administration and Vietnam

William H. Chafe

When John F. Kennedy assumed the presidency in January 1961, the United States had several hundred military advisers in South Vietnam supporting the anti-Communist regime of Ngo Dinh Diem. Diem, with U.S. backing, had refused to participate in reunification elections called for by 1954 international peace accords made after France withdrew from its former colony. By the early 1960s his rule was being challenged by the National Liberation Front (NLF, also called the Vietcong), rebel forces supported by the Communist-led North Vietnam. By the time Kennedy was assassinated in November 1963, the United States had sixteen thousand troops serving as military advisers in South Vietnam—and Diem himself had been killed in a military coup that was quietly supported by the United States. Many people have since asked why Kennedy escalated U.S. involvement in Vietnam—and whether he would have continued to do so had he lived and been reelected in 1964. Historian William H. Chafe, dean and professor at Duke University, charts the evolution of Kennedy's Vietnam policies and places them within the context of the cold war against China and the Soviet Union.

Excerpted from *The Unfinished Journey: America Since World War II*, 4th edition, by William H. Chafe. Copyright ©1986, 1991, 1995, 1999 by Oxford University Press, Inc. Used by permission of Oxford University Press, Inc.

The Kennedy policy toward Vietnam emerged during 1961 as a product of four interrelated perceptions, all directly connected to the Cold War itself. First, was the conviction, shared by Kennedy and most of his foreign policy advisors, that communism remained a monolithic conspiracy spearheaded by China and the Soviet Union and committed to newly aggressive efforts to dominate the world. Still traumatized by the "loss" of China, the stalemate in Korea, and the McCarthyite mystique about "softness" in the State Department, the foreign policy establishment was intent on preventing any further defeats, especially in Asia. Dean Rusk, Kennedy's secretary of state, believed that [China] . . . was sponsoring aggression throughout the Asian subcontinent. The new secretary of state, one aide noted, "was possessed of a special mania about China and of a knack for arguing by dubious analogy." For Rusk, compromise in Vietnam was equivalent to appeasement at Munich, with China simply a modern-day surrogate for Hitlerite Germany. Nor was he alone in his perceptions. As Walt Rostow, a White House foreign policy advisor observed in 1961, the situation in the world was exactly comparable to the early 1940s when freedom was suffering setbacks everywhere. It was time to "turn the tide," Rostow declared, and Vietnam was a good place to start.

Second, the perception of communist intentions seemed confirmed by Nikita Khrushchev's endorsement of "wars of national liberation" as a means of promoting communism's global strategy. In a rambling eight-hour speech delivered in January 1961, the Soviet premier had advanced the new doctrine, probably with the intention of warning China that the Soviet Union would not sit idly by while its growing adversary flexed its muscles. But in Washington, the declaration was understood as a clear signal that the Russians were extending their confrontation with the United States into new arenas and, hence, escalating the struggle for global dominance.

Third, a series of reversals in other Cold War crises persuaded the Kennedy administration that a strong stand—

somewhere—was imperative, lest the world, and the Sino-Soviet bloc, become convinced that the United States was a weak, waning power. In April 1961 the Castro government in Cuba had humiliated the United States by crushing a CIA-sponsored invasion at the Bay of Pigs. Three months later in Vienna, Khrushchev and Kennedy met at the summit, where the Soviet leader exhibited an attitude of near contempt for his American counterpart, taunting him about wars of national liberation in Southeast Asia and throwing down the gauntlet on Berlin. Some observers noted a "siege mentality" developing at the White House, with the president himself asking his advisors "What's gone against us today?" As Kennedy told the *New York Times* columnist Arthur Krock, it was imperative that Khrushchev not "misunderstand Cuba, Laos, etc. to indicate that the United States is in a yielding mood on such matters as Berlin." In such a context, a strong policy in Vietnam became necessary, not only because the administration believed in the domino theory, but because it needed to take a stand somewhere, even 9,000 miles away, to show the Soviet Union that America was not ready to roll over and play dead.

Fourth, and finally, American involvement in Southeast Asia provided the new administration with a "laboratory" to test its own new strategy of "flexible response" to Soviet aggression. Convinced that the Eisenhower administration's reliance on nuclear deterrence and massive retaliation was inappropriate in a world full of trouble spots of differing dimensions, Kennedy and his foreign policy advisors embarked on a major buildup of conventional forces and counterinsurgent techniques. As [Kennedy advisor] Roger Hilsman observed, "The way to fight the guerrilla was to adopt the tactics of the guerrilla." New frontiersmen shuttled back and forth to Fort Bragg, exultant about the possibility that Green Berets—an elite antiguerrilla force—could become the vanguard for turning back insurgent forces in Third World countries. "It is somehow wrong to be developing these capabilities but not applying

them in a crucial theatre," Walt Rostow said. "In Knute
Rockne's old phrase, we are not saving them for the junior
prom." By deploying such forces in areas like Vietnam,
General Maxwell Taylor observed, the United States could
prove to the Soviets that wars of national liberation were
not "cheap, safe, and disavowable [but] costly, dangerous,
and doomed to failure."

## Deepening U.S. Involvement

For all these reasons, the Kennedy administration concluded by the fall of 1961 that America's involvement in
Vietnam must be deepened. The "credibility" of the United
States as a great power was on the line. As Kennedy told
[economist and ambassador] John Kenneth Galbraith,
"There are just so many concessions that one can make to
the communists in one year and survive politically." Galbraith particularly remembered his saying, "We just can't
. . . have another defeat this year in Viet Nam." Clearly, the
administration felt on the defensive, needing to find a way
of signaling to the Soviets that containment still functioned
as an effective policy, and needing a place to demonstrate
the new tactics being devised in Washington to forge an aggressive foreign policy. During those first few months in office, [National Security advisor] McGeorge Bundy recalled,
"We [were] like the Harlem Globetrotters. Passing forward, behind, sideways and underneath. [But] nobody
[had] made a basket." Partly as an accident, but mostly as
a logical extension of everything else that had happened
during the first six months of the Kennedy administration,
Vietnam became the battleground on which the United
States would attempt to make a point with the Russians,
demonstrating the administration's commitment "to pay
any price, to bear any burden, in the defense of freedom,"
so that its word elsewhere would not be taken lightly.

What [journalist] David Halberstam eloquently described as the "quagmire" of American involvement in
Vietnam emerged gradually during the first months of
1961, and then accelerated quickly with a November deci-

sion to commit substantial American troops for the first time to that distant country. In the process a fateful pattern of bureaucratic compromise and political equivocation developed that would cripple American policy for the next eight years. Ironically, Eisenhower had never mentioned Vietnam to Kennedy in his preinaugural briefing, concentrating instead on the crisis in Laos. But within ten days after taking office, Kennedy received startling information from General Edward Lansdale on the rapid erosion of support for the Diem regime. "This is the worst one we've got, isn't it?," Kennedy replied. By the end of March, intelligence officers notified Kennedy that "an extremely critical

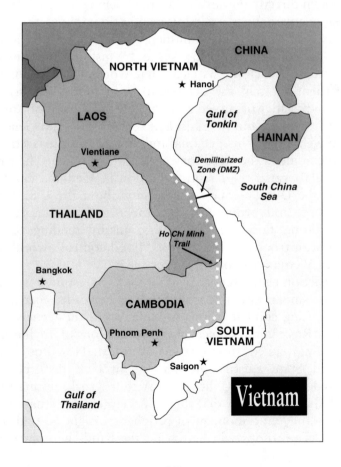

period [for Saigon] lay immediately ahead." Establishing a special task force on Vietnam, Kennedy proceeded to order five hundred Green Berets to Vietnam, authorized clandestine operations against the North, and dispatched Vice-President Lyndon Johnson on the first of a never-ending series of fact-finding missions to Southeast Asia. For the first time, active use of American combat troops was considered as a viable option. Still, in Walt Rostow's words, Kennedy was pursuing a policy of "buying time with limited commitment of additional American resources."

By the fall of 1961, such a policy no longer seemed adequate. Rapidly increasing Vietcong attacks appeared to threaten directly the survival of the Diem regime, while the Saigon government itself raised questions about the seriousness of America's commitment. Although Lyndon Johnson had described Diem as the "Winston Churchill of Southeast Asia," it was clear that words were no longer sufficient to stem the deterioration of morale. Many of Kennedy's advisors urged a major new investment of American resources, and the president sent Rostow and General Maxwell Taylor, his personal military advisor, to Vietnam to recommend the steps that needed to be taken. Their report elaborated the chaotic situation in Vietnam, emphasized the Diem regime's uncertainty about the U.S. commitment, and proposed using the occasion of a recent devastating flood in Vietnam to justify sending 8,000 American troops—allegedly for "flood control" work—to South Vietnam to bolster the regime.

Reaction to the report typified the U.S. response in a series of similar situations over the next decade. Fearful of committing combat troops in violation of the Geneva accords, Rusk initially rejected the suggestions of Taylor and Rostow. Kennedy himself was skeptical. How could the United States justify interfering "in civil disturbances caused by guerrillas," he asked Arthur Krock, noting that "it [is] hard to prove that this [isn't] largely the situation in Viet Nam." In a moment of prophetic insight he told one aide: "The troops will march in; the bands will play; the crowds will cheer; and in four days everyone will have forgotten. Then we will be told we have to send more troops. It's like taking a drink. The effect wears off, and you have to take another." The military, in contrast, recognized that 8,000 troops would be inadequate to the task and estimated that over 200,000 soldiers would be required.

Afraid to do nothing yet wary of doing too much, Kennedy eventually accepted a recommendation for compromise from Rusk and McNamara. The United States would join in a "limited partnership" with Saigon in a "sharply increased joint effort to avoid a further deterioration in the situation in South Vietnam." A combination of additional troops, American technology, and political reform would operate to forestall disaster and create a "turning point" in the struggle. A massive influx of helicopters would give South Vietnamese forces the necessary mobility to contain Vietcong guerrillas. Aircraft manned by U.S. pilots would fly support missions. American advisors inserted at critical points in the Vietnamese bureaucracy would streamline the administration of the South Vietnamese government. And the creation of new schools, better medical service, and land reform would ensure the loyalty of the Vietnamese people to the Diem government. It was all a policymaker's dream, each component designed to achieve, economically and efficiently, U.S. objectives. Although advisors like [W. Averell] Harriman and [Chester] Bowles warned against further support for a "repressive, dictatorial and unpopular regime," Kennedy was ultimately persuaded that American credibility required action. "That son-of-a-bitch [in Moscow] won't pay any attention to words," he had said in the summer. "He has to see you move." By December [1961], the United States had stationed more than 3,000 troops in Vietnam, four times the number there a year earlier. They would serve, in Taylor's words, as "a visible symbol of the seriousness of American intentions." They would also constitute a downpayment on a never-ending demand for more troops in order to preserve the initial investment. Kennedy's initial intuition had been correct, his later decisions a devastating error.

At first, Kennedy's action appeared to pay dividends. South Vietnamese troops launched a major offensive supported by American helicopters and aircraft. "Roaring in over the treetops," Roger Hilsman noted, "[the helicopters]

## A South Vietnamese Diplomat Defends U.S. Intervention

*The controversy in the 1960s over the wisdom of U.S. intervention in Vietnam lives on in conflicting historical interpretations of the period. Bui Diem, South Vietnamese ambassador to the United States from 1967 to 1972, provides his own perspective on U.S. intervention in a 1987 book cowritten with David Chanoff.*

For critics of the Vietnam War, the original decision to intervene was wrong, a result, as one of them put it, of a "steady string of misjudgments." It was wrong because American policymakers in the sixties failed to assess correctly the vital interests of the United States, because they exaggerated the geopolitical importance of Vietnam, and because they had an inflated concept of American capabilities.

Although it is neither my business nor within my competence to pass judgment on how the United States defined its interests at that time, it is my impression that such arguments are made on a distinctly *a posteriority* basis. I remember vividly the political atmosphere in the United States in the summer of 1964, the summer of the Tonkin resolution and Barry Goldwater's nomination, when I first visited this country. At that time the Johnson administration and practically the entire Congress were in favor of the commitment to defend Vietnam (the resolution passed in the Senate, 98 to 2, and in the House, 416 to 0). And so, *mirabile dictu,* were the national news media.

Moreover, the context of international affairs in that period provided good reasons for this nearly unanimous opinion, reasons that went beyond the specific perception of North Vietnamese ag-

were a terrifying sight to the superstitious Vietcong peasants. In those first few months the Vietcong simply turned
and ran—and, flushed from their foxholes and hiding
places, and running in the open, they were easy targets."
But in a nation full of swamps and forests, hiding places

---

gressiveness. It was then the aftermath of the Communist attack in
Korea, and China's Communist leaders were broadcasting the
most belligerent and expansionistic views, even as they attempted
to establish a Peking-Jakarta axis with Indonesia's pro-Communist
President Sukarno. For the fragile governments of Southeast Asia
the situation seemed serious indeed. Although twenty-five years
later it became fashionable among some Americans to belittle
Communist threats to the region's stability, among the responsible
governments at the time there was deep anxiety.

Even for those South Vietnamese who thought they saw the
inherent dangers in American intervention, there was still nothing illogical about it. The American interest in Vietnam, even its
land intervention, seemed a natural extension of U.S. policies in
Europe (the Marshall Plan, the Berlin airlift, Greece) and Asia
(Korea) aimed at preventing the expansion of combined Soviet
and Chinese power (at least until the early 1960s, no one could
imagine that the two Communist giants would become antago-
nists). And for the Europeans who were able to rebuild their
countries and save their democratic institutions, for the Germans
in Berlin, for the Greeks, and for the South Koreans, those policies were not wrong. Nor were they based on misjudgments of
geopolitical realities. In Vietnam the policy failed. But that is not
to say that it was wrong there either. The disastrous mistakes that
were made were mistakes in implementation rather than intention. But the thrust of the policy of containment and protection,
that I do not think can be faulted. It is, on the contrary, something for Americans to be proud of.

Bui Diem with David Chanoff, *In the Jaws of History*. Boston: Houghton Mifflin, 1987.

were easy to find, particularly when the local populace offered shelter—even if under duress—to Vietcong guerrillas. "You have to land right on top of them or they disappear," one American remarked. Moreover, South Vietnamese army troops were reluctant to engage the enemy. They relied increasingly on helicopter gun ships, and when they did fight, suffered a startling series of defeats.

In the meantime, the Kennedy policy foundered on the same shoals that had crippled all previous American efforts in Vietnam—the repressive and unresponsive nature of the Diem government. Refusing to insist on political reform and redistribution of land, Washington found itself bolstering a government in Saigon that consistently alienated the Vietnamese people. If Diem was the best that Americans had, he was not good enough. South Vietnamese troops made no distinction between Vietcong and innocent civilians. The use of napalm and chemical defoliants angered villagers, and a new campaign to relocate peasants from land they venerated simply increased popular hostility to the Saigon government. Moreover, most American money for services to the people was siphoned off into the coffers of corrupt Saigon officials, never reaching its intended beneficiaries. Diem, his brother, Nhu, and Nhu's wife—nicknamed the "Dragonlady" after a well-known cartoon character—became increasingly tyrannical and isolated. Although American military reports from the field contained a barrage of statistics that persuaded Washington officials that the war was being won, figures detailing enemy body counts and secure villages bore almost no relationship to reality. When reporters in Vietnam sent back dispatches to their home newspapers detailing the true situation, they were blasted as disloyal. "Why don't you get on the team?," one military official asked a critical journalist.

By the spring of 1963, the rosy optimism of earlier reports began to wane. A new fact-finding mission concluded that the war would "probably last longer than we would like [and] cost more in terms of both lives and money than we had anticipated." Although there were now 15,000

American troops in Vietnam, the war appeared to be stalemated. A massive chasm separated Pentagon reports of success and journalistic accounts of despair and failure. It became increasingly clear that, far from being able to alter the repressive policies of Diem, American aid simply drove him further into his own counsels. Whatever his intentions, Kennedy, like Eisenhower before him, had become hostage to a government in Saigon that in every way gave the lie to American propaganda that this was a battle for freedom and democracy.

The "sink or swim with Diem" policy exploded into crisis in the late spring of 1963 when Buddhists all over Vietnam rebelled against government repression. In response, Diem unleashed brutal reprisals, even ordering troops to fire into crowds of demonstrators. When a number of Buddhist monks dramatized their protest by setting themselves afire on Saigon's streets, Madam Nhu belittled their martyrdom, calling it a "bonz barbecue." Her insensitivity and contempt simply redoubled domestic anger against Diem and sparked worldwide protest. All over the globe, the CIA reported, governments and protest groups were condemning the United States for supporting a regime that brutally suppressed human rights. No longer was it possible for Washington to delude itself into thinking that victory was at hand.

Kennedy responded by appointing Henry Cabot Lodge to be his new ambassador to Saigon and by sending still another fact-finding mission to Southeast Asia. Lodge, Madam Nhu declared, came almost as a "pro-consul." Indeed, the former ambassador to the United Nations and vice-presidential candidate fit the description. A Boston Brahmin, Lodge coldly and calculatedly assessed the situation, intent on shaping policy in a firm manner that tolerated no equivocation or delay. Kennedy's fact-finding team, in turn, came back to Washington with advice that only reinforced Kennedy's reliance on his new ambassador. While General Victory Krulak assured the president that the war was going well and that Diem posed no serious problem, State Department advisor Joseph Mendenhall reported virtual chaos in Saigon. "You two did visit the same country, didn't you?," Kennedy asked.

## The Removal of Diem

Lodge quickly came to the conclusion that Diem had to be replaced. On the eve of his arrival, Diem, in total contradiction to a pledge he had made to outgoing Ambassador Frederick Nolting, ordered a massive assault by special forces units against the Buddhists and then blamed army generals for ordering the attack. Angry and disenchanted, Vietnamese military officers approached Lodge to ask whether the United States would support a coup. When Lodge reported the generals' approach to Washington, State Department advisors, with approval by phone from the president, sent back a cable declaring that if "Diem remains obdurate [and refuses to remove Nhu], then we are prepared to accept the obvious implications that we can no longer support Diem. You may tell appropriate military commanders we will give them direct support in any interim period of breakdown [of the] central government mechanism."

Kennedy now entered a period of critical decision-making. Although Kennedy's advisors, upon reconsideration, questioned the wisdom of the earlier cable, Lodge persisted. "We are launched on a course from which there is no respectable turning back: the overthrow of the Diem government," the ambassador cabled. In response, Secretary of State Rusk told Lodge that Kennedy "will support a coup which has a good chance of succeeding but plans no direct involvement of U.S. Armed forces." At the appropriate time, Lodge was given authority to announce suspension of aid to the Diem regime, which in turn would be a signal to the generals of U.S. compliance with their plans. General Paul Harkins was authorized to establish "liaison with the coup planners and to review plans," while Lodge was told to do whatever he had to do to "enhance the chance of a successful coup." Clearly, the United States was intimately involved in the decision to depose Diem.

In the meantime, Kennedy seems to have faced for the

first time the possibility that further American involvement in Vietnam would prove disastrous. According to former White House aide Kenneth O'Donnell, the president by late summer of 1963 had recognized the self-defeating nature of American participation in the war. Yet he was unable—or unwilling—to act immediately to extricate the United States from the situation. "If I tried to pull out completely now from Viet Nam," he allegedly told [Senator] Mike Mansfield, "we would have another Joe McCarthy red scare on our hands." In meetings of presidential advisors in late August, Attorney General Robert Kennedy raised the issue of whether the United States should any longer participate in the Vietnam venture—the first time anyone had asked *the* fundamental question about the war. General Charles de Gaulle [French president] simultaneously was pursuing a plan whereby the United States would pull out of Vietnam and sanction creation of a coalition government, including Diem, that would be acceptable to the North Vietnamese.

But for whatever reason, Kennedy rejected the option of withdrawal and proceeded inexorably along a course that would only further deepen U.S. complicity and responsibility for the fighting. Lodge received authorization anew to assure Vietnamese generals of American support in a coup attempt. While Kennedy publicly stated in September that "in the final analysis it is their war" and that, if the Vietnamese were not willing to fight, there was no amount of American support that could win a victory, he also declared that "for us to withdraw from that effort would mean a collapse not only of South Viet Nam but Southeast Asia. . . . I believe [in the domino theory]. . . . If South Viet Nam went, it . . . will give the impression that the wave of the future in Southeast Asia [is] China and the communists." On the night of November 1, 1963, with CIA officers at South Vietnamese army headquarters, the coup took place, Diem was arrested, and he and his brother were murdered. Just three weeks later, Kennedy himself was assassinated in Dallas.

## Assessing Kennedy's Vietnam Policies

Although Kennedy supporters continued to argue that the president, had he lived, would never have tolerated a continuation of American participation in the Vietnam debacle, the fact remains that Kennedy and his advisors had charted a course that step by step involved the United States inextricably deeper in the Vietnam tragedy. As Ambassador Maxwell Taylor later recalled, "Diem's overthrow set in motion a sequence of crisis, political and military, over the next two years which eventually forced President Johnson in 1965 to choose between accepting defeat or introducing American combat forces." Whatever the wisdom or error of the decision to depose Diem, American support for the coup carried with it responsibility for standing by those who had promoted it and for providing ever-increasing amounts of support as a desperate way of staving off ultimate defeat. As the authors of one U.S. government analysis reported, "the role played by the U.S. during the overthrow of Diem caused a deeper U.S. involvement in Viet Nam affairs. . . . By virtue of this interference, . . . the U.S. had assumed a significant new responsibility for the new regime, a responsibility which heightened U.S. commitment and deepened U.S. involvement." The die had been cast. However much Kennedy may have started to question the wisdom of the entire Cold War frame of reference, he and his Cold War advisors remained responsible for a fateful and tragic extension of the war—one that would lead to incalculable disaster.

# Lyndon B. Johnson Escalates American Involvement

Robert D. Schulzinger

The Vietnam War emerged from relative obscurity to become one of the decade's most divisive issues during the presidency of Lyndon B. Johnson, who held office from November 1963 to January 1969. In 1964 and 1965, Johnson made a series of decisions that greatly escalated America's involvement. He initiated sustained bombing campaigns against North Vietnam and introduced U.S. combat ground troops (as opposed to military advisers) to the conflict. Robert D. Schulzinger, a history professor at the University of Colorado at Boulder, traces the development of Johnson's Vietnam policy and describes the internal debates within the Johnson administration over Vietnam. He argues that Johnson placed a high priority on seeking political support for his Great Society domestic programs in weighing his options on Vietnam. Unwilling to concede defeat or to risk Chinese or Soviet intervention, the president sought to fight a limited war and was less than candid in telling the American public about the increasing military commitments in Vietnam.

---

While the Kennedy administration had undertaken a reassessment of its tactics in Vietnam in September and Oc-

Excerpted from "'It's Easy to Win a War on Paper': The United States and Vietnam, 1961–1968," by Robert D. Schulzinger, in *The Diplomacy of the Crucial Decade*, edited by Diane B. Kunz. Copyright ©1994 Columbia University Press. Reprinted by permission of Columbia University Press via the Copyright Clearance Center.

tober [1963], the basic policy remained victory in the civil war over the NLF.* Until the end Kennedy told [South Vietnam president Ngo Dinh] Diem that he gave "absolute priority to the defeat of the Communists." He maintained the same position publicly. In remarks prepared for delivery in Dallas on the afternoon of November 22 he would have maintained that Americans "dare not weary of the task" of supporting South Vietnam no matter how "risky and costly" that support might be. Yet by November 1963 the White House recognized a trilemma in U.S. policy toward Vietnam: doing more, doing less, or doing the same all entailed enormous risks.

Johnson became president promising continuity with his predecessor's personnel and policies. Keeping the advisers proved easy: Johnson told each White House staff member how vital he was to the success of the new administration. Determining precise policy proved far more difficult in the case of Vietnam. From November 1963 until July 1965 Johnson alternated between activism and passivity in setting Vietnam policy. He took a series of steps, some smaller, some larger, which, taken together, made the war a fully American affair.

The advisers Johnson retained had an interest in the success of the policy of American intervention to determine the government of South Vietnam. They agreed that abandonment of the U.S. commitment to Vietnam would represent a setback in the Cold War competition with Communism. Reversing the course of additional involvement in Vietnam also held domestic political perils. According to national security adviser McGeorge Bundy, "if we should be the first to quit in Saigon" Johnson would face the same sort of damage that President Harry Truman and Secretary of State Dean Acheson encountered when the Korean War went badly. The [military] coup of November 1, 1963 [overthrowing President Diem] did not foster the political

---

* National Liberation Front; political and military insurgents against the South Vietnam government supported by the Communist government in North Vietnam

stability or renewed South Vietnamese war effort expected by planners who had recommended American participation in Diem's ouster. Complicity in the coup had breached a significant threshold. Now Americans were willing to say directly who they wanted to take charge in Saigon and what policies they should pursue. Other Vietnamese factions, dissatisfied with the authorities, now justifiably could look to Washington for support. Faced with what Ambassador [Henry Cabot] Lodge characterized as the deep "dry rot and lassitude" within the government of South Vietnam, the new Johnson administration looked for ways to stiffen the nerve of the authorities in Saigon.

In January 1964 Johnson's militant advisers decided that the war had reached the point of a "definitive crisis." Walt Rostow warned of widespread defeatism in South Vietnam that could contribute to "the greatest setback to U.S. interests in the world scene in many years." To reverse the sense that the United States lacked a "viable concept for winning the war" he advocated "a direct political-military showdown with Hanoi" before the end of the year. Johnson would not go so far in an election year, hoping to keep the Vietnam story off the front pages and the evening news before election day. Johnson did not directly discourage his subordinates from pursuing an assertive Vietnam policy, but hoped for a delay in any showdown with the North. He seemed to agree with national security adviser McGeorge Bundy's caution that the worst political damage would come from appearing to "quit Saigon." With the situation so desperate, the time was not ripe to contemplate a peaceful settlement. "*When* we are stronger," Bundy wrote "*then* we can face negotiations."

In late January 1964 the Pentagon helped engineer another coup in Saigon, replacing General [Duong Van] Minh with General Nguyen Khanh. Americans in Saigon and Washington spent the next six months looking for ways to demonstrate United States support for the government of South Vietnam. [Secretary of Defense Robert] McNamara and [General Maxwell] Taylor returned to Vietnam in

March and May. They reported that "the situation has unquestionably been growing worse" since September 1963. The Viet Cong controlled 40 percent of the territory and the Saigon government was discouraged about the morale of the ARVN [Army of the Republic of (South) Vietnam] fighters. General Khanh told the Americans that only some "glamorous, dramatic victory," perhaps involving a U.S.-led invasion, would rally the South Vietnamese. Neither General William Westmoreland, the new U.S. commander in the South, nor President Johnson would contemplate action against the North in the spring. Westmoreland thought that such activities would divert the ARVN from less theatrical, but more productive actions clearing the NLF from the area around Saigon and the Mekong River Delta. Wanting to run in November as a leader of a country at peace supported by a wide popular consensus Johnson resisted too. He remembered how Chinese intervention in the Korean war had nearly ruined the Truman administration, and he would not approve moves that might provoke a similar intervention in Vietnam.

American policymakers still believed that the Saigon government needed assurances from Washington to boost morale. In June the president's principal advisers floated the idea of a congressional resolution supporting American air or ground action against the north. The State Department prepared a draft of such a resolution, but Johnson declined to submit it. Congress was debating a wide-ranging civil rights bill, an important element on Johnson's domestic agenda. Johnson also did not want to draw attention to Vietnam before the Republican convention met in mid July. The Republicans nominated Senator Barry Goldwater, who had accused Johnson of inaction in Vietnam during the spring primary season.

## The Gulf of Tonkin Incident

In early August, however, two controversial incidents off the coast of North Vietnam revived the idea of introducing such a congressional resolution and provided excuses for the first air strikes by U.S. forces against the North. Two U.S. destroyers, the *Maddox* and the *C. Turner Joy*, had conducted so-called De Soto patrols in connection with a covert operation, OPLAN 34-A. In De Soto patrols the American vessels supported the activities of the South Vietnamese navy by conducting surveillance, sometimes within the 12 mile coastal limits claimed by North Vietnam, along the North Vietnamese coast bordering the Gulf of Tonkin. The destroyers approached the coast in order to provoke the operators of coastal radar installations to activate their machines. The radars would then emit radio signals that would reveal their location to the sophisticated electronic equipment on the American ships. In response, the *Maddox* and the *C. Turner Joy* would notify the accompanying South Vietnamese patrol boats of the position of the North's radar, allowing the South Vietnamese to attack.

These De Soto patrols provoked the North Vietnamese navy to attack the *Maddox* on the night of August 2. Two nights later the commander of the *C. Turner Joy* believed that his destroyer also was under attack and ordered his gunners to return fire. They did so but hit nothing, probably because there were no North Vietnamese ships in the area and no attack had occurred. Nevertheless, Johnson ordered air strikes against four North Vietnamese bases and submitted to Congress the resolution prepared earlier in the spring. McNamara testified before Congress that both the *Maddox* and the *C. Turner Joy* had been attacked, although at the time he knew that only scanty evidence existed of the second attack. He also clearly did not tell the truth when he assured lawmakers that "the *Maddox* was operating in international waters and was carrying out a routine patrol of the type we carry out all over the world at all times."

McNamara's testimony and the conviction, expressed by Secretary of State Dean Rusk, that "an immediate and direct reaction by us is necessary," carried the day in Congress. On August 7 both houses passed the Gulf of Tonkin Resolution authorizing the president to "take all necessary

# Johnson's Escalation
# and the Antiwar Movement

*President Johnson was unable to limit the political repercussions of American involvement in Vietnam. Historians James S. Olson and Randy Roberts describe the effects that his decisions to escalate the war had on the emerging antiwar movement in 1965.*

The decision to Americanize and militarize the conflict in Vietnam jump-started the antiwar movement in the United States, broadening its narrow base to include new elements in American society. Student groups, New Leftists, and civil rights activists took a critical look at the war. More than thirty other antiwar organizations sprouted in 1965, and they were represented by the National Coordinating Committee to End the War in Vietnam, an umbrella organization established in August in Madison, Wisconsin.

American universities proved to be fertile ground for the antiwar movement. . . . At the University of Michigan in Ann Arbor, several faculty members organized a "teach-in"—patterned after the famous 1960 civil rights "sit-ins"—for March 24, 1965.

---

measures to repel any armed attack against the forces of the United States and to prevent any further aggression." The resolution also authorized the president "upon the request of any nation in Southeast Asia, to take . . . all measures including the use of armed force to assist" in its defense and resistance against aggression or subversion. The vote in the House of Representatives was unanimous, while in the Senate only two Democrats, Ernest Greuning of Alaska and Wayne Morse of Oregon, voted no. The resolution's extraordinarily broad grant of authority had no time limit. Later Johnson would use it to justify the greatly expanded American role in the war.

The Tonkin Gulf Resolution and the limited air strikes against the North did little to fulfill the planners' hopes of bolstering the morale of General Khanh's government. The

More than 3,500 students attended the teach-in, where faculty members discussed the nature of the war. Similar teach-ins occurred at campuses across the country in the spring of 1965, culminating with the "National Teach-In" at 122 colleges and universities on May 15, 1965. . . .

Other students ventured beyond talk. Some turned in their draft cards, others burned theirs. They played "tit-for-tat" with the government. As Johnson escalated the war, they escalated theirs. Berkeley students formed a draft resistance movement. "To cooperate with conscription is to perpetuate its existence, without which the government could not wage war," announced an antiwar leader. Even more concretely, activist Dennis Sweeney wrote, "I choose to refuse to cooperate with the selective service because it is the only honest, whole, and human response I can make to a military institution which demands the allegiance of my life." Johnson was a president facing two wars—both undeclared and both tearing at the heart of his domestic programs.

James S. Olson and Randy Roberts, *Where the Domino Fell: America and Vietnam, 1945–1995*. 2nd ed. New York: St. Martin's Press, 1996.

moody and impatient Khanh wanted the United States to mount a continuing bombing campaign. Assistant Secretary of State for Far Eastern Affairs William P. Bundy thought that Khanh's chances of remaining in power were only 50-50. He told Johnson that "even if the situation in our own view does go a bit better, we have problems in maintaining morale."

Yet the resolution and the air raids of August removed Vietnam from the political debate during the 1964 election in the United States. Johnson followed the advice of his assistant Bill Moyers to "keep the public debate on Vietnam to as low a level as possible." Goldwater dropped his earlier condemnations of Johnson's timidity. The president broadcast an air of moderation toward the war, refusing to recommend either withdrawal or intensification. Most of his listeners believed that he wanted to keep the United States out of a full-scale shooting war while at the same time preventing a Communist victory. Most supported that course. He made one major campaign speech on Vietnam in which he sounded moderate while leaving considerable room for a deeper U.S. commitment at a later date. He said that only "as a last resort" would he "start dropping bombs around that are likely to involve American boys in a war in Asia with 700 million Chinese." He could not predict the future, he said, but "we are not going north and drop bombs at this stage of the game, and we are not going south and run out and leave it for the Communists to take over."

## The Americanization of the War

The point of no return for the United States came in 1965. By June Johnson had taken a series of decisions that transformed the fighting into an American war. In July the president presided over a celebrated discussion with his key advisers about whether to increase the number of U.S. ground forces by 100,000 and call up the reserves. These discussions ratified earlier decisions to increase the American involvement in the air and ground war. They represented the last chance to reverse course, but by the time they occurred Johnson had so deeply committed the United States to the fighting that it seemed far easier to Johnson and his advisers to go forward than to diminish their involvement.

Throughout this period of gradually increasing American involvement the Johnson administration strived to keep the participation limited. Planners expected to break the will of the North Vietnamese, force them to stop the NLF fighters, without at the same time provoking retaliation from the Soviet Union or China. Most officials thought that limiting the geographical extent of the war would lessen the impact on the American public, sustaining support for it. Johnson and his advisers did not want the war to get out of hand: to "get the American people too angry" as [Secretary of State] Dean Rusk put it. An aroused public might demand greater force and the administration would lose control of management of the war. It became nearly impossible to limit the war and wage it effectively. Every step up the ladder of escalation alarmed the Soviets and Chinese and soon provoked reactions from a growing antiwar movement at home.

Political instability had persisted in South Vietnam after the U.S. presidential election of 1964. In December Senator Mike Mansfield warned Johnson that "we remain on a course in Vietnam which takes us further and further out onto the sagging limb." The succession of military regimes drove Johnson nearly apoplectic. "I don't want to hear any more of this coup shit," he exploded to aides. A continuous series of high-level visits went from Washington to Saigon and returned with the conclusion that the war was nearly lost. The morale of the ARVN had continued to sink as the initiative in the battle passed to the NLF fighters. ARVN field commanders and the government in Saigon seemed paralyzed with fear that the United States would not support them. In this atmosphere U.S. military advisers continued their search for morale boosters for the Saigon regime. General Maxwell Taylor, appointed ambassador to Vietnam in the summer of 1964, told Johnson early in 1965 that a program of air raids, lasting longer than the retaliatory strike of the previous August, would "inject some life into the dejected spirits" in Saigon. Johnson was willing to try, but recognized that the air raids had more to do with encouraging the flagging spirits in Saigon than changing the military fortunes of the war. He predicted to Taylor that "this guerrilla war cannot be won from the air." Taylor thought it would buy time and "bring pressure on the will of the chiefs of the Democratic Republic of Vietnam [North Vietnam]. As practical men, they cannot wish to see the fruits of ten years of labor destroyed by slowly escalating air attacks."

## Bombing North Vietnam

The program of sustained bombing of the North, code named Operation Rolling Thunder, began in February

[1965]. On February 7 NLF fighters fired artillery at the barracks of American marine base at Pleiku in the central highlands of Vietnam, destroying ten planes and killing eight Americans and wounding 126. American officials considered the attack another episode in a series, but they believed that the cumulative impact of assaults on Americans would panic the already demoralized South Vietnamese. After first ordering a single retaliatory strike against the North, Johnson authorized Rolling Thunder on February 13. The bombing was extensive. In April U.S. and South Vietnamese air force and navy planes flew 3,600 monthly sorties against fuel depots, bridges, munitions factories, and power plants in the North.

As had been the case for the previous several years, the results of the offensive did not meet expectations. In early March national security adviser McGeorge Bundy presented Johnson his gloomy assessment that "the chances of a turn around in South Vietnam remain less than even." Morale of the South Vietnamese government did not rebound sharply, because the infiltration of supplies and troops continued virtually unabated from the North to the South. North Vietnam quickly adapted to round-the-clock bombing. There were few industrial targets in the north and the North Vietnamese used darkness and cloud cover to rebuild destroyed highways and railroad bridges. Aware that Rolling Thunder offered little more than a temporary respite from the Viet Cong's ability to strike at will against the ARVN, General Westmoreland called for the American troops to conduct ground operations on their own throughout the South. The time had come, he told the president in March "to put our own finger in the dike."

Johnson still resisted a complete Americanization of the war. Speaking at Johns Hopkins University in April he offered "unconditional negotiations" with North Vietnam to end the war. He promised a development agency modeled on the Tennessee Valley Authority to serve nations along the Mekong River. Hanoi responded by demanding that the United States quit Vietnam and the South accept the program of the NLF to end the war. A few low-ranking officials in Washington, fretful about the direction the war was taking, thought that Hanoi had not flatly turned Johnson down, only provided "a statement of final objectives." Yet Johnson and his top advisers chose to regard the North Vietnamese statement as a rejection of calls to negotiate, setting the stage for the final, decisive escalation of U.S. participation in the war.

## The Enclave Strategy

In early May, McNamara, Taylor, and Westmoreland met in Honolulu. Reluctantly agreeing that bombing alone would not force the North and the NLF to stop their war against Saigon, they decided that American forces had to fight the war on the ground in the South if the Saigon government were to have a chance to stabilize. Still, concerned about the implications of Americans fighting throughout the South, they called for 40,000 additional U.S. soldiers to fight within fifty miles of American enclaves on the coast of Vietnam.

The enclave strategy lasted barely a month. The NLF operated at will in the remainder of the South and the Saigon government, now led by Air Marshall Nguyen Cao Ky, lost more authority daily. Westmoreland requested an additional 150,000 troops to carry the war throughout the South. McNamara returned to Vietnam and decided that Westmoreland was right. He recommended that Johnson approve sending an additional 100,000 men to Vietnam and ask Congress to authorize the potential call up of an additional 236,000 reservists. He told the president that "The situation in South Vietnam is worse than a year ago (when it was worse than a year before that). After a few months of stalemate, the tempo of the war has quickened."

McNamara framed two starkly unappealing choices: (1) To cut U.S. losses and leave under the best conditions possible—"almost certainly conditions humiliating the United States and damaging to our future effectiveness on the world scene." (2) To continue with present level of U.S. forces, approximately 75,000. That would make the U.S.

position progressively weaker and "would confront us later with a choice between withdrawal and an emergency expansion of forces, perhaps too late to do any good." Rejecting both, McNamara concluded that Johnson could do nothing but follow his third option: "Expand promptly and substantially the U.S. military pressure against the Viet Cong in the South and maintain military pressure against the North Vietnamese in the North." While no guarantee of eventual success "this alternative would stave off defeat in the short run and offer a good chance of producing a favorable settlement in the longer run."

## July Meetings on Vietnam

In late July, Johnson consulted with his principal advisers on the future of American involvement in the ground war. In a series of meetings Johnson appeared frustrated with the inability of the South Vietnamese to make progress, bewildered at the unresponsiveness of the North to his proposals for negotiations, and skeptical about the usefulness of the dispatch of additional United States troops. Most of all, however, he agreed with nearly all of the advisers that the costs of an NLF victory were unacceptably high, because it would shake world confidence in American credibility. Secretary of the Navy Paul Nitze, primarily interested in maintaining good relations with Europe and appearing strong to the Soviet Union, remarked that "the shape of the world will change" were the United States to acknowledge that "we couldn't beat the VC." Secretary of the Army Stanley Resor concurred that "we can't go back on our commitment. Our allies are watching carefully."

The only course tolerable to Johnson was continuation of a gradual buildup of U.S. forces—the very policy that had not succeeded in defeating the NLF or bolstering the morale of the South Vietnamese government for the previous year. He hoped to keep the buildup quiet and present it as a continuation of policy, not a dramatically increased American commitment. He expected that by downplaying the significance of the new commitment he would avoid a divisive public debate and prevent the sort of public war weariness that had wrecked the Truman administration during the Korean war. At the height of his authority with Congress, he feared that congressional discussion of Vietnam would interfere with passage of his ambitious program of domestic reform legislation, the Great Society. . . .

Only one of Johnson's principal advisers, Under Secretary of State George Ball, openly voiced dissent from the prevailing willingness to go forward with 100,000 more soldiers. He thought that the United States could not win in Vietnam without risk of drawing China, and possibly even the Soviet Union, into the fighting. Ball thought that public opinion would not tolerate a long war. The longer the war went on and casualties mounted there would be demands by an impatient public "to strike at the very jugular of North Vietnam." Ball thought that even greater dangers to U.S. credibility existed should the war go on for more than a year. "If the war is long and protracted, as I believe it will be," he said "then we will suffer because the world's greatest power cannot defeat guerrillas.". . .

No other advisers joined with Ball in expressing such pessimism in the public meetings. Sensing that Johnson believed the risk of a Communist victory greater than the challenges of greater commitment, they recommended sending the troops McNamara thought were needed. . . .

Eventually the president and all of his advisers with the exception of Ball, and possibly [Clark] Clifford, concurred that adding 100,000 Americans to the 90,000 troops already in Vietnam would stave off defeat without provoking a backlash against the war in Congress or with the public. Johnson and most advisers hoped to characterize the doubling of troops as only a continuation of current policy. To that end they rejected McNamara's request to call up reserves. Even so, Johnson's advisers worried about the implications of the Americanization of the war. Horace Busby, one of Johnson's most politically astute advisers, told the president that it was "self-deceptive" to claim that the troop buildup represented only an extension of what the U.S. had done in the past several years. Yet Johnson encouraged such deception, hoping to maintain the wide consensus in support of his policies.

Johnson informed congressional leaders on July 27 of the decision to send another 100,000 soldiers but not to call up reserves. Most Democratic and Republican leaders expressed support. . . .

He announced the dispatch of additional troops at a low-key mid-day press conference on July 28, 1965. For the rest of 1965 the White House continued to insist that the additional troops did not change American policy in Vietnam, and Johnson stressed the Great Society as the centerpiece of his administration's accomplishments. When Secretary of the Treasury Henry Fowler complained that the fighting strained the economy and had caused prices to rise, the White House warned him to keep his views quiet. "What the President doesn't want to do," Bill Moyers told Fowler, "is, in essence, say to the business community that we have declared war in Vietnam." Keeping the buildup quiet, however, backfired dramatically. The stealth with which Johnson announced the additional commitment of American troops contributed later to a wide belief that administration officials did not tell the truth, and a wide "credibility gap" opened.

Whether declared or not, the United States was fully at war after July 1965. The decision to send an additional 100,000 troops by the end of 1965 did not stop the buildup. During 1966 and 1967 the number of U.S. soldiers in Vietnam rose from 190,000 to 535,000. Many were conscripts, and perhaps as many as half of those who ostensibly volunteered did so because they faced induction through selective service. Yet this huge expeditionary force could not prevail against the NLF and several hundred thousand regulars from the North Vietnamese People's Liberation Army.

# The Tet Offensive Transforms the American Debate over Vietnam

David W. Levy

In late January and early February 1968, during Tet, the Vietnamese New Year holiday, North Vietnamese troops and South Vietnamese rebels (the Vietcong) launched major attacks throughout South Vietnam, including its capital of Saigon where a squad of Vietcong troops stormed the grounds of the American embassy. Virtually all of the attacks were immediately beaten back with heavy Vietnamese losses, making Tet a tactical victory for the United States and South Vietnam. However, David W. Levy, a professor of U.S. history at the University of Oklahoma, argues that the Tet Offensive resulted in a psychological defeat for the United States because it seemed to lend credence to antiwar arguments about the futility of the U.S. war effort. The antiwar movement quickly utilized Tet to reinforce its arguments that America should withdraw from Vietnam. President Lyndon B. Johnson conducted a major reassessment of the war effort after Tet and rejected a demand from his generals for two hundred thousand more troops. Levy also recaps events of the tempestuous presidential campaign of 1968 in which Vietnam was a dominant issue, including the stunning withdrawal of Johnson from the race, the violent events surrounding the Democratic National Convention in Chicago, and the ulti-

Excerpted from David Levy, *Debate over Vietnam*, pp. 143–52. Copyright ©1991 by The Johns Hopkins University Press. Reprinted by permission of The Johns Hopkins University Press.

mate victory of Richard Nixon, the Republican candidate who spoke of a "secret plan" to end the war.

News of the Tet offensive hit America a little like one of those "earthquake bombs" being used in Vietnam to uproot forests and make landing fields. On the last day of January 1968, during the customary cease fire to celebrate the lunar new year, the Communists launched surprise attacks from one end of South Vietnam to the other. Within twenty-four hours they assaulted five of the country's six largest cities; they also hit thirty-six out of forty-four provincial capitals and more than a hundred other places, including key American army and air force installations. The most shocking news came, confusedly, out of Saigon itself. The enemy entered the capital in force and, in addition to some neighborhoods, struck the huge airport complex at Tan Son Nhut, President [Nguyen Van] Thieu's palace, the government radio station, and the ARVN [Army of the Republic of (South) Vietnam] General Staff Headquarters. A small team of Vietcong sappers even blew its way onto the grounds of the American embassy and held out against the marines through the night. "The only thing that could have been more dramatic," remarked a Chicago professor on the day after the start of the offensive, "would have been if they had burst into [Ambassador Ellsworth] Bunker's private office and shot him as he sat at his desk signing letters." Senator [Eugene] McCarthy, campaigning in New Hampshire, told a crowd: "A few months ago we were told sixty-five percent of the population was secure. Now we know that even the American embassy is not secure."

The enemy paid a fearful price for the Tet offensive. Tens of thousands of North Vietnamese and Vietcong troops were killed in the effort, and the Vietcong political operation was badly damaged. Their hopes for a civilian uprising against the Thieu-Ky regime never materialized. With the exception of the occupation of Hue, which resulted in a bloody battle of three weeks and the destruction of the old city, their gains on the ground were short lived. American forces handled themselves superbly and, in most places, reversed enemy gains and "mopped up" the resistance within the week. With a few exceptions, even the ARVN fought doggedly and well. General [William C.] Westmoreland, President Johnson, and other military and political officials issued calming and optimistic assessments of the situation.

## The Impact of Tet

But the full impact of Tet could not be measured by the confident reports of regained ground and devastating enemy body counts. The effect of the episode on American public opinion was titanic; indeed, the Tet offensive was probably the single most important event in reversing American support for the war. It seemed to substantiate the contentions of the war's opponents. Two of the most publicized stories of that traumatic week, for example, raised again the moral ambiguity of the whole effort. On the evening of February 2 twenty million Americans watching the Huntley-Brinkley Report on NBC saw General Nguyen Ngoc Loan, chief of the South Vietnamese police, draw his pistol, put it to the head of a terrified, captured Vietcong, hands tied behind his back, and pull the trigger. It was an act of such naked brutality, so at odds with civilized notions of justice and decency, that it served graphically to confirm the charges that America's allies in Vietnam were brutal men, morally indistinguishable from the brutal men on the other side. And then came the best known remark of that week, the comment, on February 7, of an American major at the village of Ben Tre in the Mekong Delta: "It became necessary to destroy the town in order to save it," he told Peter Arnett of the Associated Press. The village of thirty-five thousand had been attacked by twenty-five hundred enemy troops, and in order to kill them the bombers were called in. To opponents of the Vietnam war, the quote served as a summary of the entire policy; it seemed as though the United States was destroying the whole country in order to save it.

If the morality of the war was called into question by those two moments of Tet, its costs were also graphically illustrated to millions of people back home. The picture of the slain American boys on the embassy grounds (eleven hundred Americans died during the first two weeks of February); the haunted, wide-eyed faces of marines at Hue or in the Cholon District of Saigon, fighting house to house to retake lost ground; the sight of the American wounded, writhing in agony as they awaited evacuation to hospitals; the heart-breaking pictures of thousands of new, bewildered refugees; the estimate that the rural pacification program had been set back at least six months and that in many places it would mean starting over practically from scratch—all seemed to verify the claims of those in the antiwar movement who argued that the whole thing was simply not worth it. Finally, the contention of those opposed to the war that American leaders were inept or, even worse, that they were neither trustworthy nor honest seemed amply confirmed. How could they have been taken by surprise like this? How could the president and the generals and the others—if they were honest men—have given the country, only three or four months ago, such glowing reports of progress, such assuring predictions?

To military experts, therefore, Tet was a substantial, even a crushing, victory for America. To them (and to some scholars who have studied the matter closely), the media coverage was worse than an inaccurate overreaction; it was irresponsible sensationalism of the worst sort, and it severely undercut the ability of the United States to fulfill its responsibilities in Vietnam. To opponents of the war, on the other hand, the Tet offensive was persuasive proof of what they had been saying all along. It provided, moreover, an opportunity, however regrettable the circumstances, to convince the American people of the immorality and the futility of this war. The antiwar attack on the administration's Vietnam policy poured forth on every conceivable front.

Even before Tet, SDS [Students for a Democratic Society] had announced "Ten Days of Resistance" for April, and the year-old Student Mobilization Committee set out to organize a strike of one million high school and college students. Clergy and Laymen Concerned about Vietnam raised anew the moral issue by gathering in Washington in February to hold a prayer service at Arlington Cemetery and to issue its four-hundred-page book, *In the Name of America,* an inquiry into "the conduct of the war in Vietnam by the armed forces of the United States," raising questions about American behavior with respect to principles of law and morality. More pragmatically, the Business Executives Move for Vietnam Peace called for an end to the war simply because "when a policy hasn't proved productive after a reasonable trial it's sheer nonsense not to change it." Meanwhile the Congress was growing more restive. After new hearings that culminated in February, Fulbright and about half of his Foreign Affairs Committee concluded that the Gulf of Tonkin Resolution had been an overreaction that had been obtained through "misrepresentation." There were strident but futile calls, both for its repeal and for a full congressional investigation into our Vietnam policy. Most ominous of all, in the wake of Tet some who had been supportive or neutral in opinion began to express their doubts: Walter Cronkite of CBS, Frank McGee of ABC, the *Wall Street Journal,* and others. Even the president's so-called "Wise Men," that group of close, veteran advisers, developed serious second thoughts after Tet. Upon reassessing the situation at the end of March, one of them, Dean Acheson, concluded that "we must begin to take steps to disengage."

## President Johnson and Vietnam

The meeting of "the Wise Men" was only one part of a major reassessment of the war by the Johnson administration. The enemy's impressive showing, General Westmoreland's well-publicized request for still another two hundred thousand men, and the recognition that public support for both the president and the policy was crumbling rapidly and doing so in an election year provided the cause and the backdrop for extensive discussions in February and March. These discussions—organized by Clark Clifford, who had just replaced Secretary of Defense Robert McNamara and begun his thorough review of all aspects of the war—were the most intense since the decision to Americanize the war in July 1965. They resulted in a number of decisions. The administration turned against the Westmoreland recommendation to expand the war and rejected his request for additional men. Westmoreland himself was brought home and replaced by General Creighton Abrams. The administration concluded, moreover, that much more of the fighting would have to be borne by the ARVN; there would be substantial material aid from America, but efforts would now have to be in the direction of a general de-escalation and the extrication of the country from the quagmire. These moves, writes historian George Herring, "represented a significant shift in American policy—a return, at least in part, to the principle that had governed its involvement before 1965 and adoption, at least in rudimentary fashion, of the concept of Vietnamization, which would be introduced with much fanfare by the Nixon administration a year later."

Rarely in American history has a president had a rougher time than Lyndon Johnson had in the first four months of 1968. Not all of it had to do with Vietnam. On January 23 the North Koreans captured the intelligence ship *Pueblo,* thus opening a long period of tension with yet another east Asian nation. During the first week of March, the National Advisory Commission on Civil Disorders, formed by the president the previous year to analyze the rash of race riots plaguing the nation's cities, issued its somber report. As if to give credibility to the commission's warnings about racial injustice and the creation of a biracial society, news of Martin Luther King, Jr's., assassination came on April 4, and rioting, burning, and looting exploded in 168 cities and towns across America, one of the worst instances occurring just three blocks from the White House. More than seventy thousand army and national guard troops were called to riot duty. Other problems faced the president: a serious "gold drain" to foreign nations, a suddenly alarming inflation rate, and bad publicity in connection with a rumored tax increase. But even with the problems assailing Johnson, the mounting political challenge against a sitting president, from within his own party, was still something quite extraordinary. On March 12 Senator McCarthy, capitalizing on the general discontent and with the enthusiastic help of thousands of antiwar college students who canvassed the state door-to-door, won 42 percent of the vote and twenty of twenty-four electors in the New Hampshire Democratic primary. It was taken as a stunning defeat for the president, and four days later things got even worse: the popular senator from New York, Robert Kennedy, announced that he too would seek the nomination on an antiwar program.

In a major speech to the nation on March 31, probably delivered primarily to quiet domestic antiwar protest, President Johnson took pains to appear as a man of peace and principle. He was ordering, he announced, a major reduction in the bombing of North Vietnam without demanding any reciprocal move by the enemy; he hoped that some gesture on its part would enable him to dispense with the bombing entirely. He was eager for peace talks at any time and in any place, he said, and if they should occur, America would be represented by Averell Harriman. Then, thirty-five minutes into the speech, Johnson stunned all those viewers who were still watching on that Sunday night: "I shall not seek, and I will not accept, the nomination of my party for another term as your president." By withdrawing from the contest, he said, he hoped to emphasize the sincerity of his quest for peace. He could now make his decisions in the best interests of the country without worrying about the next primary or the views of political rivals. Predictably, some peace activists reacted to Johnson's announcement with unrestrained joy, others with sarcastic skepticism; but almost everyone realized that suddenly everything was changed.

There continued to be demonstrations, of course; after six years of trying to end the war, they proceeded out of a kind of habit. In early April a few antidraft rallies were held, but they were quickly eclipsed by the King assassination and the ensuing riots. The Student Mobilization's effort, the Ten Days of Resistance, occurred later in that month. There were numerous campus activities of various sorts—according to one accounting, more than two hundred in the first six months of 1968—but it is difficult to tell how many of these were concerned with Vietnam and how many with civil rights or with narrowly local matters. The most widely noticed protest of the season took place at Columbia University, where students led by SDS president Mark Rudd occupied some buildings until the police removed them forcibly after a week, but that dramatic episode had more to do with local issues than with the war. The plain fact was that after Johnson dropped out of the presidential race, attention turned almost entirely to politics, and seeing little prospect for a change in policy through the Republican party, antiwar activists directed their efforts to the Democrats. Increasingly they left the peace movement to organize rallies, man phones, and walk neighborhoods for Gene McCarthy or Bobby Kennedy. Not even Kennedy's assassination on June 5, the night of his victory in the California primary, changed the focus. All eyes were on the showdown, the Democratic National Convention scheduled for Chicago during the last week of August.

## The Chicago Convention

Americans had never seen a political convention like the one in Chicago in 1968. The city, under its tough mayor, Richard J. Daley (who, during the King riots in April, had ordered police to shoot-to-wound looters and shoot-to-kill arsonists), was an armed fortress. Chicago's twelve thousand police were put on twelve-hour shifts; six thousand soldiers at nearby Glenview Naval base were held in readiness; five thousand national guardsmen were deployed; and hundreds of plainclothes detectives, Secret Service men, sheriffs deputies, state police, and infiltrators were braced for the worst. There were no shortages of squad cars, tear gas and gas masks, night sticks, riot helmets, small arms, and shotguns. The Amphitheater, where the convention was to be held, was protected by a cyclone fence topped with barbed wire; elaborate procedures were devised to insure that only the authorized could get into the hall. For weeks before the event the most radical antiwar spokesmen had indulged in language that would have made anything less than maximum readiness irresponsible. The talk ranged from snarling traffic, disrupting the convention, and forcing confrontations with the authorities, all the way to preventing the convention from occurring, poisoning the city's water supply, setting fires in neighborhoods, and stirring up armed rioting in the huge black ghetto on the city's south side.

The actual debate over Vietnam took place, in Chicago, in two vastly differing settings. The convention itself faced the issue. As a concession to the minority of delegates supporting Eugene McCarthy or George McGovern (who had entered the race after Robert Kennedy's assassination and had inherited much of Kennedy's support), the convention permitted a full-scale, three-hour discussion of the war on national television. At issue were a Vietnam plank for the platform that had been dictated by the White House and a plank, critical of administration policy, drafted by followers of McCarthy and McGovern. After a dozen speeches repeating the usual arguments and making the usual appeals, and amid a boisterous, unruly, and rude assemblage of cheering and booing delegates on both sides, the majority plank, endorsed by Johnson's heir-apparent, Vice President [Hubert H.] Humphrey, prevailed by a vote of 1,568 to 1,041. The melee revealed, for all the nation to see, the deep divisions within the Democratic party over the war. Following the debate the Democrats chose Humphrey to be their standard bearer in the campaign ahead.

The second "debate" took place on the streets. It was wild, brutal, and inarticulate. Those who afterwards wanted to assess blame for the gross excesses could find plenty enough to go around. Along with those who came to Chicago to exercise their right to dissent and who wanted to work "within the system" as conscientious citizens of a free society, were some who came to cause trouble. Frustrated by years of futile efforts to stop the war, now, at last, refusing to worry about how their actions would be received by middle America, determined to force a confrontation, these few carried on their sport in the streets and parks of Chicago. They smoked dope and made love with equal abandon and equal openness; they burned American flags and waved Vietcong ones; they carried rude signs and held ill-organized, chaotic "actions" in various quarters of the city. They pelted the police with eggs and rocks, referred to them as "pigs" and "Fascists" and "cocksuckers," and cast aspersions about the sexual practices of their wives and mothers. They constituted a flowing, amorphous, combustible element. They monopolized media attention, provoking terror and hatred among those Americans who still believed in order, and they were able to quite overwhelm the more respectable, reasoned, and dignified opponents of the war. Meanwhile, the police were behaving no better. They committed countless acts of sadistic brutality, engaged in what a later investigation termed "a police riot," clubbed and gassed defenseless and innocent people— young and old, men and women, protesters, bystanders, journalists, tourists, and residents of Chicago who got caught in the middle. They charged crowds of dumbfounded onlookers, pushed people through the plate-glass windows of the Conrad Hilton Hotel, and aimed their nightsticks at heads and groins with unrestrained viciousness. They did these things in full view of the cameras, and when the reports and the pictures reached the delegates inside the Amphitheater, the outrage was hard to contain.

## The 1968 Election

The campaign itself was a fitting climax to a year as harrowing as 1968. The Republicans chose the reborn Richard

M. Nixon—defeated for the presidency in 1960, defeated for governor of California in 1962, and supposedly retired from politics—to attempt the impossible: bring the party back from its devastating defeat of 1964. Nixon and his running mate, Spiro Agnew, the governor of Maryland, emphasized unifying the American people after the orgies of civil disorder during the preceding four years. They would, they said, restore confidence in America and represent the concerns of the vast majority of silent Americans who were dismayed by what their country had become. Nixon was well positioned in the debate over Vietnam. The man who led the denunciation of Truman for having lost China and who stalked Alger Hiss to the bitter end had impeccable credentials as an uncompromising foe of communism. He took the position that Vietnam should not be a campaign issue because of the sensitive status of preliminary Paris peace talks. He advocated "an honorable peace," and there was a good deal of talk about his "secret plan" for bringing it about; but the details remained sketchy.

The contest was complicated by the presence of a third candidate, Governor George Wallace of Alabama, who also attempted to capitalize on the general discontent with social disorder and the policies of Democratic liberals and intellectuals. He once threatened to run over any demonstrator stupid enough to lie down in front of *his* car and offered to throw the intellectuals and their briefcases into the Potomac after he was elected president. By demanding "law and order" and attacking "the welfare state," Wallace was able to appeal subtly to a latent racism that he found equally present among southern rural folks and northern blue-collar workers. His position on Vietnam was not much different from that of his running mate, former General Curtis LeMay, who suggested bombing North Vietnam "back to the stone age" and once remarked that America suffered from "a phobia about nuclear weapons."

As always, the Vietnam issue was hardest for the Democrats. They left Chicago with a shattered party and with very bitter feelings toward one another. Some antiwar

Democrats blamed Humphrey, as much as Mayor Daley, for the violence and brutality in the streets. Not even Humphrey's record as a consistent champion and innovator of liberal causes could save him from the Vietnam quandary. He had to walk the impossible line between supporting the Johnson policies and winning the allegiance of the war's critics. He trailed badly in the polls from the beginning. During the campaign he edged cautiously away from the president by advocating a complete bombing halt, and McCarthy begrudged him a tardy and lukewarm endorsement. Not even Johnson's announcing a complete bombing halt a week before the election could close the gap, although it helped, and some observers thought that Humphrey might have pulled out a victory had the campaign lasted another week or ten days.

As it was, Nixon was elected with 43.4 percent of the vote, the smallest share of any winner since 1912; Humphrey got 42.7 percent; and Wallace, the rest. The Democrats took both houses of the Congress. The war in Vietnam was now the responsibility of a Republican president, and it remained to be seen if he could bring it to an end. And how soon.

## How Events in 1968 Affected Public Opinion

1968 had affected the debate over Vietnam in important ways. At the end of 1967, as we have seen, around 45 percent of the American people thought the war had been a mistake and around 10 percent favored immediate withdrawal. At the end of 1968 almost 60 percent thought the war was mistaken and almost 20 percent favored getting out immediately. Some of that shift had come, no doubt, because events confirmed the contentions of antiwar critics: the increasing brutality during and after Tet emphasized the moral questions; the calls to pour ever more men and money into that little country provoked fresh consideration about the real importance of Vietnam to the national security; and the sight of Americans fighting each other on the streets of Chicago and in other cities lent substance to the argument that this war was dangerously dividing the country. But if some moved against the war because they were persuaded by arguments, it is likely that more did so because they were just weary of it, frustrated by it, angry at how long it was apparently going to take. These inchoate feelings were also fed by the events of 1968.

# The Antiwar Movement

David Steigerwald

An inescapable aspect of the 1960s was the movement against the Vietnam War. David Steigerwald argues that the antiwar movement was, contrary to stereotype, a diverse grouping of various organizations and individuals representing a cross section of the United States. He describes the origins and beliefs of the various branches of the antiwar movement, including moderates, traditional pacifists, campus radicals, and hippies. The main means of protest were draft resistance and protest marches; he depicts in detail the October 1967 antiwar demonstration at the Pentagon. Steigerwald, a history professor at Ohio State University, assesses the impact of the movement and concludes that it had only limited success in influencing U.S. policy in Vietnam.

It is difficult to speak of the opponents of the war as a united "movement." They were a widely varied group of citizens, gathered together in numerous groups and often at odds with one another over strategy and analysis. There was no single leader and no group dominated—only one person, the longtime pacifist radical, A.J. Muste, had general credibility. Those who flocked into or associated with one or several of the organizations were just as varied and hailed from all ranks and areas of American life: clergy, teachers, suburban housewives, students, union members,

Excerpted from *The Sixties and the End of Modern America*, by David Steigerwald. Copyright ©1995 by St. Martin's Press, Inc. Reprinted with permission from Bedford/St. Martin's Press, Inc.

country folk. It is true that the antiwar movement over-lapped with political radicalism, but it is equally true that sixties radicalism and the movement were distinct, in spite of the best efforts of the media and the government to de-pict them as one and the same. By 1967 the stereotypical "peacenik" was a drug-using hippie with no respect for au-thority or country; in fact, the antiwar movement was a cross section of the nation. For the sake of discussing with some coherence an entity that was not necessarily coherent, however, we might distinguish five branches of the antiwar movement, each of which had its own analysis of the war.

## Composition of the Movement

First, there were the moderates, who included mainstream antinuclear activists from the National Committee for a Sane Nuclear Policy (SANE) with Social Democrats of var-ious types. To the moderates, Vietnam was an aberration best dealt with through respectful, even deferential criti-cism. Unlike most others within the movement, moderates never demanded a unilateral U.S. withdrawal and habitu-ally balanced criticism of the United States with demands against the North Vietnamese.

Second there were traditional pacifists, whose roots lay in the honorable tradition of the twentieth-century Ameri-can peace movement, where Protestant reformism mingled with radical humanism. Opposed to war on basic principle, the pacifists sought to build on links between the civil rights movement, left-wing labor groups, and other tradi-tional progressives, although by 1965 they believed the war had become the paramount issue in American life. By that point as well, most pacifists agreed with A.J. Muste's con-clusion that moderation was no longer possible and that the war exposed a national corruption so deep that nonvi-olent revolution was necessary.

A third branch, the principal organization of campus radicals and the most aggressive group of organizers, the Students for a Democratic Society (SDS), shared much with the pacifists, particularly the conclusion that the establishment was beyond redemption. They were not necessarily committed to nonviolence, however, were harsher and often more sanctimonious in their criticism, and based their fundamental views not on Christian principles but on contemporary ideas about personal alienation and the technocratic society.

Fourth, on the movement's fringe, holdovers from the Old Left were joined with younger fringe radicals organized in what *Village Voice* writer Jack Newfield termed the "Hereditary Left," self-avowed communists given to a dogmatism and factionalism more in keeping with the 1930s than the 1960s. Never influential within the movement, they saw the war in simple terms as imperialistic genocide and advocated what they thought was the party line of Soviet or Chinese foreign policy.

By 1967 a fifth wing, the hippies, emerged mostly from SDS ranks, reflecting the growing influence of cultural radicalism within the American left. To the hippies, the war represented the predictable violence of the straight establishment. The solution was simple: everyone had to lighten up and have fun, as Abbie Hoffman recommended in his primer, *Revolution for the Hell of It* (1969). . . .

## Draft Resistance

For the movement as a whole, the two favored means of protest by 1965 were draft resistance and protest marches. Draft resistance came in several forms—refusing induction, picketing or disrupting draft boards or induction centers, or, for some, fleeing into exile. Resistance was a form of radical individual opposition to the war, for unlike participation in a march or signing a circular letter, refusing military induction was a direct confrontation between a young man and his government. Resistance was laden with ethical and political meaning: to resist the draft was to reject the standard understanding of patriotic duty, even of masculinity, and carried with it both a willingness to endure the ridicule and hatred of fellow citizens and an obligation to redefine patriotism.

The most common act of draft resistance was draft-card burning, which was often done in groups during organized protests. The first "burners" defended their actions on the grounds of the post-Holocaust Nuremberg Laws, which held individuals responsible for participating in the crimes of their government. Convinced that the war was indeed criminal, the burners maintained that they were obliged by accepted global ethics and international law to refuse the draft. Theirs were unprecedented acts, but few of the first burners were prosecuted. One who was, Tom Cornell, a Catholic antinuclear activist, burned his first card in 1960 and eventually burned ten, by his estimate—"I think I have the record," he later speculated. In response to the first collective burnings, Congress, angered by the "filthy, sleazy beatnik gang . . . thumb[ing] their noses at their own government," as some members called the protesters, increased the penalty for draft-card destruction and stepped up prosecutions. The first burner to be convicted, David Miller, refused to accept a suspended sentence and was given two and a half years in prison. By 1968 the average sentence for draft evasion had risen to 37 months, up from 21 in 1965, while the number of prosecutions peaked in 1972 at 4,906.

The prospect of serving time for resistance gave pause to some. Even student radicals in SDS were reluctant to advocate outright resistance at first, preferring instead to call for some form of alternative service, ideally through domestic work in ghettos. But on balance the hesitancy with which most activists approached open resistance to selective service came from their understanding of how grave the act was, and, if anything, there was considerably more courage than cowardice among draft resisters.

Organized, collective resistance escalated with the radicalization of the movement, so that by the end of 1966 SDS and other groups began rallying around the antidraft slogans, "Hell no, we won't go!" and "Not with my life you don't!" Antidraft groups popped up on eastern campuses and in New York and Boston; in early 1967, a group engineered a mass card burning in Central Park. West Coast activists convened an organization, simply called the Resistance, based on the principle that even accepting deferments was a form of criminal compliance with the system. The Resistance organized a mass card turn-in that fall. More than a thousand cards were turned in during ceremonies in eighteen cities, after which SANE leaders Dr. Benjamin Spock, the famous baby doctor, and William Sloane Coffin, Yale University chaplain, along with three companions, submitted them to the Justice Department. Justice officials refused to accept the cards, but Coffin, Spock, and the others were charged with and eventually found guilty of conspiracy to disrupt selective service. Meanwhile, the Catholic priest Philip Berrigan and a group of friends broke into a Baltimore customshouse, poured blood over draft files, and accepted arrest, an act that Berrigan, his brother Daniel, and seven others repeated several months later, this time using homemade napalm to burn files.

Organized resistance reached its high point in the mid-October 1967 Stop-the-Draft Week. In the Bay area, Berkeley's militant students, community groups, and the Resistance aimed to shut down the large induction center in Oakland. When the nonviolent tactics of the pacifists failed, militants took over and conducted a huge street demonstration of perhaps 10,000 people, some of whom came prepared to fight. The march to the induction center turned into a running battle with Oakland police. Moving from block to block, throwing up street barricades when they could, and falling back when police approached, the crowd fought what activists quickly glamorized as a successful guerrilla action. Although the Oakland induction center was never shut down, the hand of the militants was strengthened, for the Oakland battle inspired the dreams of activists nationwide.

If Stop-the-Draft Week was the organizational zenith of draft resistance, it also tended to eclipse the core of such resistance, individual acts of noncompliance. Draft resistance had escalated to match the war, so that draft-card burning became lost in the acceleration of protest—paradoxically, at a time when individual resistance in all forms was peaking. By 1970 resistance reached such lengths that some states struggled just to muster their selective service quotas; from September 1969 to March 1970, over half of the men called in California refused to show up, and the state had to call 18,000 in order to meet its 7,800-man quota. There are no firm numbers on how many men refused to register nationally, but there were at least several hundred thousand and perhaps as many as 2 million. For tens of thousands of those who lost deferments, exile, usually in Canada but occasionally in Europe, became their fate.

## Antiwar Demonstrations

Besides draft resistance, the antiwar movement was committed to regular demonstrations, the organization of which often generated competition between groups. . . .

The best the movement could manage was to paste together successive umbrella organizations. Beginning with the National Coordinating Committee to End the War in Vietnam in late 1965, followed by several reincarnations under the banner of the Mobilization to End the War (MOBE), antiwar activists consistently organized large, even historic demonstrations, but more often than not the coordination was minimal, the leadership loose, and the activists at cross purposes.

The Pentagon march of October 1967 was ample testimony here. Inspired by the apparent success of the Oakland demonstration's "mobile tactics," the National Coordinating Committee embraced the concept of moving "from protest to resistance." The committee invited hippie leader and Oakland organizer Jerry Rubin to take the movement into "the business of wholesale disruption and widespread resistance and dislocation of the American society," in Rubin's words. The huge throng of over 100,000 that descended on Washington included all sides of the movement. The event was to run for several days, with a series of celebrity speeches and a march to the Mall, all capped off with a march across the Potomac to the Pentagon. This rough schedule seemed almost the extent of organization, however; there was no central leadership and people appeared, as Norman Mailer put it in his famous description of the march, *Armies of the Night* (1968), "unaffiliated or disaffiliated." The march was deprived of its symbolic leader, A.J. Muste, who had died the previous February. Exact plans were "hard to concretize," Dave Dellinger later explained, other than to say it would be a mix of "Ghandi and guerrilla," a synthesis of the new radicalism and the old pacifism.

## March on the Pentagon

What happened became a centerpiece of movement mythology. On Saturday afternoon, October 21, the demonstrators sat through the usual speeches by the political and cultural stars at the Lincoln Memorial. Then some 50,000 laid siege to the Pentagon, where they indulged in the most fantastic of scenes. The marchers made their way along a prescribed route to the north parking lot of the complex. They came face to face with a line of military MPs. Everyone went about the business of disruption after their own fashion. "There was no leadership," one protester said, "that was what was so beautiful." SDSers handed bullhorns around to anyone who wanted to make a speech. The celebrities led their own contingents in another round of spontaneous oratory mixed with impromptu press conferences. The hippies settled in for an attempt to levitate the building through group meditation. A small group broke through the police line and found its way into the Pentagon, where they were roughly rounded up. Protesters sang to the troops, called for them to "join us!," and stuck flowers in gun barrels. According to movement mythology, "two, possibly three MPs defected or attempted to defect." "We had come to the Pentagon to confront the war makers," one participant wrote, "only to discover that many armed men in uniform are just like us." Mailer thought "the air was violent, yet full of amusement." Another activist thought "it most resembled . . . a football game when spectators rush the goal posts." Utopia had met Hell and for a moment prevailed.

People came and went as the day turned into a chilly autumn night. Several thousand intended to camp out. Evidently bored with the vigil, the news media packed up and went home. Then the real action began. Regular paratroopers, backed by federal marshalls, moved toward the crowd, which attempted to hold its line by nonviolent tactics of locking arms and sitting down. The regulars went easy on the demonstrators, embarrassed perhaps by being used against nonviolent fellow citizens. The marshalls were an altogether different class, and they made a serious assault, dragging protesters out of their lines and beating them with billy clubs. They reportedly singled women out for particular abuse, reckoning that male protesters would attempt to rescue them and make themselves vulnerable to added beating. Through the "massacre," as Mailer called it, a Vietnam veteran named Gary Rader grabbed a bullhorn and appealed in military cadence to the troops; over the attempts of a nearby officer to drown him out, Rader conducted a swift teach-in about Vietnam. The arrests continued until only a hundred or so were left to see the dawn.

Activists proclaimed the Siege of the Pentagon an unqualified success. They alleged that the establishment's brutality had been exposed, that a heartfelt sympathy between the movement and the troops had been established, and that the diversity of genius embodied in the movement's variety had been successfully focused without compromising anyone's principles or belittling anyone's fears. The establishment was somewhat less enthusiastic. The president [Lyndon B. Johnson] and his family had driven around the remnants of the protest on Sunday to see "what a hippie looked like" but otherwise tried to ignore the event. Congressional conservatives denounced the whole business as a communist plot, a line of reasoning that Johnson may have privately encouraged. The general impression of the march, fostered by the national media, was that the counterculture had arrived in its most obnoxious manner, and from that point on public sympathy for the movement consistently decreased.

## Assessing the Antiwar Movement

The antiwar movement was a qualified failure. Certainly, it was much less successful than its symbolic counterpart, the civil rights movement. There is no tangible evidence that the administration felt direct pressure from the movement, and it is painfully obvious that no policy was reconsidered. Nor can the movement claim to have had more than a modest effect on U.S. electoral politics, which, if anything, tilted rightward beginning with the 1966 off-year elections. Johnson paid for the war with his political life, but his debtors were not the activists; he was a good enough politician to count on the media and the radicals themselves to discredit the movement in the eyes of the public. He was right on this score. The movement never gained public sympathy after 1967 when it in effect conceded the struggle over its public image.

Marginalized in the larger scheme of national politics, the peace movement floundered after 1968. Nixon's promises to win "peace with honor," the policy of Vietnamization that reduced U.S. casualties after 1969, the revision of the draft, and federal harassment of activists took the steam from the movement, though by no means was it destroyed. As Charles DeBenedetti, the foremost student of the peace movement, has concluded, "in this war no victory was decisive, at home or abroad." Some of the largest demonstrations took place in response to the persisting war. In April 1969, one hundred thousand or more marched again in Washington; the next spring, in response to the invasion of Cambodia, over 1 million college students struck all across the nation. The campus revolts brought outbreaks of violence, especially from authorities. During melees associated with the protests, Ohio National Guardsmen killed four students at Kent State University; guardsmen killed two at Jackson State in Mississippi while storming a dormitory. Through 1970, draft resistance turned into something like guerrilla war as fringe groups began bombing federal facilities and selective-service offices, at times egged on by FBI infiltrators and informants. A self-anointed band of radicals at the University of Wisconsin capped off a series of bombings by blowing up the university's Army Mathematics Research Center, killing an innocent young physicist. In April 1971 a peace coalition organized the largest of all marches, which brought perhaps half a million to Washington. Several weeks later, another, more radical group descended on Washington with the intention of shutting down the city by sitting in streets and government buildings, but they were routed by police, much to President Nixon's satisfaction.

Radical pacifists like Dave Dellinger not only regretted the violence of antiwar activists on principle but also knew it was self-defeating. The size of the Nixon-era demonstrations belied the poor organization of the movement as a whole. No new converts were being made. Indeed, the political lines solidified after 1968. The liberal center, the very existence of which had prevented the war from becoming an "us-versus-them" issue, had dissolved, and the war had become "us-versus-them." So the Nixon administration believed; so the radicals believed. What progress opponents of the war made came through the most mundane of channels, congressional action, and could not honestly be connected to the antiwar movement. SANE, along with a few other persisting moderates, mounted lobbying campaigns in support of several bills designed to overturn the Gulf of Tonkin Resolution [authorizing the president to order military action in Vietnam], restore congressional control over war making, and force Nixon to set a specific date for total U.S. withdrawal.

Still, there is little question that the movement kept the issues of Vietnam in the public's mind, even if the public did not want to recognize them. Activists prevented the government from waging war without proper checks—though one might well compare Vietnam to Korea and argue that the government might have withdrawn from Vietnam anyway.

The successes of the movement, as [historian] George Herring concludes, were "limited and subtle." "Perhaps most important," he writes, "the disturbances and divisions set off by the antiwar movement caused fatigue and anxiety among the policymakers and the public, and thus eventually encouraged efforts to find a way out."

CHAPTER 4

# The Civil Rights Movement and Minority Protest

AMERICA'S DECADES

# The Struggle for Civil Rights

Clayborne Carson

The black civil rights movement that captured the nation's attention in the 1960s had its immediate roots in two developments of the previous decade. In 1954 the U.S. Supreme Court in the case of *Brown v. Board of Education* ruled that segregated schools were unconstitutional. Racial segregation had been challenged in court by the National Organization for the Advancement of Colored People (NAACP). Then in 1955 black citizens of Montgomery, Alabama, boycotted city buses to protest race discrimination in the city's bus service. The boycott brought into prominence a young black minister, Martin Luther King Jr., who went on to found the Southern Christian Leadership Conference (SCLC). These organizations, joined by the younger activists of the Student Nonviolent Coordinating Committee (SNCC), became important parts of the civil rights movement of the 1960s. Clayborne Carson, a history professor at Stanford University, provides a brief overview of the civil rights movement during this time. He recounts important milestones of the movement, including the sit-in protests of 1960, the Birmingham demonstrations of 1963, and the March on Washington that same year. Carson concludes that the civil rights movement transformed American society by ending official forms of racial segregation and removing barriers to black voting.

Excerpted from "Civil Rights Movement," by Clayborne Carson, in *The Reader's Companion to American History*, edited by Eric Foner and John A. Garraty. Copyright ©1991 by Houghton Mifflin Company. Reprinted by permission of Houghton Mifflin Company. All rights reserved.

The modern period of civil rights reform can be divided into several phases, each beginning with isolated, small-scale protests and ultimately resulting in the emergence of new, more militant movements, leaders, and organizations. The *Brown* decision demonstrated that the litigation strategy of the National Association for the Advancement of Colored People (NAACP) could undermine the legal foundations of southern segregationist practices, but the strategy worked only when blacks, acting individually or in small groups, assumed the risks associated with crossing racial barriers. Thus, even after the Supreme Court declared that public school segregation was unconstitutional, black activism was necessary to compel the federal government to implement the decision and extend its principles to all areas of public life rather than simply in schools. During the 1950s and 1960s, therefore, NAACP-sponsored legal suits and legislative lobbying were supplemented by an increasingly massive and militant social movement seeking a broad range of social changes.

The initial phase of the black protest activity in the post-*Brown* period began on December 1, 1955. Rosa Parks of Montgomery, Alabama, refused to give up her seat to a white bus rider, thereby defying a southern custom that required blacks to give seats toward the front of buses to whites. When she was jailed, a black community boycott of the city's buses began. The boycott lasted more than a year, demonstrating the unity and determination of black residents and inspiring blacks elsewhere.

Martin Luther King, Jr., who emerged as the boycott movement's most effective leader, possessed unique conciliatory and oratorical skills. He understood the larger significance of the boycott and quickly realized that the nonviolent tactics used by the Indian nationalist Mahatma Gandhi could be used by southern blacks. "I had come to see early that the Christian doctrine of love operating through the Gandhian method of nonviolence was one of the most potent weapons available to the Negro in his struggle for freedom," he explained. Although Parks and

King were members of the NAACP, the Montgomery movement led to the creation in 1957 of a new regional or-

*The August 28, 1963, March on Washington drew two hundred thousand participants to the nation's capital. It was here that Martin Luther King Jr. gave his famous "I Have a Dream" speech.*

ganization, the clergy-led Southern Christian Leadership Conference (SCLC) with King as its president.

## 1960s Protests

King remained the major spokesperson for black aspirations, but, as in Montgomery, little-known individuals initiated most subsequent black movements. On February 1, 1960, four freshmen at North Carolina Agricultural and Technical College began a wave of student sit-ins designed to end segregation at southern lunch counters. These protests spread rapidly throughout the South and led to the founding, in April 1960, of the Student Non-Violent Coordinating Committee (SNCC). This student-led group, even more aggressive in its use of nonviolent direct action tactics than King's SCLC, stressed the development of autonomous local movements in contrast to SCLC's strategy of using local campaigns to achieve national civil rights reforms.

The SCLC protest strategy achieved its first major success in 1963 when the group launched a major campaign in Birmingham, Alabama. Highly publicized confrontations between nonviolent protesters, including schoolchildren, on the one hand, and police with clubs, fire hoses, and police dogs, on the other, gained northern sympathy. The Birmingham clashes and other simultaneous civil rights efforts prompted President John F. Kennedy to push for passage of new civil rights legislation. By the summer of 1963, the Birmingham protests had become only one of many local protest insurgencies that culminated in the August 28 March on Washington, which attracted at least 200,000 participants. King's address on that occasion captured the idealistic spirit of the expanding protests. "I have a dream," he said, "that one day this nation will rise up and live out the true meaning of its creed—we hold these truths to be self-evident, that all men are created equal."

Although some whites reacted negatively to the spreading protests of 1963, King's linkage of black militancy and idealism helped bring about passage of the Civil Rights Act of 1964. This legislation outlawed segregation in public facilities and racial discrimination in employment and education. In addition to blacks, women and other victims of discrimination benefited from the act.

## Seeking the Right to Vote

While the SCLC focused its efforts in the urban centers, SNCC's activities were concentrated in the rural Black Belt areas of Georgia, Alabama, and Mississippi, where white resistance was intense. Although the NAACP and the predominantly white Congress of Racial Equality (CORE) also contributed activists to the Mississippi movement, young SNCC organizers spearheaded civil rights efforts in the state. Black residents in the Black Belt, many of whom had been involved in civil rights efforts since the 1940s and 1950s, emphasized voter registration rather than desegregation as a goal. Mississippi residents Amzie Moore and Fannie Lou Hamer were among the grass-roots leaders who worked closely with SNCC to build new organizations, such as the Mississippi Freedom Democratic party (MFDP). Although the MFDP did not succeed in its attempt to claim the seats of the all-white Mississippi delegation at the 1964 National Democratic Convention in Atlantic City, it attracted national attention and thus prepared the way for a major upsurge in southern black political activity.

After the Atlantic City experience, disillusioned SNCC organizers worked with local leaders in Alabama to create the Lowndes County Freedom Organization. The symbol they chose—the black panther—reflected the radicalism and belief in racial separatism that increasingly characterized SNCC during the last half of the 1960s. The black panther symbol was later adopted by the California-based Black Panther party, formed in 1966 by Huey Newton and Bobby Seale.

Despite occasional open conflicts between the two groups, both SCLC's protest strategy and SNCC's organizing activities were responsible for major Alabama protests in 1965, which prompted President Lyndon B. Johnson to introduce new voting rights legislation. On March 7 an SCLC-planned march from Selma to the state capitol in Montgomery ended almost before it began at Pettus Bridge on the outskirts of Selma, when mounted police using tear gas and wielding clubs attacked the protesters. News accounts of "Bloody Sunday" brought hundreds of civil rights sympathizers to Selma. Many demonstrators were determined to mobilize another march, and SNCC activists challenged King to defy a court order forbidding such marches. But reluctant to do anything that would lessen public support for the voting rights cause, King on March 9 turned back a second march to the Pettus Bridge when it was blocked by the police. That evening a group of Selma whites killed a northern white minister who had joined the demonstrations. In contrast to the killing of a black man, Jimmy Lee Jackson, a few weeks before, the Reverend James Reeb's death led to a national outcry. After several postponements of the march, civil rights advocates finally gained court permission to proceed. This Selma to Montgomery march was the culmination of a stage of the African-American freedom struggle. Soon afterward, Congress passed the Voting Rights Act of 1965, which greatly increased the number of southern blacks able to register to vote. But it was also the last major racial protest of the 1960s to receive substantial white support.

## New Militancy

By the late 1960s, organizations such as the NAACP, SCLC, and SNCC faced increasingly strong challenges from new militant organizations, such as the Black Panther party. The Panthers' strategy of "picking up the gun" reflected the sentiments of many inner-city blacks. A series of major "riots" (as the authorities called them), or "rebellions" (the sympathizers' term), erupted during the last half of the 1960s. Often influenced by the black nationalism of Elijah Muhammad and Malcolm X and by pan-African leaders, proponents of black liberation saw civil rights reforms as insufficient because they did not address the problems faced by millions of poor blacks and because African-American citizenship was derived ultimately from the involuntary circumstances of enslavement. In addition, proponents of racial liberation often saw the African-American freedom struggle in international terms, as a movement for human rights and national self-determination for all peoples.

Severe government repression, the assassinations of Malcolm X and Martin Luther King, and the intense infighting within the black militant community caused a decline in

## The FBI Investigates
## Martin Luther King Jr.

*Martin Luther King Jr., winner of the Nobel Peace Prize in 1964, was perhaps the single most influential leader of the civil rights movement.* Former New York Times *reporter Charles Kaiser writes that King's prominence made him an adversary of J. Edgar Hoover, the powerful head of the FBI. Hoover, Kaiser writes, attempted to "neutralize" King by spreading accounts of the civil rights leader's private life to newspapers.*

[King's] treatment by the Federal Bureau of Investigation was perhaps the single worst domestic scandal of both the Kennedy and the Johnson administrations. Many years later, William Sullivan, the bureau's former chief of domestic intelligence, told Congress that "no holds were barred" in the FBI's effort to "neutralize" King as an effective civil rights leader. The bureau used the same techniques against King it applied to "Soviet agents."

King's nemesis was Sullivan's boss, J. Edgar Hoover, the FBI director who served—and often cowed—eight successive presidents. . . . Appointed in 1924, Hoover died in office forty-eight years later. He rose to power after directing mass arrests of radicals during the first "Red scare" after World War I, and anticommunism was the obsession he never abandoned. . . .

Hoover insisted that King was a menace because two of his key advisors were or had been Communists, even though there was protest activity after the 1960s. The African-American free-dom struggle nevertheless left a permanent mark on American society. Overt forms of racial discrimination and government-supported segregation of public facilities came to an end, although de facto, as opposed to de jure, segregation persisted in northern as well as southern public school systems and in other areas of American society. In the South, antiblack violence declined. Black candidates were elected to political offices in communities where

---

never any evidence that they used King to promote the aims of the party. It was inconceivable to Hoover that anyone who spoke regularly to a Communist was not also his pawn. . . .

The evidence his agents accumulated of King's extramarital affairs infuriated Hoover: To him this behavior was a good and sufficient reason for his ruthless persecution of the civil rights leader. The bureau made multiple attempts to leak details of King's private life to the *New York Times,* the *Los Angeles Times, Newsweek,* the *Chicago Daily News,* and the *Atlanta Constitution,* among other publications, but none of them would print what the FBI offered. . . .

[In 1964], the bureau's campaign of character assassination reached its nadir: It sent King an anonymous letter threatening him with dire consequences—unless he committed suicide. His wife, Coretta, was the first to open the letter; enclosed with it was a tape of highlights gleaned from the bureau's frequent bugging of the activist's hotel rooms. . . .

The CIA and Army Intelligence also spied on the civil rights movement. And King was only the most prominent target of the extensive campaign of intelligence, provocation, and disruption directed at civil rights activists by the FBI. In 1968 the bureau boasted of "3,248 ghetto-type racial informants" who provided it with a steady stream of information.

Charles Kaiser, *1968 in America: Music, Politics, Chaos, Counterculture, and the Shaping of a Generation.* New York: Grove, 1988.

---

blacks had once been barred from voting, and many of the leaders or organizations that came into existence during the 1950s and 1960s remained active in southern politics. Southern colleges and universities that once excluded blacks began to recruit them.

Despite the civil rights gains of the 1960s, however, racial discrimination and repression remained a significant factor in American life.

# The Rise of Black Militancy

Thomas R. West and James W. Mooney

The character of the black civil rights movement changed over the course of the 1960s. While the movement in the decade's early years had emphasized integration, interracial cooperation, and nonviolence, many black activists in the latter half of the 1960s rejected cooperation with whites, stressed black empowerment rather than racial integration, and condoned violence. Historians Thomas R. West and James W. Mooney describe this evolution, focusing on the activities of the Student Nonviolent Coordinating Committee (SNCC). Its growing militancy, its embrace of the slogan "black power," and its decision in 1967 to expel all whites led to friction between SNCC and more conservative civil rights organizations including the National Association for the Advancement of Colored People (NAACP), and Martin Luther King's Southern Christian Leadership Conference (SCLC). West and Mooney also note the influence of the Nation of Islam and its most famous representative, Malcolm X, on African Americans in the 1960s.

The civil rights movement had its internal distinctions, the NAACP being perceived as committing itself to careful judicial procedures while the Southern Christian Leadership Conference spoke with the voice and acted with the passion of evangelical Christianity. The movement as a whole, however,

Excerpted from the introduction to *To Redeem a Nation: A History and Anthology of the Civil Rights Movement*, edited by Thomas R. West and James W. Mooney. Copyright ©1993 Brandywine Press. Reprinted by permission of Brandywine Press.

went by its compound ethic: against unjust law and custom, set your conscience; when law is just, demand obedience.

Much of the same applies as well to the Student Nonviolent Coordinating Committee (SNCC), a group that did some of the toughest rights work of the times. Yet from the beginning SNCC had an edge of anger and rebellion that set it apart.

A founder of SNCC was Ella Baker, a critic of the Southern Christian Leadership Conference for what she thought to be its heavy-handed domination of the movement. She wanted a thoroughly democratic movement, and SNCC, formed soon after Greensboro and never having a membership of more than a few hundred, was designed to operate not through conventional leadership but through continuous democratic participation on the part of all members. SNCC was active in the freedom rides. Its most notable work was in Mississippi during the early 1960s.

There, facing the constant possibility of violence from white thugs and police and subject to arrest at the whim of local officials, SNCC activists encouraged black Mississippians to register for the vote. The purpose was not only to increase registration but to awaken among black people an awareness of their latent power and independence. It was difficult to persuade the black community that the gain was worth the risk; and beyond the fear of physical retaliation was the recognition that officials were going to find excuses to reject registrants anyway. A powerful force in the movement was Bob Moses of New York, an introspective young black intellectual who, in keeping with his own personality as well as SNCC's commitment to democracy, refused to act the part of a commander and instead encouraged those around him to make decisions.

In time the project decided to hold a separate unofficial primary vote nominating candidates for state positions, while the rights workers also continued their efforts to open up the official registration process. The candidates so chosen would have no chance in the real contest, and at any rate the procedure brought the threat of harassment by police, who did not like to see black Mississippians doing anything that suggested political activity. But the unofficial registration would not be in the hands of local officials determined to reject black applicants. And the participation of black Mississippians could increase their self-confidence, at the same time showing the rest of the country their determination to become politically empowered. In 1963 their Freedom Vote nominated Aaron Henry of the NAACP for governor. For lieutenant governor they chose Edwin King, a white minister and veteran of civil rights actions who would maintain the integrationist faith into a future in which others had forsaken it.

## Freedom Summer

Then, in 1964, the Mississippi project carried out the idea of bringing in northerners, most of whom would be white, to help voter registration. Some hostility to the recruitment of northern whites foreshadowed the future of the organization. But SNCC recognized both that the extra volunteers would be a material help and that the presence of comparatively affluent young whites was sure to draw national attention. During Freedom Summer of 1964, some thousand volunteers came south: the typical volunteer was a northern white college student. The murder of three SNCC workers—Michael Schwerner, Andrew Goodman, and their black companion James Chaney—dramatized for people outside the southern states the condition of Mississippi.

That summer the project sent to the Democratic National Convention at Atlantic City delegates chosen in another unofficial tally, this time drawing from eighty to ninety thousand black votes. These dissidents called themselves the Mississippi Freedom Democratic Party (MFDP). The delegates claimed that as representatives of a vote more democratic than that which had chosen the official Mississippi slate, they were more fit to receive acceptance at Atlantic City as the true Mississippi delegation. Fannie Lou Hamer was one of them, and she gave an eloquent speech before the credentials committee at the Convention, recounting her arrest and beating for having tried to register. Part of it was televised. But Lyndon Johnson, who upon the assassination of John Kennedy had succeeded to the presidency and was certain to receive at the Convention the Democratic nomination for the coming presidential election, held a live news conference and thereby managed to preempt the television channels before Mrs. Hamer had finished speaking. Johnson and other organizers of the Convention, liberal but fearful of antagonizing white voters in the South, wanted the MFDP to have as little visibility at Atlantic City as possible, and offered the Freedom Democrats nothing immediate beyond token compromise. Lyndon Johnson was nominated overwhelmingly as the party's presidential candidate. He went on to win the national election by a large margin against the Republican candidate Barry Goldwater, and as President he worked impressively for civil rights. But the memory of the treatment his political handlers at Atlantic City had accorded the MFDP continued to embitter SNCC along with others in the civil rights movement, and was instrumental in bringing about a material change in its character.

That change included a rejection of established political liberalism. Relations between liberals and civil rights activists had been tenuous anyway. Washington had shown itself to be sympathetic to the movement but uncomfortable with actions that it considered politically dangerous to the Democratic party. Perhaps it was unreasonable of the rights forces not to understand that a government and a political party have many considerations to balance and can rarely make a complete commitment to any one goal. But resentment was a natural reaction to the frustrating caution of establishment liberals. The party's handling of the MFDP at Atlantic City was bad. By every political measure, Lyndon Johnson was sure to be the winner in November, and the liberals could have afforded the very small risk that would have come with granting substantial recognition at the Convention to one of the most spirited and politically deserving efforts of the time. Instead, it turned a difficult ally into an enemy.

SNCC went further. Rejecting political liberalism, it became increasingly distant from whites in general, liberal and radical as well as conservative. Not adopting an explicitly racist language against whites, militants were claiming that whites were incapable of understanding the black experience, that blacks must concentrate on cultivating their own racial pride and power. SNCC during the time of the Mississippi project itself intended to nurture black communal power and self-dependence. Now self-dependence was turning into self-enclosure. . . .

The turn that black militancy had taken after the 1964 Democratic Convention and even earlier was now clearly going to qualify or complicate rights activities for some years to come. The next large rights action, in Mississippi in June 1966, made that clear.

After James Meredith was shot on a lonely walk across Mississippi in the cause of racial equality, a march called by King and other rights leaders crossed the state demanding that federal marshals be assigned to the protection of black voter registration. King's intention was to unify the movement. But militants, most notably Stokely Carmichael of SNCC, brought to the march their determination to draw a line between blacks and even the most committed of white supporters. Some hostility among black marchers was directed not at Mississippi racism but at the whites among them. A film of the event records a moment of nonviolent self-containment on the part of a white woman demonstrator who walks resolutely onward while a black youth beside her chants his rejection of whites.

Besides King, a core of seasoned rights figures remained to keep alive the vision of an interracial society and to concentrate on concrete social, economic, and political problems. They included Whitney Young of the Urban League, King's associate in the Southern Christian Leadership Conference Ralph Abernathy, the young Jesse Jackson, and Roy Wilkins of the NAACP. Wilkins was to be a persistent critic of the direction black militancy was taking. But SNCC made a decisive break. Calling itself the Atlanta Project, a group within the organization was proclaiming white people to be incapable of understanding the struggle of blacks and urged the expulsion of whites from SNCC. Fannie Lou Hamer was repelled at the hostility toward whites she discovered in SNCC, which in 1967 voted by a narrow margin to expel all whites, the measure to become effective the following year. By this time as well, the organization was abandoning its ethic of nonviolence.

## Black Power and Other Phrases

Among a number of phrases soon to be in confused and at times interchangeable use among black militants and observers of them is "black militant" itself, a term that could cover just about anyone who is black and militant on the racial issue. We employ it here, somewhat unsatisfactorily, to apply to blacks who stress not so much an end to racial division as the development of black unity and action. "Black consciousness" and "black pride" are among the most elusive of the other terms. They do not have to point to anything more than the degree of self-awareness to be expected within any ethnic group, and could look back, for example, to the Harlem Renaissance. In this usage they suggest another term current in the sixties: "black culture." Or "black consciousness" could represent a belief that deep within their collective psyche blacks share a consciousness, an experience inaccessible to outsiders—a belief that comes close to denying to the individual black man or woman an individual mind and will and a personal identity freely constructed.

"Black power," again, has possible contrary meanings, referring to no more than the building of a power base of a kind desirable to any group, or to no less than the acquisition of power to be wielded defensively or aggressively against the rest of society. "Black separatism" is clear enough: it designates the intent to withdraw as far as possible from the white world. It is near in signification to the slightly softer "black nationalism," referring to a phenomenon going back at least as far as to [1920s black activist] Marcus Garvey.

That the word "black" itself has become prominent in recent usage in place of the once-common "Negro" or "colored" is probably attributable mostly to insistence on the part of the black power movement. Employment of the word was intended as a strong and clear statement of the distinctiveness of black Americans. Still more recent, at least as a term in wide usage, is "African American," designating an ancestry and ethnicity as does "Irish American" or "Polish American."

## The Nation of Islam

In its more antiwhite meanings, black power had a predecessor in Elijah Muhammad's Nation of Islam, a group popularly called the Black Muslims. The sect had preached a doctrine combining a few scraps of the actual Moslem faith with a bizarre and fanciful mythology purporting to demonstrate that the white race is a devilish and degenerate offspring of black ancestors. Elijah Muhammad's followers were to prepare for the day when whites would be destroyed and blacks would inherit the earth. The organization practiced a stern code in sexual matters, personal hygiene, and the avoidance of drugs and alcohol. Its most famous leader was Malcolm X (he had rejected his family name "Little": believers held that in time blacks would learn their true names). He was a former hustler who after conversion to the teachings of the Nation of Islam demonstrated power in oratory and debate. After a break with Elijah Muhammad early in the 1960s and in the course of a trip to Mecca, as is expected of Moslems, Malcolm X encountered the true Islamic religion and discovered there an ethic of interracial harmony. For the short period that remained to him, he presented a radical modification of his old convictions, urging separate economic and political development among black Americans but insisting that they could live at peace with whites of good will. In 1965 he was assassinated. Followers of the Nation of Islam were convicted of the murder.

The newer crop of militants who for one reason or another rejected the mainline civil rights movement were widely varied in belief and practice. The Black Panthers, active particularly in California in the late sixties and counting among their leaders Huey Newton, Bobby Seale, and Fred Hampton, were distinctive particularly for a semi-military mode of conduct and for hostility to the police. The Panthers were recognizable for a style of dress: black jackets and black berets. Differences in tone and emphasis racked SNCC. Agreeing that blacks must be the vanguard of revolution and whites at best followers, James Forman insisted that white racism was ultimately a function of class rather than of skin color. Under black leadership in the United States and that of other colored peoples throughout the world, Forman argued, a revolution including enlightened whites could win a future free of class oppression, imperialism, and racism.

Even in the absence of such incidents as that of the backhanded treatment accorded the Mississippi Freedom Democratic Party at the 1964 Convention, an eventual end would have been inevitable for the spirit of the Montgomery [bus] boycott and the Greensboro sit-ins. Nonviolent action, accompanied when necessary by civil disobedience, was effective against specific offensive white-supremacist laws and practices. It was almost useless when the problem was to address some stubborn social or economic condition having racist roots but requiring complex measures of law and bargaining.

# Urban Riots Place Cities Under Siege

Allen J. Matusow

In the first half of the 1960s the nonviolence teachings of civil rights leader Martin Luther King Jr. were influential in the civil rights movement. Most of the violence relating to the black protest for equality took the form of attacks on activists by reactionary whites. In the second half of the decade, however, black violence became a major concern when a series of racially motivated riots and disturbances engulfed major U.S. cities, including Los Angeles in 1965, Detroit in 1967, and numerous cities following the assassination of King in 1968. Allen J. Matusow, a history professor at Rice University, analyzes the riots and describes how Americans, especially the police and black activist leaders, responded to them.

---

The archetypical ghetto riot of the 1960s was Watts, which so closely resembled most of the others that to understand its character was to understand theirs also. Most of the 300,000 residents in the ghetto of southeast Los Angeles lived in neat homes along spacious streets. But, underneath the pleasant surface, the usual depressing conditions prevailed—segregated schools, an unemployment rate twice that of the national average, inadequate transportation to decent jobs. In Watts, the neighborhood at the core of the

Excerpted from *The Unraveling of America: A History of Liberalism in the 1960s*, by Allen J. Matusow (New York: Harper & Row). Copyright ©1984 by Allen J. Matusow. Reprinted by permission of the author.

sprawling ghetto, the social order was in the process of disintegrating—four persons in ten were poor, 38 percent of the families were headed by women, 47 percent of the children under eighteen lived in broken homes. The site of the worst fury, Watts gave its name to the great riot that began on August 11, 1965, in an ordinary encounter between white policemen and the blacks who hated them. Officer Lee Minikus of the California Highway Patrol stopped a car driven by Marquette Frye, a twenty-one-year-old unemployed black man, on a main thoroughfare near the Watts neighborhood. When Frye, who had been drinking, resisted arrest, a crowd gathered, forcing police to summon reinforcements. Within an hour a thousand blacks were on the street hurling rocks and bottles at the cops and shouting "Burn, Baby, Burn!" the hip slogan of a local disc jockey, the Magnificent Montague. Thus did Officer Minikus and Marquette Frye become historical personages by virtue of having caused, in the phrase of the sociologists, "the precipitating event.". . .

That first night along Avalon Boulevard youths attacked cars driven by whites, beat up white newsmen, and battled the police. On the next night the looting and burning began. Calmly and without shame, people smashed the windows of liquor, grocery, and department stores and helped themselves to whatever they could carry. By the third day, as rioting spread throughout southeast Los Angeles, a dull orange haze from a thousand fires hung over the city. On the streets of Watts crowds milled about amid a carnival atmosphere, exhilarated by their collective act of defiance and proud that at last they were forcing attention to be paid. With the arrival of the National Guard early in the morning of the fourth day, the authorities began to gain the upper hand, and the fire and the fury slowly burned themselves out. "Now we're on the top, and they're on the bottom," declared Police Chief William H. Parker. The toll: 34 killed, 1,072 injured, 977 buildings damaged or destroyed, 4,000 persons arrested.

The McCone Commission, appointed by the governor of

California to study the riot and named after its chairman, former CIA director John McCone, explained Watts as most conservatives would explain all the other riots—as a "senseless" explosion by a handful of alienated blacks. This was a thesis no knowledgeable observer endorsed. Surveys of the riot area revealed that at one time or another at least 30,000 blacks had participated in the looting, burning, and sniping, while approximately 60,000 more had been in the streets as supportive spectators. Rioters and spectators together formed a majority of the riot-age population (14–65 years old). Moreover, the typical rioter was not socially on the margin—i.e., "riff-raff"—but a young man somewhat better educated than the typical nonrioter and holding a job. Sociologists called the character type of which the rioter was representative "the New Ghetto Man."

## The New Ghetto Man

Bred on the asphalt pavements of the northern cities, this new man bore scant resemblance to the stereotypical black—docile and submissive—of plantation days. Proud of his race, politically hip, savvy to discrimination, tolerant of violence, the New Ghetto Man reached maturity in the 1960s, which explained why centuries of repressed black anger erupted when it did. The riots were the new man's contribution to the black protest movement, his announcement that he would not passively submit to a life of discrimination and poverty. The announcement contained clear nationalist overtones. Whites were the target of the rioters' wrath, especially whites in the ghetto who had humiliated, cheated, or exploited them. Thus rioters chased white passersby, fought white police, and meted out their version of justice to thieving white merchants. The most arresting fact about Watts—and most of the other riots—was this: Looters and arsonists moved along the streets destroying white-owned stores but ordinarily sparing stores with signs reading "Negro-owned" or "Blood." Scornful of the black middle class and the traditional black leadership, the rioters heeded no counsel except their own violent

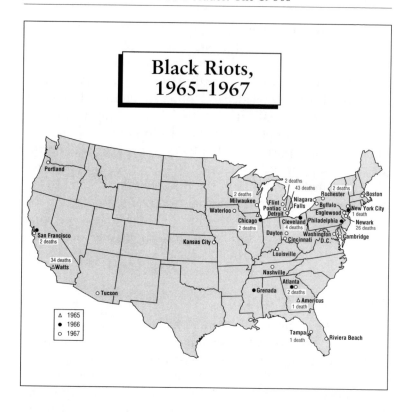

impulses. Martin Luther King was on the streets during the riot, preaching nonviolence. The rioters ignored him. Mervyn Dymally, who represented Watts in the state legislature, urged his constituents to stay cool. One New Ghetto Man handed him a bottle, saying, "If you're with the people, throw it."

Black riots became such a regular feature of the decade that their annual appearance soon ceased to occasion surprise. By official count 43 racial disorders occurred in 1966 and 164 during the first nine months of 1967, the year when the insurrectionary fever peaked. Thirty-three of the 1967 disorders were serious enough to require the intervention of the state police; eight required the National Guard. Two of them—Newark and Detroit—were cataclysms on the scale of Watts.

The rioters of Newark manifested remarkable discipline, looting white-owned businesses but not black, smashing windows but avoiding arson since black families usually lived above the wooden stores. Newark also featured a counterriot by "peace-keeping" forces, a form of violence all too common in the decade. National Guardsmen—white, ill-trained, and terrified of snipers—proved a trigger-happy lot. "Down in the Springfield Avenue area it was so bad," reported Police Director Dominick Spina, "that, in my opinion, Guardsmen were firing upon police and police were firing back at them. . . . I really don't believe there was as much sniping as we thought." Spina watched two columns of unprovoked Guardsmen riddle a housing project with bullets. By the time they finished, three women were dead. Meanwhile, police and soldiers charged down streets, shooting up black-owned stores that had been spared by the looters. Early in the morning of the fourth day, uncertain what to do, New Jersey governor Richard J. Hughes privately summoned [New Left activist] Tom Hayden to ask his advice. Hayden, who had spent three years organizing the Newark ghetto and the past few days "looking at the streets of violence," recalled warning the governor that if he did not pull back the Guard, "the troops are gonna massacre more people, and you're going to go down in history as one of the biggest killers of all time." A few hours later, Hughes withdrew the Guard, and calm returned to Newark.

Less than a week later, on July 23, 1967, the worst American riot in a century erupted in Detroit. Beginning the usual way, with a police incident, it rapidly spread through fourteen square miles of black slums. But Detroit was different from the major riots that preceded it, for here disciplined violence gave way to the sheerest nihilism. Rioters looted black stores and white stores, burned down businesses and burned down homes. Middle-class Negroes in big cars joined with the poor in hauling off merchandise. Carefree kids, excited by the fires, sacked and burned for the pleasure of it, appearing to one observer to be "dancing amidst the flames." Police and National Guardsmen were helpless in the face of this massive breakdown of public order—or else fed the furies of the people by their own excesses. George Romney had no choice except to become the first governor of the decade to request the intervention of federal troops. Shortly after midnight on July 25, Lieutenant General John L. Throckmorton, who had served General [William C.] Westmoreland as an aide in Vietnam, began to deploy 4,700 paratroopers from Fort Bragg and Fort Campbell to pacify Detroit. The carnage of the riot, when it ended, was stunning in magnitude—43 dead, 7,000 arrested, 1,300 buildings destroyed, and 2,700 businesses looted. Surveying his city, Mayor Jerome Cavanagh grimly remarked, "It looks like Berlin in 1945."

## A Perverse Interpretation of Riots

Intoxicated by the blood and fire, militant [black] nationalists concluded in 1967 that rioters were urban guerrillas engaged in a nationalist revolution to free the black colony. Theirs was a perverse interpretation. Spontaneous uprisings against deeply felt grievances, the riots were neither revolutionary nor even consistently nationalist. Rioters harassed the white man, but even snipers did not try to kill him. Wrath was directed less against whites in general than against those whites whose presence in the ghetto had aroused local antagonism—i.e., white cops and shopkeepers. Rioters were less hostile to the National Guard than to the local police and downright friendly to federal troops. They attacked retail stores but left untouched public institutions like schools, hospitals, banks, and government buildings. They looted not in the name of socialism but because looting was one way to acquire the material possessions that they believed, in typical American fashion, would make them happy. They did not invade nearby white neighborhoods, engage in terrorism, or manifest the slightest interest in mounting a sustained struggle against the government. Torn between a desire to assert control over their own turf and the hope for full participation in America, they wanted above all to deliver a message to their white fellow citizens: progress halting, patience gone. Gabriel Pope (the name was a pseudonym), one of the new ghetto men figuring prominently in Robert Conot's fine book on Watts, *Rivers of Blood, Years of Darkness,* expressed the ambivalence of the rioters and summed up their purpose:

We'll give this country a chance. We'll give 'em a chance to make up for what they've done in the past, we'll give 'em a chance to say "We know we've done you wrong, and we're gonna do our best to change it!" But I'm not gonna have nobody tell me what to do. . . . I'm gonna be the master of my life, and if they try to run over me, I'm gonna demolish them! And next time, baby, let me tell you, it's not gonna be a gentle war like it was, it's not gonna be the soul people doing all the bleeding. . . . If we get pushed again, it's gonna be goodbye, baby.

# The Chicano Movement

Carlos Muñoz Jr.

African Americans were not the only minority group to engage in political protest activity in the 1960s. Inspired in part by the civil rights and "black power" movements, Native Americans, Puerto Ricans, and other ethnic minority groups organized movements and protests to end discrimination, fight for political recognition, and foster ethnic pride. In the following excerpt from his study *Youth, Identity, Power: The Chicano Movement*, Carlos Muñoz Jr. recounts the activities of Mexican-American students and activists during the 1960s. Among the significant figures he examines is labor union organizer César Chavez and Sal Castro, leader of the 1968 Los Angeles high school student strike. He argues that they inspired a new generation of student activists who believed that older Mexican-American political leaders were too accommodating to white society. Activists in the 1960s created a "Chicano Power Movement" with an ethnic nationalist ideology. Muñoz is a professor of ethnic studies at the University of California at Berkeley.

---

The politics of the 1950s were not conducive to radicalism anywhere, especially to participation in social struggles that could be easily characterized as 'communist inspired'. Like other young people of their generation, Mexican

---

Excerpted from *Youth, Identity, Power: The Chicano Movement*, by Carlos Muñoz Jr. (New York & London: Verso). Copyright ©1989 Carlos Muñoz Jr. Reprinted by permission of the publisher.

American student activists—the few in existence—were influenced by the politics of super-patriotism generated by the war against Hitler and fascism and reinforced by the Cold War against new enemies, Stalin and communism. . . .

The politics of the times notwithstanding, the anti-Mexican racism in the larger society, although not as ugly as it had been during the 1920s and 1930s, compelled a few of the more progressive of them to speak out in defense of their people in the context of the liberal reformist political tradition typified by the LULAC [League of United Latin American Citizens] organization and further developed and refined by the new middle-class and professional organizations of the post–World War II era. Veterans played central leadership roles in those organizations. Their political consciousness was shaped by patriotic Americanism and the anticommunism then permeating society. They did not reject their Mexican origins but, like the generation of the 1930s, emphasized the American part of their Mexican American identity. In their minds, political accommodation and assimilation were the only path toward equal status in a racist society. Integration in education and at all levels of society would result, they believed, in the acceptance of their people as first-class citizens.

They acknowledged that Mexican Americans were victims of racism, but they did not promote a nonwhite racial identity for their people. Instead, they promoted the image of Mexican Americans as a white ethnic group that had little in common with African Americans. . . .

When John F. Kennedy declared his candidacy for president in 1960, he called leaders of the Mexican American middle-class and professional organizations for help. The Kennedy campaign thus marked the entry of this leadership into national politics. They played an important role in the campaign through the Viva Kennedy Clubs they organized in the southwestern states. The Kennedy campaign also recruited Mexican American college student activists into the Viva Kennedy Clubs and they became visible as well in middle-class organizations. Most important, it marked the beginning of a new era of politics that was to eventually produce the Chicano Generation: Mexican American student activists who would embark upon a new quest for identity and power characterized by a militant and radical politics.

## The Politics of the 1960s

The politics of the early 1960s differed markedly from those of the 1950s. The Kennedy presidency followed by the Johnson administration marked the end of McCarthyism and the beginning of a liberal political era in national politics. Liberalism nurtured the aspirations for political change on the part of African Americans and created cracks in the system of racial oppression in the South. The dramatic emergence of the civil rights movement generated reform in education and politics. Although chiefly aimed at benefiting African Americans, the movement created a political atmosphere beneficial to Mexican American working-class youth, for it gave them more access to institutions of higher education. Their access to college was no longer limited to patronage by the YMCA and the Protestant and Catholic churches, as had been the case in the 1930s, nor was it limited to veterans with G.I. Bill benefits, as it had largely been in the 1940s. There were now hundreds of youth of Mexican descent attending college as a direct result of federal educational programs made possible by the civil rights movement and implemented especially during the Johnson administration.

The growing numbers of Mexican American students on college campuses did not come close to representing a significant proportion of the Mexican American population: Mexican American youth remained severely under-represented. Neither did they produce a visible Mexican American student activism. But from those numbers came a few student activists who, between 1963 and 1967, participated in some activities and organizations of the civil rights movement. Some of them became active indirectly or directly as members of the Student Nonviolent Coordinating Committee. . . .

Others participated in the 1963 March on Washington

organized by Dr. Martin Luther King, Jr. and the Southern Christian Leadership Conference. . . . At San Jose State College in Northern California, a few Mexican American students joined a campus protest when a Black student was denied admission. . . .

## Other Developments

Several other events occurred which, in addition to the civil rights movement, also had great impact on Mexican American student activists in the early 1960s. These included the dramatic emergence of the farmworkers struggle in California led by César Chávez, the land grant struggle in New Mexico led by Reies López Tijerina, and increasing discontent on the part of the Mexican American middle-class leadership with the Democratic Party and other dominant political institutions.

On 16 September 1965, the anniversary of Mexican independence from Spain in 1810, the National Farm Workers Association (NFWA) met at a local Catholic church hall in Delano, California and voted to join the striking Filipino grape pickers in the area. Four days later, members of the NFWA led by César Chávez joined their Filipino brothers and sisters on the picket lines with shouts of 'Viva La Causa!' Luis Valdez wrote the 'Plan de Delano' which proclaimed 'the beginning of a social movement in fact and not pronouncements.' The 'Plan de Delano' defined the farmworker struggle as a nonviolent revolution 'for social justice' led by the 'sons of the Mexican Revolution' and called for the unity of all poor farmworkers across the nation:

> The strength of the poor is also in union. We know that the poverty of the Mexican or Filipino worker in California is the same as that of all farm workers across the country, the Negroes and poor whites, the Puerto Ricans, Japanese, and Arabians; in short, all the races that comprise the oppressed minorities of the United States. . . . We want to be equal with all the working men in the nation . . . to those who oppose us be they ranchers, police, politicians, or speculators,

we say that we are going to continue fighting until we die, or we win. WE SHALL OVERCOME.

Student activists, especially those on some of the larger college and university campuses in California, were moved by the upwelling of the farmworkers' struggle to begin support activities on behalf of the farmworker movement. . . .

On 5 June 1967, another major event took place that had an important impact on Mexican American student activists. It occurred in Tierra Amarilla, New Mexico where Reies López Tijerina had been leading a struggle to recapture lands that had been stolen from the Hispano people (Spanish-Americans who were direct descendants of the original Spanish colonizers of New Mexico). Tijerina had founded the Alianza Federal de Mercedes as the organizational vehicle of that struggle. On 5 June, a group of armed men from the Alianza took over the county courthouse, taking twenty hostages who they held for about an hour and then released. A jailer and a state police officer were wounded. Later Tijerina's men fled into the mountains. The National Guard was mobilized, and it carried out a massive manhunt, complete with tanks. Forty innocent Hispanos were arrested. This was the first militant armed action taken by Mexican Americans anywhere in the Southwest for over a hundred years, and it became a source of inspiration for some student activists, especially in New Mexico.

With all these events taking place between 1964 and 1967, Mexican American student activism was becoming more visible on the campus as well as in the community. Federally funded War on Poverty programs in the community became training grounds for many students, and they became participants in local community politics. . . .

By 1966, student activists, though still relatively few in number, were seriously discussing the formation of distinct Mexican American student organizations on their campuses throughout the Southwest. By the fall of 1967 organizations had emerged on several college campuses in Los Angeles and on two campuses in Texas. . . .

## Two Inspiring Leaders

The initial student support for the Chávez and Tijerina movements . . . was largely related to pride in the fact that two Mexican American leaders struggling for social justice had achieved national recognition and extensive mass media coverage. In 1967 Chávez was the first Mexican American leader to appear on the cover of *Time* magazine. He was promoted by the mass media and his followers as the 'Mexican American Dr. Martin Luther King, Jr.' since he was also a disciple of the Ghandian philosophy of nonviolence. . . .

Support for Chávez also stemmed from the reality that most Mexicans and Mexican Americans had been farmworkers at some time in their lives. But the stark reality had to be faced that the farmworker movement was far from being a broad civil rights effort; Chávez was a union organizer and lent his increasing prestige and astute leadership abilities only to farmworkers—or to efforts that he saw as in the immediate interests of farmworkers. He consistently shunned responsibility for leading a movement broader than a union for farm workers, and he told student leaders that the issue of educational change was not on his agenda. Many of his followers, however, . . . continued to embrace Chávez as the leader of all Mexican Americans and eventually as one of the leaders of the Chicano Movement.

Despite the inspiration provided by César Chávez and the farmworkers movement, student activists found it difficult to organize students solely around the issues related to the struggle of the farmworkers. The attention given to the farmworker movement by liberal politicians like the Kennedys and by the mass media contributed greatly to the movement's rise and the making of Chávez into a respected national leader. But it also reinforced the existing stereotype of all Mexican Americans as farmworkers. Although strongly supportive of the Chávez and Tijerina movements, student leaders on urban campuses were well aware that the vast majority of their people lived in cities. They therefore felt the need to build an urban movement to address the issues faced by the majority of Mexican Americans. Neither César Chávez and the farmworkers nor Reies Tijerina and the farmers of northern New Mexico truly addressed the needs of urban youth.

## Identity Crisis

Rodolfo 'Corky' Gonzáles did. Gonzáles, founder and head of the Crusade for Justice, a civil rights organization in Denver, Colorado was in his early forties but younger than Chávez and Tijerina; in addition he was a product of an urban *barrio*. He had parted company with the Mexican American middle-class organizations he had worked closely with in the past and now spoke directly, and forcefully, to the issues facing the youth. His charisma captured the imagination of young activists, students and non-students alike. . . .

In 1967 he wrote an epic poem entitled *I Am Joaquín*. . . . *I Am Joaquín* did not offer its readers a well-defined radical ideology, but it did provide a critical framework for the developing student movement through its portrayal of the quest for identity and its critique of racism. More than a poem, it was an ambitious essay that attempted to dramatize key events and personalities from important moments of Mexican and Mexican American history, beginning with the indigenous ancestors prior to the Spanish conquest. It ended with the adamant assertion that people of Mexican descent and their culture would continue to endure. . . .

The most significant aspect of *I Am Joaquín* was that it captured both the agony and the jubilation permeating the identity crisis faced by Mexican American youth in the process of assimilation. . . .

This search for identity and the dilemmas that it posed are the key to understanding the Chicano student movement of the 1960s. To a large degree, the movement was a quest for identity, an effort to recapture what had been lost through the socialization process imposed by US schools, churches, and other institutions. In order to create a new identity, as an alternative to the one defined by the Mexican-American

Generation, the more militant student leadership sensed the need to take on that socialization process. . . .

## The Rise of Student Militancy

On the morning of 3 March 1968, shouts of 'Blow Out!' rang through the halls of Abraham Lincoln High School, a predominantly Mexican American school in East Los Angeles. Over a thousand students walked out of their classes, teacher Sal Castro among them. Waiting for them outside the school grounds were members of UMAS [United Mexican American Students] and various community activists. They distributed picket signs listing some of the thirty-six demands that had been developed by a community and student strike committee. The signs protested racist school policies and teachers and called for freedom of speech, the hiring of Mexican American teachers and administrators, and classes on Mexican American history and culture. As might be expected, the signs that caught the attention of the mass media and the police were those reading 'Chicano Power!', 'Viva La Raza!', and 'Viva La Revolución!'. By the afternoon of that day, several thousand more students had walked out of five other *barrio* high schools to join the strike. The strike brought the Los Angeles city school system, the largest in the nation, to a standstill and made news across the country; a *Los Angeles Times* reporter interpreted the strike as 'The Birth of Brown Power.' Over ten thousand students had participated by the time the Los Angeles 'blow-outs' ended a week and a half later.

But the strike accomplished something much more important than shaking up school administrators or calling public attention to the educational problems of Mexican American youth. Although not one of its original objectives, the strike was the first major mass protest explicitly against racism undertaken by Mexican Americans in the history of the United States. As such, it had a profound impact on the Mexican American community in Los Angeles and in other parts of the country, and it generated an increased political awareness along with visible efforts to mobilize the community. This was manifested in the revitalization of existing community political organizations and the emergence of new ones, with youth playing significant leadership roles.

Overnight, student activism reached levels of intensity never before witnessed. A few Mexican American student activists had participated in civil rights marches, anti-Vietnam War protests, and had walked the picket lines for the farmworker movement. But the high school strike of 1968 was the first time students of Mexican descent had marched en masse in their own demonstration against racism and for educational change. It was also the first time that they had played direct leadership roles in organizing a mass protest. The slogans of 'Chicano Power!', 'Viva La Raza!', and 'Viva La Revolución!' that rang throughout the strike reflected an increasing militancy and radicalism in the ranks of UMAS and other student organizations. The nature of these concerns and the momentum built up among Mexican American students—both in high school and on college campuses—broke the ideological bonds that characteristically keep student organizations, and students in general, from questioning authority and the status quo. Membership grew as those organizations and their leaders became protagonists in struggles for change in Mexican American communities. The strike moved student activism beyond the politics of accommodation and integration which had been shaped by the Mexican-American Generation and the community's middle-class leadership.

However, it was not student activists who conceived of the strike; the idea originated with Sal Castro, the teacher at Lincoln High School who had walked out with his students. Like Corky Gonzáles, he had become disillusioned with the Democratic Party and with Mexican American middle-class leadership. . . .

A product of the *barrio* schools in East Los Angeles, Castro returned to the neighborhood as a teacher only to find that racism toward Mexican American youth remained virulent. . . . He worked hard to make reforms within the school bureaucracy but was not able to accomplish much. Like other middle-class leaders, he saw that the civil rights movement ignored Mexican Americans and that they were low on the agenda of the War on Poverty and in education reform plans. But unlike most other middle-class leaders, Castro came to the conclusion that his people needed their own civil rights movement and that the only alternative in the face of a racist educational system was nonviolent protest against the schools. He therefore prepared to sacrifice his teaching career, if necessary, in the interest of educational change for Mexican American children. The strike made Castro one of the movement's leaders.

The strike of 1968 went beyond the objectives of Castro and others concerned only with improving education. It was the first loud cry for Chicano Power and self-determination, serving as the catalyst for the formation of the Chicano student movement as well as the larger Chicano Power Movement of which it became the most important sector. . . .

The movement was given further impetus by other events that took place in 1968, the year that was the turning point of the decade. The antiwar movement became a potent political force in national politics as mass protest against the war in Vietnam dramatically increased. Simultaneously, on the battlefields of Vietnam, US troops were being overrun in the Tet offensive, the largest Vietnamese attack of the war. As a result the Johnson administration was forced to agree to peace talks held in Paris later that year. It was also the year that Dr. Martin Luther King, Jr., led the Poor People's March on Washington, which included a contingent of Mexican Americans. Later in the year Dr. King and Senator Robert F. Kennedy were assassinated.

Even more important, 1968 was also the year of international student uprisings from Paris and Berlin to Tokyo to Mexico City. In Mexico City, the site of the Olympics that year, over four hundred students were massacred by the Mexican army. In Paris, students battled police and brought the entire city to a standstill, touching off a month-long nationwide general strike of ten million workers. Between 1968 and 1969, Mexican American student militancy intensified as more and more of them became convinced that they were part of an international revolution in the making.

From the ranks of these militant students came artists, poets and actors who collectively generated a cultural renaissance and whose work played a key role in creating the ideology of the Chicano movement. . . .

The student strikes in the community and on the college campus, in conjunction with the political upheavals of the late sixties, thus generated the framework for the eventual transformation of student activist organizations into a full-blown student movement with clear social and political goals and an ethnic nationalist ideology that came to be known as cultural nationalism.

# CHAPTER 5

# Youth Protest and the Counterculture

## AMERICA'S DECADES

# The Radical Youth Movement

Norman L. Rosenberg and Emily S. Rosenberg

Norman L. Rosenberg and Emily S. Rosenberg are professors of history at Macalester College in St. Paul, Minnesota. In the following viewpoint, they examine the outpouring of protest and dissent during the 1960s among college students and other young people. An influential minority of the young became radical political and social activists because they were disaffected from the liberalism that informed the policies of John F. Kennedy and Lyndon B. Johnson and suspicious of American institutions including the federal government. For many, political activism became a source of personal fulfillment as well as a means of changing society. While leftists of previous decades were primarily inspired by Marxist and Communist teachings, members of the "New Left"—a term used by 1960s radicals to distinguish themselves from their radical forerunners—were influenced by a variety of sources. These included maverick professors such as Herbert Marcuse and C. Wright Mills, "Beat" poets and writers of the 1950s, civil rights workers, and folk and rock singers such as Bob Dylan. One result of this activism was frequent campus unrest as students protested against university policies ranging from complicity with the U.S. military to restrictive lifestyle rules. The Vietnam War also inspired many students and young people to participate in political demonstrations—if not necessarily to sustained political activism.

Excerpted from *In Our Times*, by Norman L. Rosenberg and Emily S. Rosenberg. Copyright ©1995 by Prentice-Hall, Inc. Reprinted by permission of Prentice-Hall, Inc., Upper Saddle River, N.J.

The revolt against liberalism was one of the most important phenomena of the 1960s and early 1970s. For better or for worse, the loosely structured political and cultural radicalism touched almost every area of American life and left a significant impact upon institutions and ideas.

## Roots of Radicalism Among the Young

Young people's enthusiasm for John Kennedy led most supporters of the New Frontier to expect that the 1960s would be a decade of steady liberal reform. But even before JFK's death, some young people were becoming disillusioned with his gradualism and with liberalism itself. The young radicals, many of whom were white and from relatively affluent, middle-class homes, began to denounce American institutions and values and to seek their own alternatives to the highly rationalized world of big-government liberalism. The potpourri of sources from which disaffected young people sought insight and inspiration reflected the diversity of this new radicalism. Unlike the "old left" of the 1920s and 1930s, which looked primarily to Marxism, radicals of the 1960s sampled a variety of social theories. "Beat" writers, Eastern mystics, academic mavericks, and folk-rock songwriters helped provide the movement's eclectic intellectual base.

While the middle-class protesters of the 1960s were still opening their school day by saluting the flag, the Beat poets and novelists of the 1950s had already dismissed American society as an "air-conditioned nightmare." Jack Kerouac's novel *On the Road* (1957) glorified the drifter, the rebel who resisted the temptation to conform. The poems of Allen Ginsberg denounced materialism and middle-class morality and celebrated the satisfactions of marijuana, Eastern mystical religions, and homosexual love. In their best works, Beat poets such as Ginsberg and Gary Snyder displayed a free-flowing style that epitomized their rejection of restrictive cultural forms. Part hipster and part huckster, Ginsberg kept alive the spirit of the Beat movement, becoming a revered elder-in-residence to the radicals of the 1960s.

While the Beats protested America's supposed cultural sterility the maverick sociologist C. Wright Mills attacked its political system. Although Mills taught at Columbia University, his lifestyle—he would roar up to his office on a motorcycle—and his political ideas clashed with the urbane liberalism that dominated leading colleges. Mills's writings helped popularize theories that became the New Left's central tenets: that an undemocratic "power elite" dominated American society; that liberalism had lost its social consciousness and become an ideology of the status quo; and that most liberal intellectuals merely offered rationalizations for an illiberal society. Mills also condemned United States foreign policy as an extension of the same corrupted values: He warned that a small group of politicians, military officials, and business leaders enjoyed virtually unchecked power. An activist as well as a scholar, Mills visited Cuba and wrote a short book praising Fidel Castro's social experiments. After his death in 1962, Mills became one of the radical movement's most revered saints.

The critique of American liberalism received greater philosophical development in the works of Herbert Marcuse. A German-born Marxist, Marcuse attacked the sophisticated technology and economic prosperity that liberals praised so highly. The United States, according to Marcuse, was a quasi-totalitarian "technocracy." Real power lay with the "technocrats"—the experts in government, business, science, and other dominant institutions, who defined social policies and national priorities. In such a one-dimensional society, people became slaves to a technological imperative. The political process offered no real choice: Voters could choose only among candidates who endorsed the same social and economic policies and who ultimately relied on the same group of technocrats. People had become enslaved to a mass-production, mass-consumption economic system that satisfied only "false" needs—new automobiles, electronic gadgets, and thousands of other products that provided no real sense of happiness or personal fulfillment. Disaffected young people borrowed from Marcuse and his many popularizers, and terms such as *false consciousness* and *technocracy* became parts of the radical vocabulary. Marcuse, like Mills, endorsed the thesis that the liberal "good guys"—including the people who ran the big universities and the big government in Washington—were really the villains. Some young people came to see liberalism as a new form of conservatism; others saw it as a kind of suave totalitarianism, one that enslaved people with images and illusions rather than with guns and concentration camps.

Paul Goodman, a multifaceted social critic, also helped to popularize the theory that supposedly liberal institutions actually repressed Americans, especially young people. In *Growing Up Absurd* (1960) and a variety of essays, Goodman argued that educational institutions stifled young people's healthy natural instincts and subtly indoctrinated them with the values and skills of a badly flawed society. Order and regularity, he claimed, took precedence over spontaneity and creativity; memorization of meaningless data became more important than critical thought; the interests of teachers and administrators outweighed the needs of students. Goodman applied his anarchist critique to all of American society, contending that large bureaucratic institutions run by technocratic "experts" rarely performed their appointed tasks. . . .

## Experiences in the Civil Rights Movement

Their own experience in the civil rights movement of the later 1950s and early 1960s also propelled some young people, white as well as black, toward an open break with liberalism. Lacking great financial resources, the early civil rights movement relied upon youthful volunteers who could perform time-consuming jobs: preparing leaflets, running mimeograph machines, and marching in demonstrations. All these activities brought young people together in a common cause. Often travelling long distances and sleeping in makeshift accommodations, civil rights workers discovered a camaraderie and commitment that seemed to be missing elsewhere in America. Working together, young people found personal fulfillment in a crusade that they hoped would change the entire society.

At the same time, many of these young activists began to view the American political system as hopelessly corrupt and liberal political leaders as impediments to real social change. Attending school during the era of the cold war, young white volunteers had been brought up on idealized descriptions of American democracy, and the realization that black people suffered all types of legal discrimination and racist harassment proved disquieting. Seeking immediate solutions, civil rights workers inevitably confronted hostile or cautious political leaders. Segregationists in Alabama and Georgia would make no concessions, and even liberal politicians such as John Kennedy stressed the need to move slowly and to avoid sudden changes in race relations. On many occasions southern crowds beat up civil rights workers while FBI agents simply looked on and took notes. After confronting the racial hatred of Oxford, Mississippi, or Cicero, Illinois, many young activists charged that liberals offered Band-Aid solutions for deep national wounds. Segregation and racism, young civil rights workers charged, were evils that no decent society would tolerate.

## Beyond Liberalism and Toward a New Left

Not all young people protested, and the new radicals constituted only a minority of those between eighteen and twenty-five. Others remained true to the liberal spirit of John Kennedy, voting for Lyndon Johnson and going off to fight a war for "democracy and freedom" in Vietnam. Many young people bitterly resented long-haired "hippie" protectors, and they embraced the consumer products and the nine-to-five jobs scorned by the radicals. Talk of a "generation gap" obscured the equally large fissure within the youth generation itself and ignored the small yet significant group of older radicals who joined the Movement. But the young people who protested seemed to overshadow their peers in much the same way they dominated the media in the 1960s. Deeply disturbed by the direction of American society and convinced that they could find alternatives, the youthful rebels became the symbols of their generation.

What distinguished the young radicals from others of their age? Drawing upon several studies of college students, the psychologist Kenneth Keniston argued that the rebels were "psychological adults" but "sociological adolescents." Contrary to conventional wisdom, Keniston found that protesters tended to be excellent students, usually in the humanities, who suffered no great psychological difficulties. But as the products of affluent or solidly middle-class homes, they possessed the freedom, as well as the desire, to postpone settling into permanent social roles. Instead of leaping into an established career pattern, the young radicals wanted to adopt a less conventional role—that of social activist and agitator for political change. The fact that many believed their parents shared many of their ideals, but were forced to compromise them in their day-to-day lives, only intensified their desire to remain free from settled, adult routines.

To the young dissenters, liberalism's failures seemed more important than its admitted successes. Liberals *had* produced greater material affluence, but at a price: Most jobs seemed boring; life lacked adventure and excitement; racial discrimination oppressed millions of people; and personal relationships seemed as artificial as the products by which "straight" people measured their success. The cool, rational world of John Kennedy appeared to lack genuine feeling and to substitute eloquent rhetoric for meaningful social change. In contrast, a stance of opposition seemed to offer hope for immediate personal fulfillment as well as the chance for basic social change. Through a commitment to radicalism young people could instantly complete Paul Simon's "dangling conversations" or explore Bob Dylan's "smoke rings of the mind."

During the late 1950s and early 1960s a small group of college students helped to spark a revival of radical politics in the United States. At various universities—especially the

University of Wisconsin at Madison, the University of California at Berkeley, and the University of Michigan—youthful graduate students began to explore the relationship between "radical scholarship" and social activism. How could university professors avoid the kind of "scholarly dispassion" that radicals considered a means of justifying a repressive status quo? In time, a number of graduate students came to see themselves as prototypes for a new breed of college teacher: In the style of C. Wright Mills they would awaken campus life and bring new vitality to radical thought. Other university students took more direct action. In the San Francisco Bay area, students from Berkeley joined older radicals to demonstrate on behalf of such causes as dissolution of the House Un-American Activities Committee, abolition of capital punishment, and elimination of racial discrimination. Young people were also active in the South, helping miners fight the large coal companies in Hazard County, Kentucky, in addition to working for various civil rights organizations.

## Students for a Democratic Society

The predominately white Students for a Democratic Society (SDS) which began as an arm of the old left's League for Industrial Democracy, epitomized the New Left. SDS's Port Huron Statement of 1962, written largely by Tom Hayden, argued that America needed a dramatically new social and political system in which people "share in those social decisions determining the quality and direction" of their lives. In contrast to the liberal political order—one that "frustrates democracy by confusing the individual citizen, paralyzing policy discussion, and consolidating the irresponsible power of military and business interests"—SDS espoused "participatory democracy." The search for a true participatory democracy, the Port Huron Statement argued, was "governed by two central aims: that the individual share in those social decisions determining the quality and direction of his life; that society be organized to encourage independence in men and provide the means for their common participation." Though the Port Huron Statement contained clear hints of the radicalism that SDS would soon embrace, the manifesto of 1962 remained essentially a leftist-liberal document. It sounded no call for revolution and endorsed specific political programs only slightly to the left of the Fair Deal-New Frontier agenda.

SDS's leaders initially viewed community organizing as the first step toward participatory democracy. Poor people fell victim to better-organized elites, SDS argued, because they could not exert political pressure commensurate with their numbers. SDS branched out from the college campuses—many of its early leaders came from the University of Michigan—and launched grass-roots programs among the urban poor. By moving into the ghettos SDS hoped to stimulate the formation of new organizations and to channel poor people's discontent into local politics. In cities such as Newark, New Jersey, SDS mounted drives against urban renewal and in support of better housing, more jobs, and school lunch programs. The first SDSers displayed a missionary zeal. While cultural radicals were smoking dope, the SDSers bragged that they were turned on to political organizing. But despite their commitment, they quickly discovered the difficulties of organizing poor people, especially for a group committed to participatory democracy. Drawn mostly from white, middle-class families, young SDS members, unlike veteran organizers such as Saul Alinsky, were too impatient. Seeking a more congenial environment, SDS shifted its emphasis back to the college campus, the heart of the youth revolt in the 1960s.

## Campus Protests

The first serious campus protest occurred at the University of California at Berkeley in the fall of 1964. When university officials tried to limit political activity by radical students, protesters charged that the university's administration was bowing to pressures from right-wing business leaders in the Bay Area and destroying free speech on campus. As protests against the new university restrictions escalated and a temporary truce collapsed, mass rallies, takeovers of university buildings, and raids by local police highlighted the Berkeley Student Revolt. A number of campus groups, not all of whom represented New Left factions, joined under the banner of the Free Speech Movement. Thus, the earliest protests represented more of an attack upon the bureaucratic routine of Berkeley than a revolt against the entire university structure. In early December 1964 student protesters began wearing computer cards as name tags; militants soon called a campus-wide strike. Student leaders claimed that almost three-quarters of the student body—and a sizable portion of the faculty—supported the three-day walkout.

The Free Speech Movement gradually took a turn toward cultural and political radicalism. A young New Yorker who had drifted West to "check out the scene" arrived with a simple protest sign—FUCK. (Some people claimed that the letters really stood for "Freedom Under Clark Kerr," the president of the University of California.) His example encouraged a group of imitators, the "word-mongers," who helped give Berkeley an even more lurid reputation among the already unsympathetic. By the spring of 1965 many of the campus issues that had precipitated the first student protests had been largely forgotten or replaced by larger political concerns, especially the war in Vietnam.

## Grievances Against Big Universities

The unrest at Berkeley provided a scenario that repeated itself on many large college campuses during the rest of the 1960s. Increasingly, the tone and the aims of the protesters grew more militant. In banding together to fight college administrators and their outside supporters—James Kunen, a student observer of the 1968 disturbances at Columbia, called them "the biggies"—young people often discovered a new sense of community. As the civil rights workers in Mississippi had done earlier, they developed a kind of garrison mentality, viewing themselves as victims of a faceless power structure.

The modern "multiversity" provided a perfect target. Big universities displayed what radicals considered the major sins of modern liberalism: an emphasis on competitiveness, reliance on bureaucratic structures, petty restrictions on personal lifestyles, and an apparent feeling that bigger inevitably meant better. Many nonradicals shared some of these concerns. Sensitive young students, many of whom had been reared in families that stressed openness and concern for their children's feelings, felt especially frustrated by the impersonality and routine of universities such as Berkeley and Columbia. They complained that large, impersonal lectures and haphazard discussion sections exemplified the multiversity's assembly-line approach to education. Many students felt reduced to IBM numbers, subject to the whims of giant computers, and dependent on faceless bureaucrats who ran the multimillion-dollar operations. Even the University of California's liberal president Clark Kerr considered himself primarily the administrator of a large "benevolent bureaucracy," a huge enterprise that produced knowledge instead of consumer goods. "The university and segments of industry are becoming more alike," Kerr observed in 1960. Finally most students resented what they considered invasions of their personal freedoms by university officials. Women, even those who were legally of age, had to observe dress codes and dorm hours on most college campuses during the early 1960s; men at many state universities were required to take two years of ROTC; and faculty-dominated committees censored student publications. Dissidents began to demand that universities abandon or relax these restrictions, reduce the number of required courses, and offer programs "relevant" to mid-twentieth-century society.

When student muckrakers examined the multiversity's role in American society they found additional grievances. Professors conducted classified research for the Defense Department; Harvard chemists, not Dow Chemical, had developed napalm. Seeking additional space for new buildings, athletic stadiums, and parking lots, universities sometimes expanded into neighboring black ghettos and pushed out the residents. Some private universities, radicals also discovered, owned inner-city properties and qualified as genuine slum landlords. To make the indictment complete, big universities rarely admitted black students; when they did, recruitment efforts centered on talented black athletes and a few top-flight minority students. Viewed from within, the multiversity seemed to offer mind-numbing courses and senseless regimentation. Seen as part of liberal society, it appeared to aid war and racism.

Student and faculty pressures brought significant changes and a few strategic retreats by the old guard. Most colleges relaxed lifestyle restrictions, abolished compulsory ROTC, adjusted curriculum requirements, made special efforts to recruit minority students, and established separate minority-studies programs. A few professors even encouraged social activism by permitting students to substitute "relevant" outside projects for more traditional assignments. Although a number of spectacular "busts" temporarily halted protests, many campuses continued to serve as staging areas for forays against the outside world. At many urban universities large groups of street people provided additional troops for campus demonstrations and swelled the ranks of the "student" opposition. A radicalized university, activists began to hope, would be an important tool for changing the larger society.

## Protesting Against the Vietnam War

The protests against growing American involvement in the war in Vietnam demonstrated the value as well as the limitations of the university in radical politics. The crusade against the Vietnam war did not begin on the campuses, but dissent within the academic community gave the antiwar movement an influential forum. Early in 1965, after President Johnson mounted an all-out bombing campaign against North Vietnam, antiwar activists organized a nationwide series of teach-ins, meetings at which supporters and opponents of American participation in the war debated before largely student audiences. Initially some protesters hoped that the teach-ins would spark vigorous exchanges with government officials and that the confrontations might eventually change the policies of the Johnson administration. But by 1966 most militant opponents of the war were charging that teach-ins only wasted precious time. Obviously, the meetings were having little effect on President Johnson's actions, and the novelty of the gatherings was wearing thin. Although teach-ins continued sporadically throughout the 1960s—and even into the 1970s on some campuses—the antiwar movement began to desert the lecture platforms for the streets.

Antiwar demonstrations borrowed from both the tactics of the civil rights movement and the techniques of the teach-in. Beginning with a mass march, demonstrations invariably concluded with a series of speeches and entertainment by folk-rock musicians. Organizers claimed that by bringing large numbers of people into the streets they could dramatize the strength of the Movement, increase "radical consciousness," and pressure the national government to change its policies. . . .

By collecting tens of thousands of people at one demonstration, leaders of the movement could reassure themselves that all was going well. Even a fraction of a percent of the baby boom generation, when gathered in one spot, made a good-sized crowd, and a sprinkling of older people raised hopes that the movement was making converts outside its normal youth market. Such gatherings gradually became ritualized. Protesters sprawled on the grass, half-listening to familiar political rhetoric, and reminisced about previous demonstrations and "hassles." For many people marches served much the same function as religious revival meetings: The faithful assembled from across the country, felt their faith renewed, and then went back to plan for the next gathering.

The vast majority of youthful protesters strongly opposed the war and felt estranged from the liberal society, but many simply lacked interest in sustained political activity. In time, the antipathy that disaffected young people felt toward the liberal establishment was transferred to the "peace bureaucrats" in the New Left. Most cultural radicals, whom the mass media labeled *hippies*, preferred to "do their own thing."

# The Counterculture

Timothy Miller

Many young people in the 1960s rebelled against society not through political protest or activism, but by rejecting middle-class values in dress and behavior in their personal lives. Beginning especially in 1967, enclaves of a distinctive "counterculture" sprang up in the Haight-Ashbury district of San Francisco, New York's East Village, and other metropolitan areas. Timothy Miller, a professor of religious studies at the University of Kansas, examines the beliefs and values of the 1960s counterculture and its chief practitioners, called "hippies" (from "hip," a jazz musician's expression of being aware and knowledgeable). Hippies, who were mainly white children of relatively affluent families, rejected American culture as too restrictive, unjust, and boring, he argues. Miller examines the connections and differences between hippies and New Left political activists, and asserts that the counterculture can be viewed as a religious movement—albeit one that rejected most trappings of organized religion.

---

The counterculture was a romantic social movement of the late 1960s and very early 1970s, mainly composed of teenagers and persons in their early twenties, who through their flamboyant lifestyle expressed their alienation from mainstream American life. *Counterculture*, written as one word

Excerpted from chapter 1, "Introduction," of *The Hippies and American Values*, by Timothy Miller. Copyright ©1991 by The University of Tennessee Press. Reprinted by permission of The University of Tennessee Press.

or two, became the standard term for the movement (or nonmovement, as some would have it) after the appearance, in 1969, of Theodore Roszak's influential book *The Making of a Counter Culture.* Until then, several competing terms described the cultural revolt of the young; other early contenders were *alternative culture* and *the underground.*

Any culture, of course, can spawn its countercultures, and thus the hippies were part of a long tradition of cultural demurring. In many ways their most obvious and immediate predecessors were the bohemians and beatniks who inhabited earlier decades of the twentieth century. The progression from beat to hip is a fairly obvious one; the beats of the 1950s advocated dropping out of society, promoted new forms of art and literature, smoked marijuana, listened to unorthodox music (jazz), rejected traditional sexual norms, and even popularized the word "hip." One of the first books (1966) to notice the first stirrings of what would become hippie culture in the East Village of New York was plausibly entitled *The New Bohemia.*

Behind both the 1960s counterculture and its predecessor beat culture lay black America. Although the hippies were mainly white (more about that later), they were cultural outsiders, renegades who deviated from the American Way of Life. Black radicals (Malcolm X, W.E.B. duBois) were countercultural heroes because they refused to compromise with the white and prosperous Establishment. Black musicians gave heart as well as soul to hip music. (Bob Dylan and the Beatles may have been the principal cultural icons, but the energy of Chuck Berry and Little Richard wrote the grammar of rock.) Black musicians were smoking marijuana decades before white dropouts had heard of it. Norman Mailer was writing about beatniks in his 1957 essay "The White Negro," but his observations apply equally to hippies:

> It is no accident that the source of Hip is the Negro for he has been living on the margin between totalitarianism and democracy for two centuries. But the presence of Hip as a

working philosophy in the sub-philosophies of American life is probably due to jazz. . . . In this wedding of the white and the black it was the Negro who brought the cultural dowry. Any Negro who wishes to live must live with danger from his first day.

And, Mailer concluded, even the jargon of hip was shaped in major part by "the Negro jazzman who was the cultural mentor of a people."

## Hippies

The counterculture's participants, usually called hippies, found themselves cast adrift from the prevailing values of society and tried, variously, to effect major changes in majority society or to drop out of it. As the hippies saw things, the Establishment—the tired, entrenched, declining dominant system—was rotten to the core, and a new society needed to arise on the cultural dunghill. Some hippies were escapists who simply favored withdrawal from the prevailing culture; others proposed much more active opposition to and confrontation with it as a necessary step on the road to cultural freedom and progress.

The counterculture had a vocal separatist minority which rejected the dominant culture wholesale and proclaimed the necessity of creating a new, independent, egalitarian society, although the means for getting there were usually murky. Separatist rhetoric could be powerful: one notable separatist document, "The Declaration of Cultural Evolution," written in 1968 by a committee including Timothy Leary, Allen Ginsberg, Paul Krassner, and Abbie Hoffman, listed, in a style imitative of the Declaration of Independence, grievances against majoritarian society—political repression, destruction of the environment, war, and the like. The Declaration maintained that the counterculture had pointed the way to needed social changes, but that "many have been deaf to the voice of reason and consanguinity." Therefore, "human beings everywhere are, and quite properly ought to be, absolved from all allegiance to the present Cultural Arrangements insofar as they are obsolete and harmful.". . .

On the whole, however, the counterculture proposed not so much a confrontation with mainstream culture as a simple withdrawal from it. As Lawrence Lipton put it in 1968, "The hippies have passed beyond American society. They're not really living in the same society. . . . It's not so much that they're living on the leftovers, on the waste of American society, as that they just don't give a damn." Or, as Raymond Mungo wrote, "we . . . long ago commenced on our own total Moratorium on constructive participation in this society."

Withdrawal often meant heading for a hip commune. The communes, so the theory went, were not aimed at cultural confrontation, but simply were a turning away to build a new society apart from the old. Down on the commune, a hipster wrote in 1969, "We are in Amerika, but we are no longer a part of it."

From what were the hippies so alienated? Why did they see an alternative, be it confrontive or simply escapist, as necessary? The widespread sense of the counterculture was that it was simply impossible to cope with the dominant American culture any longer. America was a treadmill, a swamp of mediocrity, an emotional pressure cooker; it had become a series of meaningless institutions that transcended persons and developed lives of their own. Moreover, America had become Amerika (the German spelling evoked the Nazis), an oppressor of dissenters. Worse, it was all boring. Widespread mental illness and compulsive violence showed that there was a deep-running malaise in the culture; the rational alternative, as the hippies saw it, was simply to drop out.

But even dropping out was hard to do. Hippie communes were not welcome in many neighborhoods. Rock festivals were banned at every turn. Nonviolent psychedelic chemists ended up in prison. Establishment culture—which was, after all, in the driver's seat—was not willing to tolerate the deviant behavior of the new alternative. As one hippie wrote, "They sense a threat to their continued . . . dominance. And they are absolutely correct."

## The Generation Gap

Age did not a hippie make or unmake (there were, after all, a few older hippies and lots of young straights), but it is abundantly clear that most counterculturists were relatively young (under thirty, as the catchphrase had it) and that there was great distrust among the hippies of persons very far beyond adolescence. Many writers on both sides of the chasm depicted a "generation gap" that constituted a major battle-line between youth and adults. Theodore Roszak helped promote the concept in *The Making of a Counter Culture*, depicting as critical formative agents Allen Ginsberg's 1950s poem *Howl*, which condemned the parental generation by identifying it with the evil Moloch, and *Mad* magazine, which steadily presented a fairly consistent cynicism about "adult" culture to a very large young audience. Within the counterculture, the generation gap was much discussed. The old was moribund; revolutionary cultural change was imminent. One polemicist, Jack G. Burgess, proclaimed,

> [You are standing on a generation that] WILL NOT BE STOOD UPON!
>
> You have declared illegal virtually every establishment, event, gathering, device, and instrument we consider important and worthwhile.
>
> [BUT] YOU CANNOT STOP THE HANDS OF TIME AND YOU CANNOT STILL THE WINDS OF CHANGE!
>
> YOU ARE DYING! Time is removing you from the face of this earth.

In a more analytical frame of mind, underground writer George D. Maloney in 1968 pictured society as broadly divided by age groups into three major generations: under thirty, thirty to forty-five, and over forty-five. The problem of the thirty–to–forty-five generation, he argued, was a simple one: its members were children of the Depression, were unable to shake their preoccupation with security when prosperity returned, and thus were never much concerned with human values. Maloney saw as hopeless the impasse between "young" and "parental" generations, and proclaimed, "'Tis indeed the stuff of which revolutions are made."

The hopelessness of the parental generation was a common theme in the underground, but occasionally a note of a brighter future sounded. Andrew Kopkind, writing in *Rolling Stone* about the 1969 Woodstock festival, saw a phoenix of new culture rising from the ashes of "adult" American life:

> What is not illusionary is the reality of a new culture of opposition. It grows out of the disintegration of the old forms, the vinyl and aerosol institutions that carry all the inane and destructive values of privatism; competition, commercialism, profitability and elitism. . . .
>
> It's not a "youth thing" now but a generational event; chronological age is only the current phase.

## The Counterculture and the New Left

Although there was a widespread sense of a youth culture of opposition at least by 1967, the alternative culture was never a monolith. Within it were at least two quite different approaches to the social crisis: there was a New Left, an overtly political opposition to the dominant culture; and there was hippiedom, the world of the dropouts and cultural dissenters. Most writers analyzing the sixties have grappled with the problem of showing convergences and divergences between the "Heads" and the "Fists," as Laurence Leamer called them. Paul Goodman distinguished the two related movements in classic religious terms: the distinction involved between inward-oriented hippies and outward-oriented activists was, he said, very close to the age-old question of faith and works. The majority of hippies, while often sympathetic to the New Left, weren't much interested in politics and thus saw the counterculture and New Left as distinct movements, even though the line between them was not always precise. A substantial minority, on the other hand, saw the two groups as more alike than different, because they were both sworn opponents of the established regime; therefore, they were to be considered as fingers on one hand, distinct but sharing a common role. The visionary culture the hippies wanted to establish was based on such political ideologies as peace, racial harmony, and equality; the political crusade of the New Left was deeply romantic, and the great majority of the New Leftists lived the cultural values of the hippies, smoking marijuana, engaging in liberated sex, and often living communally.

Richard Neville created a typology, echoed in less precise terms elsewhere, that is useful here. Under the general heading of "The Movement," he saw three fundamental divisions: the New Left, the Underground (i.e., counterculture), and the "militant poor." The New Left consisted primarily of radical political activists, many of them members of organizations such as Students for a Democratic Society and the Student National Coordinating Committee. The militant poor consisted primarily of ethnic revolutionaries and activists, most notably blacks, Chicanos, and Native Americans. Finally, the Underground included "hippies, beats, mystics, madmen, freaks, yippies, crazies, crackpots, communards and anyone who rejects rigid political ideology ('it's a brain disease'). . . ." The New Left and the counterculture both manifested a sharp discontent with American society and its decadent hypocrisy, but they were nonetheless distinct groups. . . .

The differences between counterculture and New Left sometimes aroused hostility on both sides. David McReynolds wrote in 1967 of a meeting to plan an antiwar rally, at which Richard Alpert (later known as Ram Dass) delivered a long diatribe urging people to boycott the planned rally because some people there would burn their draft cards, and it would be "bad public relations for the psychedelic community to be involved in that kind of thing." McReynolds, writing up the incident, blasted Alpert: "I do not mock the man who seeks out the God within him. But I do mock the man who, in one breath, tells every youth to follow his own light and in the next breath warns him about public relations."

## Hippies and Drugs

*Terry H. Anderson, a professor of history at Texas A&M University, writes that hippies or "freaks" commonly took drugs to expand their consciousness, to rebel against the establishment, and to enhance their own sense of being different. Hippies distinguished between "dope" (marijuana and certain hallucinogens such as peyote or LSD) and other drugs such as alcohol, barbiturates, opiates such as heroin, and amphetamines ("speed").*

Dope was the freak's little helper that aided their escape from the establishment. "If it hadn't been for grass I'd still be wearing a crewcut and saluting the flag." Escape was important. Frustrated people often relieve anxieties by eating, smoking, drinking, even shopping away their worries: "I Love to Shop!" But not hippies. "Smoke dope everywhere," proclaimed one. "Dope is Great, it's fun, it's healthy. . . . Get every creature so stoned they can't stand the plastic shit of American culture."

Dope, especially LSD, also helped them expand or alter their own consciousness. . . .

Thus, by taking dope hippies felt different, Heads versus Straights, another form of Us versus Them. "Grass opened up a new space for middle class white kids," recalled Jay Stevens, "an inner space as well as outer space. It became a ritual—sitting around with your friends, passing a joint from person to person, listening to music, eating, talking, joking, maybe making out—all the senses heightened." They felt community being part of the underground. A daughter wrote:

Dear Dad:
   Dope . . . potacidspeedmetheshitboojointtripped freakfiend. . . . Flip Out. It all runs together; indivisible, etc. etc. etc. from—if you can take it—the world in which we live. Real. World. REAL

Such was the typical New Leftist attitude toward the counterculture. But there was also a periodic recognition, in some leftist circles, that the hippies made an important con-

WORLD. Our world, not yours. The world of everything, dream dance escape thought and blood. A machine has cranked us out. And our father doesn't know how to stop it, much less fix it. . . . There's a LOVE in MY WORLD for the new exciting land that was always far off the map in fifth grade geography. Things aren't always knowable and certain and stifling. To walk through it is its essence, so, Dad, let's TAKE A TRIP.

But trip on certain helpers. While no two hippies would agree, in general they used marijuana and its more potent form, hashish, to obtain a quiet euphoria and "get high," or they used hallucinogens or psychedelics such as psilocybin, peyote, and LSD to expand sensory perception and "blow the mind." Thus, dope that felt good or expanded experience was fine; others that made one sick or addicted were a "bad trip," a "bummer." Freaks might avoid depressants and substances that tended to be addicting such as amphetamines, or "speed," or narcotics such as heroin, or "smack." New drugs appeared endlessly, and underground editors ran columns like Dr. Eugene Schoenfeld's "HIPpocrates" and other articles which warned their readers, "Speed kills!" "I would like to suggest that you don't use speed, and here's why," cautioned musician Frank Zappa: "it is going to mess up your heart, mess up your liver, your kidneys, rot out your mind. In general, this drug will make you just like your mother and father."

Hippies made their own decisions, of course, and they violated the norm because they were rebels and because they enjoyed experimenting. Nevertheless, various surveys reported that at the beginning of the sixties only 4 percent of youth aged 18 to 25 had tried marijuana, and that twelve years later that figure was almost 50 percent; 60 percent for college students; and much higher at some universities.

Terry H. Anderson, *The Movement and the Sixties*. New York: Oxford University Press, 1995, pp. 259–60.

tribution to radical politics just by their existence. No less a leftist than Herbert Marcuse called the hippies "the only viable social revolution" of the day, arguing that despite their disinterest in Marxism, they were having a revolutionary impact because they opposed a repressive social system, "reject[ed] the junk they're supposed to buy now, . . . reject[ed] the war . . . reject[ed] the competitive performances."

A generation later, Marcuse's observations still hold up. As Andrew Kimbrell argued in 1988, the New Left's agenda was actually not a fundamental threat to society: civil rights of blacks, women, and others could be ensured by law, the war could be ended, the environment could be protected—all without making major inroads on the basic structure of society. After all, the New Left did not challenge the supremacy of reason, the notion that material prosperity is the supreme goal of society, the sanctity of economic growth, or the belief that spiritual values constituted an opiate, or at least were unimportant. By contrast, the counterculture

> though often acting in a drugged haze, attacked society at a more fundamental level than the New Left. Through experiments with lifestyles and philosophies, it challenged, if only by implication, the assumptions of most Americans about politics, knowledge, materialism, technology, and what constitutes the "good life."

## A White, Male-Defined Movement

The hippies were mainly children of privilege, and their outlook reflected their heritage. They glorified poverty and sometimes lived in it; they championed the rights of racial minorities and, to some extent, women. But the movement came from a prosperous, white, male-defined segment of society. Perhaps it was inevitable that those who would reject middle-class comforts had to come from comfortable backgrounds; the have-nots of society had no material luxuries to rebel against.

Black hippies were unusual. They did show up occasionally, and they were readily accepted by the white majority. Their numbers, however, were never large. Blacks interested in dissent from the prevailing culture tended to be more interested in racial-political than flower-child activities. It is noteworthy, though, that militant blacks, while critical of all who would not join the revolutionary struggle, regarded the hippies as allies, not enemies. In 1968, an editorial in the *Black Panther*, the most widely read militant black publication, defined the Black Panther Party's position in its usual mince-no-words style:

> Black brothers stop vamping on the hippies. They are not your enemy. Your enemy, right now, is the white racist pigs who support this corrupt system. . . . Your enemy is not the hippies. . . . WE HAVE NO QUARREL WITH THE HIPPIES. LEAVE THEM ALONE. Or the BLACK PANTHER PARTY will deal with you!

Certainly the counterculture was male-defined. As the following chapters will suggest, authorship in the underground press was overwhelmingly male. Women were commonly "chicks"; when they were in relationships with men, they were "old ladies." It is important to remember, however, that the heyday of the counterculture, which was in the late 1960s, came along before the prominent advent of the contemporary feminist movement, which began to attract serious, widespread attention only about 1968 or 1969, just as the counterculture was starting to wind down. At least at first, the male hippies were as disinclined as males elsewhere in society to allow women equal rights and privileges; the gap between egalitarian hippie rhetoric and male hippie actions may have had some influence on the emerging feminists, many of whom had deep roots in the counterculture. If . . . hippie ideas seem largely male-defined, it is because that was the dominant orientation of the hippies in their prime years.

## The Counterculture and American Religion

Many ethical systems are theological or religious in basis; if the hippies had an ethic, one may naturally ask whether or not they constituted a religious movement. The answer hinges mainly on how one defines *religion*. Definitions that involve institutions and rituals supporting a clearly articulated religious quest would leave the hippies out; most counterculturists did not see hipness as religious per se, even if there were religious movements (such as the dope churches and various Eastern movements) within the hip world. Definitions that involve such concepts as ultimate concern, however, could well include the hippies. The counterculture was a movement of seekers of meaning and value, a movement which thus embodied the historic quest of any religion. Like many dissenting religions, the hippies were enormously hostile to the religious institutions of the dominant culture, and they tried to find new and adequate ways to do the tasks the dominant religions failed to perform.

Some outside observers regarded the hippies as religionists, whether the hippies liked the label or not. Harvey Cox, for example, wrote, shortly after the Summer of Love (1967) . . . :

Hippieness represents a secular version of the historic American quest for a faith that warms the heart, a religion one can experience deeply and feel intensely. The love-ins are our 20th Century equivalent of the 19th Century Methodist camp meetings—with the same kind of fervor and the same thirst for a God who speaks through emotion and not through anagrams of doctrine. Of course, the Gospel that is preached differs somewhat in content, but then, content was never that important for the revivalist—it was the spirit that counted.

Hippieness has all the marks of a new religious movement. It has its evangelists, its sacred grottoes, its exuberant converts.

Similarly, religion scholar William C. Shepherd found that countercultural religiousness was patent:

Since a set of symbols, certain ritual practices, and the production of social cohesion are all marks of religious systems, it is fair to say that our counter cultural young have developed a genuine form of religiosity, indeed a quite new form for the West because it does not include doctrines or truth claims about supersensual entities.

Many within the counterculture itself also saw the movement as essentially a new religion, one which drew from many traditions, including Asian and Native American religions as well as Western Christianity and Judaism. West Coast sexual and psychedelic activist Jefferson Poland wrote, "we find ourselves (to our surprise) in a religious revival. Simple atheism is not enough." Ralph J. Gleason, the senior sage of hip, believed that religiosity could not be ignored here or anywhere: "The need to believe is there. The knowledge is implicit in life itself and the desire to believe is so overwhelming that non-belief cannot be tolerated. It is part of the life support system and it must be there."

No sense of religious purpose among the hippies meant, however, that the counterculture had any fondness for the dominant religions of America. To the hippies, the churches and synagogues were mainly hoary vehicles of Establishment thought and activity in its worst form. As one hip writer (rather awkwardly) summarized the critique,

> The churches are as flagrant violators of the natural, real religious way, the way of man in harmony with earth, water, sky and fire, and, of course, his fellows as any other institution. These supposed houses of worship, where one would hope, there might exist something analogous to an institutionalized conscience, are in fact just further examples of sham and hypocrisy. Rather than insist Christians as Christians in the barest sense the word conveys, refrain from supporting the golden calves our government spawns, its campaigns, its waste, its wars, the church instead functions as a Sunday salve . . . assuaging the blunted senses of each cowardly congregation . . . dressed its best for one more Sunday obligation.

Self-righteous centers of hypocrisy, stations for the blessing of the Establishment, wealthy organizations mainly interested in preserving themselves, havens for the narrow-minded, anachronisms utterly irrelevant to modern life—thus were the dominant religions regarded by counterculturists. The whole point of the hip rebellion was to announce the New, and the prevailing religious institutions stood foursquare for the Old. They were part of the problem, not part of the solution.

# Rock Music and Revolution

Godfrey Hodgson

The role of rock music in the various political and cultural movements of the 1960s is described in the following selection by Godfrey Hodgson, a British journalist and author. In the early years of the decade, folk musicians such as Bob Dylan, Phil Ochs, and Joan Baez gained notoriety with their songs featuring political themes. Beginning around 1965 rock supplanted folk as the leading music of the generational "revolution"—but a revolution of consciousness and culture rather than of politics. Influential groups of the mid-to-late 1960s, including the Beatles, Rolling Stones, and San Francisco–based bands such as the Grateful Dead and Jefferson Airplane developed a style of music that featured radical political rhetoric and drug references. Hodgson argues, however, that rock music is essentially a commercial product. The idea that it could revolutionize society was simply part of its skillful marketing to the younger generation.

Throughout the sixties, the changing phases of popular music did coincide uncannily with changing political moods. First came the unworldly moralizing and naive political idealism of the folk-music movement: Judy Collins, Joan Baez, Pete Seeger, and [Bob] Dylan the folk singer were at the height of their popularity between 1963 and

Excerpted from *America in Our Time*, by Godfrey Hodgson. Copyright ©1976 by Godfrey Hodgson. Used by permission of Doubleday, a division of Random House, Inc.

1965, the years of high hopes for the New Frontier and the Great Society.

Then, in 1965, came rock. The words of the folk songs had been full of radical implications. The singers themselves were men and women of the Left. They sang about peace and war, poverty and injustice, and sometimes, as in *The Times They Are A-Changin'*, they looked forward to the coming of revolution.

The rock singers sometimes sang about revolution, too. But the word meant something different for them from the literal, political revolution of such New York Marxist folk singers as Pete Seeger and Phil Ochs. The music itself was to be the revolution. In the first dizzy years of rock, in 1965 and 1966, and above all in 1967, the promise that intoxicated initiates was that of a wider revolution of consciousness and culture, of which political revolution would come as a by-product.

## Rock Music's Origins

Rock music is American on both sides of the family if you trace its pedigree far enough. Its technical elements have come down through the commercial rock-and-roll and rhythm-and-blues of the 1950s from the two deepest fountains of American popular music, black blues and white country music. But, in 1965, two traditions fused to create the rock music of the late sixties: one come back to America from Britain, and one out of San Francisco.

## The Beatles

Beginning, like so much else, in 1963, first the Beatles, and then a succession of other British pop groups, of whom the Rolling Stones eventually became almost as important as the Beatles themselves, re-exported American popular music to America and proved that their kind of it could be a commercial success on a far bigger scale than the originals it came from. Folk music, rock-and-roll, and urban blues all sold to fractional markets: to campus and coffee house and to the black "race" market. The Beatles' formula, compounded of driving rhythm, sophisticated musical craftsmanship, fresh and often exquisite melody, and literate, irreverent lyrics about real life, unlocked the American youth market as a whole. After the Beatles had made the breach, a host of imitators, British and American, poured through it.

Technical and economic factors contributed to the staggering commercial success of rock music. The improvement in electronic amplifying; the development of eight- and sixteen-track tape recorders; the spread of FM radio; the marketing shift from 45-rpm singles to 33-rpm albums (itself predicated on the new prosperity which meant that even teen-agers were used to spending four dollars on an album once a week or more and could afford elaborate stereo equipment); the rise of such aggressive new recording companies as the Ertegun brothers' Atlantic Records to compete with the stodgy giants of the industry—these made the rock boom possible.

But in the end the phenomenal success of the Beatles was due to psychological compatibility. They came from an Irish working-class background in Liverpool, where irreverence toward all established authority, and especially toward national and military authority, is endemic. They grew up knowing some of the things that young Americans were discovering with pained surprise in the 1960s: that industrial society uses people as well as makes them more affluent, that there is a good deal of hypocrisy about politicians' patriotism, that a lot of middle-class virtue is a sham. When a generation of young Americans emerged from Birmingham and Dallas, Mississippi and Vietnam, into disillusionment and cynicism, the Beatles were waiting there with a grin on their faces. They were as disillusioned and cynical as anyone, but they were cheerful about it; they had never expected that life would be any different.

It would be hard to exaggerate the influence the Beatles had on the generation of Americans who grew up in the sixties. But the Beatles were influenced by America, too, and in particular by the other stream that went into creating the vitality of rock music. That was the San Francisco influence.

## The San Francisco Bands

In San Francisco in 1965, 1966 and 1967, Jon Landau of *Rolling Stone* has written, "rock was not only viewed as a form of entertainment." It was "an essential component of a 'new culture,' along with drugs and radical politics." That hardly does justice to the fervid claims that were made on behalf of the new music. The leading San Francisco band, The Grateful Dead, was at the very center of the general ferment in the Bay Area in those years. It had played at Ken Kesey's legendary "acid tests." Augustus Owsley Stanley III had personally bought the band its equipment out of his LSD profits. And the Dead had actually lived in a commune in the Haight-Ashbury until driven out by the sheer squalor into which that neighborhood declined after 1967. The other San Francisco bands, such as the Jefferson Airplane, shared this "underground" style. In 1967, for their own various reasons, the three unarguable superstars of the new music—Bob Dylan, the Beatles, and the Rolling Stones—all stopped touring America. In their absence, after the Monterey festival of that summer, it was the "underground," San Francisco style that emerged triumphant. Soon even the Beatles were imitating the San Francisco underground style: a peculiar blend of radical political rhetoric, of allusions to the drug culture, and of the excited sense of imminent, apocalyptic liberation. After 1967 the equation between rock music and "revolution" became firmly anchored in the minds of all those who listened to the one or hankered after the other.

## The Altamont Concert

It was perhaps always an absurd idea that a new kind of music could change society as Hamelin was changed by the Pied Piper. It was in any case a short-lived idea. The episode which, more than any other, revealed the sheer nastiness that was the antithesis to the claim that rock music was liberating came at the Rolling Stones' concert at Altamont, California, in the last month of the sixties.

It was part of the Stones' carefully polished image to be "their satanic majesties," the naughtiest boys in the world. That winter, they toured the United States. Audiences and critics agreed that their music was as exciting as ever. To end the tour, they planned to give a free concert in San Francisco. It was to be a royal gesture, and at the same time their acknowledgment of the city's role in the culture that had crowned them.

The coronation was as satanic as any press agent could have wished. "Hustlers of every stripe," wrote the relatively sympathetic Michael Lydon in *Ramparts*, "swarmed to the new scene like piranhas to the scent of blood." And so did three hundred thousand for them to prey off. Lydon saw "the dancing beaded girls, the Christlike young men and smiling babies familiar from countless stories on the Love Generation." But another side of the culture was unmistakable, too: "speed freaks with hollow eyes and missing teeth, dead-faced acid-heads burned out by countless flashes, old beatniks clutching gallons of red wine, Hare Krishna chanters with shaved heads and acned cheeks."

Four people died. One, a young man with long hair and a metal cross around his neck, was so stoned that he walked unregarding into an irrigation ditch and drowned. Another was clubbed, stabbed and kicked to death by the Hell's Angels. What were those dangerous pets of the San Francisco *avant-garde* supposed to be doing at the concert? It turned out that they had been hired as "security guards" by the Rolling Stones, on the advice of none other than The Grateful Dead, the original troubadours of love, peace and flowers. "Regrettable," commented the Rolling Stones' manager, "but if you're asking me for a condemnation of the Angels . . ." It sounded eerily like President Nixon discussing Lieutenant Calley's conviction for the massacre at My Lai.

"Altamont showed everyone," wrote one of the most levelheaded of the rock critics, Jon Landau, in *Rolling*

*Stone,* "that everything that had been swept under the rug was now coming into the open: the greed, the hustle, the

## Memories of Woodstock

*Thirty years after the 1969 Woodstock Festival, photojournalist Jason Lauré wrote the following reminiscence of what is arguably the single most famous rock music event of the 1960s.*

I arrived in San Francisco at the end of the summer of love in 1967 and stayed for six months in Haight-Ashbury. We would gather in Golden Gate Park for free concerts by the Grateful Dead and Jefferson Airplane. It was there that I bought my first camera and started photographing these folks. Nearly two years later in New York, the idea of seeing old friends and meeting new ones brought me to Woodstock.

When it began, no one could have known that the Woodstock Festival—a three-day celebration of community and music—would turn into a watershed moment of American culture and a landmark of the twentieth century. Woodstock defined a generation and symbolized the differences between the World War II generation and their children. It was the largest peaceful gathering in our history, and it happened spontaneously.

Woodstock grew to half a million by word of mouth alone. Most of us heard about it from like-minded friends and simply picked up our backpacks and went. We weren't concerned about where we would sleep, how we would live, or any of the other mundane details. We were drawn by the promise of the music—the music that defined us and that still endures thirty years later. From all over the country we made our way to the tiny town of Bethel (there was no place for the festival in Woodstock proper). Fortunately, a local farmer named Max Yasgur offered his land to the organizers, giving the event a home.

Woodstock literally stopped traffic. For the only time in its history, the New York State Thruway was closed down by sheer hype. . . ." Only four months earlier, the national media, always quick to seize on some dramatic but complex event and shape its ambiguities into the oversimplified symbol of

volume. Undaunted, hippies simply left their cars on what was the best-paved parking lot around and walked the rest of the way to the site. The performers had to be helicoptered in; there was no other way in or out.

Although tickets were sold, the endless stream of people arriving gave the organizers no choice but to let them in free of charge—and it became a free festival. This was very much in keeping with the ethos of the participants: share everything, experience life, and "don't sweat the small stuff."

Music was at the heart of Woodstock. An endless roster of the best in the business performed day and night. Music was the common bond that transcended professional status, religion, education, and region. It brought us together as a community ready to change the world.

Though often characterized by the slogan "make love, not war," Woodstock wasn't an overt demonstration. There weren't any posters or rallies; it all came out through the music. Hundreds of thousands of draft-age people were facing a war that seemed endless. The festival gave them hope. Young people from small towns could see that there were half a million others just like them who were facing the same thing.

Although people watching from the outside thought it was the beginning of an era, it was in fact the end. Those of us who had lived through the sixties kept hearing about an "end of summer" event in the East. We all wanted to be there. Woodstock was to mark the culmination of that era and the end of a decade.

Since 1969, there have been attempts to re-create the spirit of Woodstock, but the defining spontaneity of that free festival remains elusive.

Jason Lauré, "Memory of a Free Festival, Woodstock Thirty Years Later," *The World & I*, August 1999.

a new trend, had celebrated the Woodstock Festival as the birth of a new "nation." Then, after Altamont, the boom jibed brutally over onto a new tack. Where the news magazines, the networks and the commentators had managed to ignore the hype, the hustle and even the mud, and had portrayed Woodstock as a midsummer night's dream of idyllic innocence, Altamont was painted as Walpurgisnacht, a witches' sabbath.

Those who were most sympathetic to the counter culture had been aware of its deep and dangerous ambiguities even long before Woodstock. It was as if, wrote Andrew Kopkind, a wholehearted convert to the alternative life style, "some monstrous and marvelous metaphor had come alive, revealing itself only in terms of its contradictions: paradise and concentration camp"—it was quite typical of the fashion of the time in radical journalism to compare a wet weekend with the Final Solution—"sharing and profiteering, sky and mud, love and death. The urges of the ten years' generation roamed the woods and pastures, and who could tell whether it was rough beast or speckled bird slouching through its Day-Glo manger to be born?" For Landau, more realistically, Woodstock was not a new birth but an ending. It was "the ultimate commercialization" of the underground culture at the very moment when it seemed to be in process of being transformed into a mass culture, and perhaps indeed into *the* mass culture. Since it demonstrated "just how strong in numbers the rock audience had become, and just how limited its culture was," he thought Woodstock "a fitting end to the sixties" and the satanic events at Altamont only a parody and an anticlimax.

## A Commercial Product

One reason why it was absurd to equate rock music with revolution, political or cultural, was because it was so very much a commercial product and one that was marketed with single-minded cynicism by individual entrepreneurs and corporate business alike. Behaving in this instance, for once, just as pragmatically as Marxist lore would have predicted, the entertainment industry put up with whatever the musicians and their admirers chose to inflict on it. It tolerated outrageous arrogance, boorishness and unreliability. It raised no demur at long hair on stage and clouds of marijuana in recording studios. It even shelled out royalties far higher than the deferential blacks and crooners who ground out the hits of the past had ever been paid. It would have put up with far more—just so long as the records kept selling. And sell they did.

In the very month of Woodstock *The Wall Street Journal,* no friend of revolution, psychic or political, looked upon rock music and found it good. Over the past several years, it reported, record sales had been rising at the rate of between 15 per cent and 20 per cent annually. The previous year, they had passed the $1-billion mark. The fundamental cause of this sales boom, no doubt, was prosperity: that very "Great Society" prosperity that the counter culture so bitterly affected to despise. But it was rock that was making those burgeoning sales. "Five years ago," the *Journal* found, meaning 1964, "Columbia Records . . . did about 15% of its business in rock. Today rock (using the term loosely) accounts for 60% or more of the vastly increased total."

In 1967 *Rolling Stone* magazine was founded, by Jann Wenner, age twenty-one, with seventy-five hundred dollars borrowed from family and friends. He could not have been a more characteristic product of the counter culture. He had dropped out of Berkeley, where he had been caught up in the Free Speech Movement. He knew Ken Kesey. He had been one of the early hippies. He had been involved with drugs. By the end of its first year *Rolling Stone* had a circulation of sixty thousand. By the end of the decade, with a circulation of over a quarter of a million, it was attracting lush advertising from the big record companies. Less than three years after it was floated, *Rolling Stone* was spending a sum of money roughly equivalent to its original capitalization in order to advertise on the back page of the New York *Times.* "If you are a corporate executive," the ad said, "trying to understand what is happening to youth today, you cannot afford to be without *Rolling Stone.*"

"Several large Establishment-oriented corporations," the New York *Times* reported as if to confirm the effectiveness of this pitch, "are interested in cashing in on the youth market that Woodstock proved exists These firms are hiring highly paid youth consultants to advise them on forthcoming trends that percolate from the deepest underground to . . . the silk-shirt hippie types from Forest Hills who do so much of the buying." "The Establishment," one underground journalist complained in 1970, "is slowly but steadily finding ways to exploit the radical movement."

To call this development revolution was to pervert language. Some of the adherents of the counter culture were uncomfortably aware of the incongruity of what was happening. They saw it, however, almost without exception, as evidence that "the Establishment" was taking their thing over. The more optimistic saw in the trend a portent of ultimate victory. The counter culture, wrote Andrew Kopkind, had grown out of the "vinyl and aerosol institutions that carry all the inane and destructive values of privatism, competition, commercialism, profitability and elitism." He conceded, however, that since the new culture had yet to produce its own, alternative institutions on a mass scale, it must be content with feeding the old system "with rock and dope and love and openness," so as to receive these precious gifts back "from Columbia Records or Hollywood or Bloomingdale's"—or, in other words, from the very "vinyl and aerosol institutions" that the new culture was supposed to be superseding.

## Music, Not Revolution

Others were unable to foresee any such spectacular conversion of the plastic Babylon. "So effective has the rock industry been in encouraging the spirit of optimistic youth takeover," wrote Michael Lydon in a bitter little essay called *Rock for Sale*, "that rock's truly hard political edge, its constant exploration of the varieties of youthful frustration, has been ignored and softened. Rock musicians, like their followers, have always been torn between the obvious pleasures that America held out and the price paid for them. Rock and roll is not revolutionary music, because it has never gotten beyond articulation of this paradox."

It was true enough that rock musicians made a beeline for the obvious pleasures of fame and fortune, and true, too, that many of them paid full price for them in the coinage of neurosis, crackup, and overdose. It is less clear that more than a handful of them ever had much of a hard political edge. Each of the three superstars of the sixties, as it happens, put himself on record on this point with brutal clarity.

"I was much more political before I started music," said Mick Jagger. "At the London School of What's-'is-Name, I was big on it, big arguments and thumping on tables—like everybody in *college*, man."

"Even though you've more or less retired from political and social protest," Nat Hentoff asked Bob Dylan in an interview for *Playboy* in 1966, "can you conceive of any circumstances that might persuade you to reinvolve yourself?"

"No," was Dylan's answer, "not unless all the people in the world disappeared."

"You say you want a revolution," sang John Lennon, "well, you can count me out."

Janis Joplin was of almost the same mind. "My music isn't supposed to make you riot," she once said. "It's supposed to make you fuck."

Rock music was never, except in the minds of a handful of its adherents, an attack on the values of "privatism, competition, commercialism, profitability and elitism." By the end of the decade it was hard even for them to deny that it had become a glorification of each and every one of those.

# The Backlash Against Social Protesters

William H. Chafe

The social turmoil of the 1960s produced a backlash among the majority of Americans who did not engage in organized protest or embrace the counterculture. William H. Chafe describes the reactions and beliefs of "middle Americans" during the 1960s in the following excerpt from his study *The Unfinished Journey: America Since World War II*. He argues that economic insecurity partly explains the antipathy many Americans felt towards black, feminist, and antiwar activists. More important, however, was the sense many felt that certain values and ideas they cherished—including patriotism, religion, and the importance of hard work—were coming under assault by those seeking radical social change. Chafe is a dean and professor of history at Duke University.

Inevitably, the turmoil of the sixties sparked a backlash of resentment. As one commentator remarked, those who endorsed radical change had forgotten Newton's third law of motion—that for every action there is an equal and opposite reaction. Even if all the social protectors were grouped together, they still comprised a distinct minority of the country. The majority, meanwhile, could not be expected to sit idly by as rebels assaulted their values and threatened their self-interest. Millions of citizens had devoted their

Excerpted from *The Unfinished Journey: America Since World War II*, 4th edition, by William H. Chafe. Copyright ©1986, 1991, 1995, 1999 by Oxford University Press, Inc. Used by permission of Oxford University Press, Inc.

lives to playing by the rules of the game—working hard, keeping the family together, advancing step by step toward a life of security and prosperity. Now, these same people believed that the rules were being changed and that a wholesale attack on middle-class respectability was in progress. Blacks who rioted in America's cities were challenging the concept of law and order. As antipoverty militants declared war on City Hall, they seemed to be undercutting all legitimate institutions of political representation. And when student protestors unfurled the Vietcong flag, called policemen "pigs," and openly flaunted their sexuality, they were assaulting institutions and mores that were central to the self-definition of countless citizens. If radical critics of America were alienated from the values of mobility, achievement, and respectability that characterized the dominant culture, many middle-class Americans were equally alienated from those who questioned customs they had been taught to cherish.

## White Ethnics

Events of the 1960s, and especially the rise of black militancy, galvanized a new self-consciousness among white ethnics. As the plea for black civil rights turned to a clamor for Black Power, members of other ethnic groups felt a challenge to their prerogatives and hard-earned victories. Many white workers had struggled for years to buy a decent house, achieve job security, and give their children an adequate education. Now, blacks seemed to be demanding all of these same things—immediately. To many, it seemed that blacks were seeking an unfair advantage. "The ethnic groups . . . don't want to penalize the Negro," observed political scientist John Roche, but "they feel strongly that the rules they came up by should apply." That meant hard work, sacrifice, and patience—qualities which white ethnics did not perceive in the Black Power movement, or in the activities of rioters in the inner city. "We build the city, not burn it down," one group of white workers declared. In the early 1960s, the vast majority of white Americans had approved of the Negro quest for justice. In 1964, only 34 percent of white Americans believed that blacks were seeking too much, too fast. By 1966, however, that figure had climbed to 85 percent as whites reacted against Black Power and urban riots. "How long," Congressman Gerald Ford asked, "are we going to abdicate law and order—the backbone of civilization—in favor of a soft social theory that the man who heaves a brick through a window or tosses a firebomb into your car is simply the misunderstood and underprivileged product of a broken home?"

Some analysts traced such sentiments to the economic insecurity of those they dubbed the "middle Americans." Earning between $5,000 and 15,000 a year and including many white ethnics, "middle Americans" were estimated to comprise 55 percent of the population. The majority were blue-collar workers, lower-echelon bureaucrats, school teachers, and white-collar employees. Although not poor, they suffered many of the tensions of marginal prosperity, including inflation, indebtedness, and fear of losing what they had worked so hard to attain. From 1956 to 1966, the rate of borrowing to purchase homes and consumer goods had risen by 113 percent, but income had increased by only 86 percent. More than two-thirds of all Americans earned under $10,000 a year by the end of the sixties, and many families were hard pressed to hold onto their "middle-class" status, particularly in an era when Vietnam war inflation brought a sudden end to increases in *real* income. Struggling to get by, many of these white Americans saw black demands and antipoverty expenditures as a direct threat to their own well-being.

But economic vulnerability and ethnic competition could explain only part of the "middle American" protest. More important was a sense of crisis in cultural values, a belief that the rules were being changed unfairly in midstream. Although most whites did not live in neighborhoods immediately threatened by urban violence or student demonstrations, everyday they witnessed on TV and read in the newspapers evidence of a concerted assault on the morals and values that had guided their lives. At just the time when the economic situation began to seem shaky, faith in the old doctrines was also being questioned. "We just seem to be headed toward a collapse of everything," a small-town California newspaper editor said.

From the perspective of such people, the radicalism of blacks, poor people, antiwar demonstrators, and "women's libbers" represented an attack on the very foundations of what they defined as the American way. Everything they had been brought up to believe in—patriotism, religion, monogamy, hard work—seemed under siege. While *their* children were drafted and sent to Vietnam, young radicals were abusing the privilege of a college education to denounce the system that had given them the opportunity to go to college in the first place. Nor were such attitudes limited to the middle-aged. Indeed, if a generation gap did exist in America, it was more likely to be found among the young themselves, between college-educated activists and those without a college degree. The sharp hostility that existed among the young generation was vividly expressed in the attitudes of Vietnam soldiers toward college demonstrators at home. "I'm fighting for those candy-asses because I don't have an old man to support me," said one soldier. To many GIs—and their parents back home—the entire antiwar movement represented an act of virtual treason, made even more unacceptable by the implicit assumption that certain people—especially blacks and the young—were privy to a higher code of justice and had no obligation to obey the rules of conventional society.

## Defending Traditional Values

By the end of 1967, therefore, the shrill attacks on "establishment" values from the left were matched by an equally vociferous defense of traditional values by those who were proud of all their society had achieved. If feminists, blacks, antiwar demonstrators, and advocates for the poor attacked the status quo with uncompromising vehemence, millions of other Americans rallied around the flag and made clear their intent to uphold the lifestyle and values to which they had devoted their lives. Significantly, pollsters Richard Scammon and Ben Wattenburg pointed out, the protestors still represented only a small minority of the country. The great majority of Americans were "unyoung, unpoor, and unblack; they [are] middle-aged, middle class, and middle minded." It was not a scenario from which dissidents could take much comfort.

CHAPTER 6

# Gender and
# Sex Revolutions

AMERICA'S DECADES

# The Sexual Revolution of the 1960s

William E. Leuchtenburg

During the 1960s numerous social and legal barriers and taboos concerning sex were weakened or eliminated, writes historian William E. Leuchtenburg in the following analysis. Several Supreme Court decisions overturned pornography laws, enabling books and motion pictures to use graphic sexual language and depictions. Affluence, mobility, and the development of the birth control pill all contributed to greater sexual experimentation for many Americans. However, some observers have argued that the 1960s marked a simple continuation of existing trends rather than a radical break in American sexual behavior.

Much of the country considered . . . promiscuity and nudity . . . peculiar to hippiedom, but in truth new attitudes toward sex antedated the rise of the counter culture and were by no means confined to the young. The postwar [World War II] years witnessed a veritable revolution in public acceptance of forms of sexual depiction and vocabulary that had hitherto been proscribed. In 1948 Norman Mailer had been compelled to resort to the euphemism "fuggin" in *The Naked and the Dead,* and as late as 1953 Otto Preminger's movie *The Moon Is Blue* was denied a seal of approval because it employed the word "virgin." But by 1966, the

Excerpted from *Troubled Feast: American Society Since 1945,* by William E. Leuchtenburg. Copyright 1983 by William E. Leuchtenburg. Reprinted by permission of Addison-Wesley Educational Publishers Inc.

bitchy language Elizabeth Taylor spoke in the film of Edward Albee's *Who's Afraid of Virginia Woolf?* was becoming conventional, and downtown movie houses would soon be screening fetishism, autoeroticism, and fellatio. In 1969 *Time* commented that "writers bandy four-letter words as if they had just completed a deep-immersion Berlitz course in Anglo-Saxon" and observed that "today, the corner drugstore sells Fanny Hill along with Fannie Farmer."

The turning point had come in 1959. In voiding the censorship of *Lady Chatterley's Lover*, the [Supreme] Court, in the words of Mr. Justice [Potter] Stewart, maintained that the First Amendment "protects advocacy of the opinion that adultery may sometimes be proper, no less than advocacy of socialism or the single tax." The film was based on D.H. Lawrence's novel of anal eroticism, published in its unexpurgated form by Grove Press that same year. Heartened by the Court's latitudinarianism, Grove Press in 1961 brought out Henry Miller's *Tropic of Cancer,* another under-the-counter item; it sold two and a half million copies and also won the benison of the Supreme Court. The Court did indicate there were still some constraints when in 1966 it sustained the conviction of Ralph Ginzburg, publisher of *Eros,* for promoting the circulation of his magazine in a pandering fashion; he had even applied for a mail permit from Intercourse, Pennsylvania. But the much-criticized Ginzburg decision proved to be an exception rather than a guideline.

## Falling Taboos

In the 1960's almost every barrier came down. That bourgeois standby, *Cosmopolitan,* ran an article on "Low-Fidelity Wives" and printed instructions for its female readers on how to achieve an orgasm. Manufacturers turned out dolls with sexual organs, and in Jeane-Claude van Itallie's *America Hurrah* giant dolls fornicated on stage. "Billy the Kid" and "Jean Harlow" simulated an act of oral intercourse before audiences for *The Beard,* while in *Dionysus 69* a troupe invited members of the audience

## Hippies and the Sexual Revolution

*Youth that came of age in the 1960s—especially hippies and other adherents of the 1960s counterculture—were at the forefront of the sexual revolution and its questioning of traditional sexual values, writes historian Terry H. Anderson. He describes some of their beliefs in the following excerpt from his study* The Movement and the Sixties.

A majority of the sixties generation . . . attempted to liberate themselves from the older generation's sexual mores. Elders had taught children Puritan values, that sex was reserved for married adults. Youth must avoid premarital sex and promiscuity, and rumors abounded that masturbation caused everything from blindness to hand warts. The sledgehammer to prevent such behavior was GUILT. Hippies rebelled, calling those ideas "hang-ups" and advocating "free love." Of course, they did not invent the idea, for armed with birth control pills the sixties generation had been experimenting at college and sexual freedom leagues had been es-

to disrobe and take part in a mock orgy. Some did. Bacchantic rock stars like Janis Joplin sang with a raw, sexual urgency, and at a Miami concert Jim Morrison of the Doors enticed female "groupies" by exposing himself. In 1970 the Federal Commission on Obscenity and Pornography brought the new era to a culmination by recommending wiping out all legal restrictions on the acquisition by adults of hard-core pornography.

The falling away of taboos on expression appeared to be accompanied by a radical change in sexual activity. Affluence and mobility encouraged experimentation and slackened the hold of folkways, and technology contributed the Pill, which virtually eliminated the fear of conception in premarital intercourse. Colleges made birth control devices available to single coeds; young unmarried mothers cited tablished earlier in the Bay Area and New York City. But freaks expanded the idea so sex seemed freer than at any time in memory. "Let's spend the night together" wailed the Rolling Stones, while Janis Joplin advised her sisters to "get it while you can." For the first time the airwaves were filled with blatant demands for sex, and while kids began wearing buttons—"Save Water, Shower with a Friend"—hippies clarified the ideas of liberation. "A legal contract for a sexual relationship is, if not out of date, at least beside the point for most of us." This was different from a college kid "getting laid," they claimed; free love meant a couple "making love," any time, any form, out of wedlock, and especially without guilt. "Make love," wrote a freak, "not to one guy or chick who you grab onto and possess out of fear and loneliness—but to all beautiful people, all sexes, all ages." They watched the film *Harold and Maude*, where a zestful woman of 79 taught a young man to be sensual, to live, and they agreed with the ideas that "If you can't be with the one you love, then love the one you're with."

Terry H. Anderson, *The Movement and the Sixties*. New York: Oxford University Press, 1995.

the model of Mia Farrow; and *Select,* a periodical for swingers, claimed a readership of one hundred thousand among a swiftly growing movement that was said to number perhaps 2 million middle-class citizens engaged in transient trysts. Sex, wrote [Sociologist] David Riesman, had become America's last frontier. In a society where many groped for identity, "sex provides a kind of defense against the threat of total apathy," and the other-directed person "looks to it for reassurance that he is alive."

Scholars contributed to the fostering of this "erotic renaissance," and the modified value system in turn made possible a warmer welcome for advanced ideas. By the 1960's there was a more hospitable audience for the precepts of earlier sages like Wilhelm Reich and Henry Miller as well as for such latter-day evangelists as Norman O.

Brown, who in *Life Against Death* celebrated the "resurrection of the body" and "erotic exuberance." In 1956 Dr. William H. Masters and Mrs. Virginia E. Johnson of Washington University in St. Louis began an eleven-year study in which they observed nearly seven hundred men and women masturbating and copulating and measured the intensity of their orgasms. "The '60's," Dr. Masters declared, "will be called the decade of orgasmic preoccupation." It was widely thought that the Pill accounted for the permutation in mood, but Edward Grossman reasoned that it was rather the altered perceptions that made the Pill possible. "The grants to set up the labs would not have been awarded, the talent to synthesize the chemistry would not have been collected, if there had not been an agreement . . . too deep to be put into words," he wrote, "a state of mind, in which sex would be separated—as far as science, will and conscience could separate it—from duty, pain and fear, from everything but pleasure."

Yet sexual liberation seems not to have been as seismic a development as some thought, or to have had all the consequences its earlier exponents claimed for it. Dr. Kinsey's successor as director of the Institute for Sex Research at Indiana University explained:

> People talk more freely about sex nowadays, and young people are far more tolerant and permissive regarding sex. But we don't think there have been changes that we could truly call revolutionary. Our studies indicate that there has just been a continuation of pre-existing trends, rather than any sudden revolutionary changes. For instance, premarital intercourse has increased, but it hasn't shot up in any inflationary way; it has been on the rise ever since the turn of the century.

Moreover, the Dionysian spirit proved less emancipating than the oracles had foretold. The campus liaisons of the "unmarried marrieds," noted one report, were "familiar, predictable and slightly boring," and a student of group sex found that swingers "have now gone from Puritanism into promiscuity without passing through sensuality." So much did libertinism resemble babbittry that in the summer of 1970 in Chicago 184 couples congregated at the First National Swingers Convention. As the French critic Raoul de Roussy de Sales once remarked, "America appears to be the only country in the world where love is a national problem."

## A Lost Consensus

Furthermore, the uninhibited displays in book stores and on movie marquees obscured the fact that there was no national concordance on sexual mores. An opinion survey in 1969 learned that 76 percent of respondents wanted pornography outlawed, and a minority report of the President's commission protested that hardcore materials had "an eroding effect on society, on public morality, on respect for human worth, on attitudes toward family love, on culture." Reverend Dr. Billy James Hargis, leader of the Christian Crusade, charged that the new morality was "part of a gigantic conspiracy to bring down America from within." "I don't want any kid under 12 to hear about lesbians, homosexuals, and sexual intercourse," the evangelist said. "They should be concerned with tops, yo-yos and hide and seek." The division in the country revealed, as *Newsweek* wrote, "a society that has lost its consensus on such crucial issues as premarital sex and clerical celibacy, marriage, birth control and sex education; a society that cannot agree on standards of conduct, language and manners."

# The Feminist Revival

Jane Sherron De Hart

In the years immediately following World War II, U.S. society fostered a domestic ideology that celebrated women's "natural" roles of wife and mother and disparaged working mothers, career women, and feminism. The 1960s marked a turning against this ideology and a revival of the feminist movement. In the following viewpoint, Jane Sherron De Hart, history professor at the University of California at Santa Barbara, identifies two distinct wings of the women's movement that came to prominence in this decade. "Women's rights advocates" were generally well-educated middle- and upper-class women who objected to the pervasive sex discrimination found in the nation's laws, banking practices, higher education, and other areas. They formed organizations such as the National Organization for Women (NOW) in 1966 to attain equal rights for women; one of NOW's main purposes was the enforcement of the 1964 Civil Rights Act that banned discrimination based on race *and* sex. In a separate development, a younger generation of women—veterans of the civil rights and antiwar movements of the 1960s—formed a more radical "women's liberation" movement consisting of a network of small groups rather than a national organization such as NOW. The believed that NOW's emphasis on legal equality outside the home was insufficient and that personal and cul-

Excerpted from "Conclusion: The New Feminism and the Dynamics of Social Change," by Jane Sherron De Hart, in *Women's America: Refocusing the Past*, 4th edition, edited by Linda K. Kerber and Jane Sherron De Hart. Copyright ©1995 by Oxford University Press, Inc. Used by permission of Oxford University Press, Inc.

tural transformation was necessary for women to attain real freedom and equality in the United States.

---

Revolutions are seldom started by the powerless. The revolution of mainstream feminists was no exception. It was begun largely by educated, middle-class women whose diverse experiences had sharpened their sensitivity to the fundamental inequality between the sexes at a time when America had been thrust into the throes of self-examination by a movement for racial equality. Some were young veterans of the civil rights movement and the New Left, steeped in a commitment to equality and the techniques of protest. Others were young professionals increasingly aware of their secondary status. Still others were older women who in their long careers as professionals or as activists had used organizations such as the American Civil Liberties Union (ACLU), the Young Women's Christian Association (YWCA) and the United Auto Workers (UAW) to fight sex-based discrimination. Included, too, were those whose outwardly conformist lives belied an intense awareness of the malaise of domesticity and the untenably narrow boundaries of their prescribed roles. To explore how they came self-consciously to appraise women's condition as one demanding collective action is to explore the process of radicalization that helped to create a new feminist movement.

## Two Distinct Groups

In its early state, a major component of that movement consisted of two different groups—women's rights advocates and women's liberationists. Although the differences between the two groups began to blur as the movement matured, initial distinctions were sharp. Women's rights advocates were likely to have been older, to have had professional training or work experience, to have been more inclined to form or join organized feminist groups. Reform oriented, these organizations used traditional pressure group tactics to achieve changes in laws and public policy that would guarantee women equal rights. Emphasis on "rights" meant extending to women in life outside the home the same "rights" men had, granting them the same options, privileges, and responsibilities that men enjoyed. There was little suggestion initially of personal or cultural transformation.

Women's liberationists were younger women, less highly educated, whose ideology and political style, shaped in the dissent and violence of the 1960s, led them to look at women's predicament differently. Instead of relying upon traditional organizational structure and lobbying techniques, they developed a new style of politics. Instead of limiting their goals to changes in public policy, they embraced a transformation in private, domestic life as well. They sought liberation from ways of thinking and behaving that they believed stunted or distorted women's growth and kept them subordinate to men. Through the extension of their own personal liberation they hoped to remake the male world, changing it as they had changed themselves. For women's liberationists as for women's rights advocates, however, the first step toward becoming feminists demanded a clear statement of women's position in society, one that called attention to the gap between the egalitarian ideal and the actual position of women in American culture. There also had to be a call to action from women themselves, *for* women, *with* women, *through* women. Redefining themselves, they had to make being a woman a political fact; and, as they did so, they had to live with the radical implications of what could only be called a rebirth.

## Women's Rights Advocates

For some women, the process of radicalization began with the appointment of a Presidential Commission on the Status of Women in 1961. Presidents, Democrat and Republican, customarily discharged their political debt to female members of the electorate, especially to those who had loyally served the party, by appointing a few token women, usually party stalwarts, to highly visible posts. John Kennedy was no exception. He was, however, convinced by Esther Peterson, the highest-ranking woman in his administration, that the vast majority of women would be better served if he also appointed a commission charged with investigating obstacles to the full participation of women in society. Peterson, who was assistant secretary of labor and head of the Women's Bureau, believed that the report of such a commission could sensitize the public to barriers to equality just as her own experience as a labor organizer had sensitized her to the particular problems confronting women workers. Citizens thus informed could then be mobilized on behalf of governmental efforts at reform. Accordingly, the commission was appointed with Eleanor Roosevelt serving as chair until her death a year later. Its report, *American Women* (1963), was conservative in tone, acknowledging the importance of women's traditional roles within the home and the progress they had made in a "free democratic society." Acknowledging also that women were an underutilized resource that the nation could ill afford to ignore, the report provided extensive documentation of discriminatory practices in government, education, and employment, along with substantial recommendations for change. Governors, replicating Kennedy's move, appointed state commissions on the status of women. In these commissions hundreds of men and women encountered further evidence of the economic, social, and legal disabilities that encumbered the nation's "second sex." For some, the statistics were old news; for others, they were a revelation. . . .

## The 1964 Civil Rights Act

Aroused by growing evidence of "the enormity of our problem," members of state commissions gathered in Washington in 1966 for the Third National Conference of the Commissions on the Status of Women. Individuals who were coming to know and rely on one another as they pooled their growing knowledge of widespread inequities, they were a network in the making. They were also women who wanted something done. This time they encountered a situation that transformed at least some of those present into activists in a new movement for women's equality. The catalyst proved to be a struggle involving Representative Martha Griffiths and the Equal Employment Opportunity Commission (EEOC), the federal agency in charge of implementing the Civil Rights Act of 1964.

Despite the fact that the law proscribed discrimination on the basis of sex as well as race, the commission refused to take seriously the problem of sexual discrimination. The first executive director of EEOC, believing that "sex" had been injected into the bill by opponents seeking to block its passage, regarded the sex provision as a "fluke" best ignored. Representative Griffiths from Michigan thought otherwise. While the bill was still in Congress she encouraged a small group of women in the House to become part of an unlikely alliance with legislative opponents of a federal civil rights act in order to keep the sex provision in the bill. Liberals objected, fearing that so encumbering a bill would prevent passage of much-needed legislation on behalf of racial equality. But despite such objections—and the ridicule of many of her male colleagues—Griffiths persisted. She urged her fellow representatives not to give black women and men advantages which white women were denied. A racist appeal, it revealed the exclusivity of Griffiths's vision of sisterhood. Her commitment to the sex provision, however, was unqualified. Once the bill passed she was determined to see the new law enforced in its entirety. When EEOC failed to do so, she lambasted the agency for its inaction in a biting speech delivered on the House floor only days before the Conference of the Commissions on the Status of Women met.

Griffiths's concern was shared by a group of women working within EEOC. Echoing an argument made the year before by a black trade unionist in the Women's Bureau, they insisted that the agency could be made to take gender-related discrimination more seriously if women had a civil rights organization as adept at applying pressure on their behalf as was the National Association for the Advancement of Colored People (NAACP) on behalf of blacks. . . .

Before the day was out twenty-eight women had paid five dollars each to join the National Organization for Women (NOW), including author Betty Friedan, who happened to be in Washington at the time of the conference.

## The Feminine Mystique

Friedan's presence in Washington was auspicious; her involvement in NOW, virtually inevitable. The author of a brilliant polemic published in 1963, she not only labeled the resurgent domestic ideology of recent decades but exposed the groups perpetuating it. Editors of women's magazines, advertising experts, Freudian psychologists, social scientists, and educators—all, according to Friedan, contributed to a romanticization of domesticity she termed "the feminine mystique." The result, she charged, was the infantilization of intelligent women and the transformation of the suburban home into a "comfortable concentration camp." Harsh words, they rang true to those who found the creativity of homemaking and the joys of motherhood vastly exaggerated. Sales of the book ultimately zoomed past the million mark.

By articulating heretofore inarticulated grievances, *The Feminine Mystique* had advanced a process initiated by more dispassionate investigations of women's status and the discriminatory practices which made that status inferior. That process was the collective expression of discontent. It is not surprising that the voices initially heard were those of women who were overwhelmingly white, educated, and middle or upper middle class. College women who regarded themselves the equals of male classmates by virtue of intellect and training were . . . more likely to develop expectations they saw realized by their male peers but not, in most cases, by themselves. The frustrations were even greater for women with professional training. The very fact that many had sought advanced training in fields not traditionally "female" meant that they were less likely to find in traditional gender roles the identity and self-esteem such roles provided other women. Moreover, when measuring themselves against fellow professionals who happened to be men, the greater rewards enjoyed by their white male counterparts seemed especially galling. Privileged though they were, such women *felt* more deprived in many cases than did those women who were in reality less privileged. By 1966 this sense of deprivation had been sufficiently articulated and shared and the networks of like-minded women sufficiently developed so that collective discontent could be translated into collective action. The formation of NOW signaled a feminist resurgence.

## The Work of NOW

The three hundred men and women who gathered in October for the organizational meeting of NOW included mainly professionals, some of them veterans of commissions on the status of women as well as a few feminist union activists, notably Dorothy Haener. Adopting bylaws and a statement of purpose, they elected officers, naming Friedan president. Her conviction that intelligent women needed purposeful, generative work of their own was reflected in NOW's statement of purpose, which attacked "the traditional assumption that a woman has to choose between marriage and motherhood on the one hand and serious participation in industry or the professions on the other." Determined that women should be allowed to develop their full potential as human beings, the organization's goal was to bring them into "full participation in the mainstream of American society NOW, exercising all the privileges and responsibilities thereof in truly equal partnership with men." To that end NOW developed a Bill of Rights, adopted at its 1967 meeting, that exhorted Congress to pass an equal rights amendment to the Constitution, called on EEOC to enforce anti-discrimination legislation, and urged federal and state legislators to guarantee equal and unsegregated education. To ensure women control over their reproductive lives, these new feminists called for removal of penal codes denying women contraceptive information and devices as well as safe, legal abortions. To ease the double burden of working mothers, they urged legislation that would ensure maternity leaves without jeopardizing job security or seniority, permit tax deductions for child care expenses, and create public, inexpensive day care centers. To improve the lot of poor women, they urged reform of the welfare system and equality with respect to benefits, including job-training programs.

Not content simply to call for change, NOW leaders, following the lead of equality advocates within the labor movement, worked to make it happen. Using persuasion, pressure, and even litigation, they, with other newly formed women's rights groups such as the Women's Equity Action League (WEAL), launched a massive attack on sex discrimination. By the end of the 1960s NOW members had filed legal suits against newspapers listing jobs under the headings "Help Wanted: Male" and "Help Wanted: Female," successfully arguing that such headings discouraged women from applying for jobs they were perfectly capable of doing. Building on efforts begun in the Kennedy administration such as the passage of the Equal Pay Act, they pressured the federal government to intensify its commitment to equal opportunity. They urged congressmen and labor leaders to persuade the Department of Labor to include women in its guidelines designed to encourage the hiring and promotion of blacks in firms holding contracts with the federal government. They persuaded the Federal Communications Commission to open up new opportunities for women in broadcasting. Tackling the campus as well as the marketplace, WEAL filed suit against more than three hundred colleges and universities, ultimately securing millions of dollars in salary raises for women faculty members who had been victims of discrimination. To ensure that women receive the same pay men received for doing the same work, these new feminists lobbied for passage of a new Equal Employment Opportunity Act that would enable EEOC to fight discrimination more effectively. . . .

Collectively such protests served notice that more women were becoming radicalized. The particular combination of events that transformed these women into feminists varied with the individual. . . . Although the number of women who understood what it meant to be the "second sex" were still only a tiny minority, they were nonetheless a minority whose energy, talents, and experience enabled them to work for changes necessary to ensure equal rights.

## A Younger Generation

The process of radicalization that transformed some individuals into liberal feminists occurred simultaneously—but in different fashion and with somewhat different results—among a younger generation of women who were also predominantly white and middle class. Many of them veterans of either the civil rights movement or of the New Left, these were the activists who would initially become identified as women's liberationists. Differing in perspective as well as style, they would ultimately push many of their older counterparts beyond the demand for equal rights to recognition that true emancipation would require a far-reaching transformation of society and culture.

The experiences awakening in this 1960s generation a feminist consciousness have been superbly described by Sara Evans in her book, *Personal Politics.* "Freedom, equality, love and hope," the possibility of new human relationships, the importance of participatory democracy—letting the people decide—were, as Evans points out, part of an egalitarian ideology shared by both the southern-based Student Nonviolent Coordinating Committee (SNCC) in its struggle for racial equality and the Students for Democratic Society (SDS) in its efforts to mobilize an interracial organization of the urban poor in northern ghettos. Membership in both organizations—"the movement"—thus reinforced commitment to these ideals among the women who joined. In order to translate ideals into reality, however, young, college-age women who had left the shelter of middle-class families for the hard and dangerous work of transforming society found themselves doing things that they would never have thought possible. Amidst the racial strife of the South, they joined picket lines, created freedom schools, and canvassed for voter registration among blacks, often enduring arrest and jailing. SDS women from affluent suburbs entered decaying tenements and were surrounded by the grim realities of the ghetto. They trudged door-to-door in an effort to reach women whose struggle to survive made many understandably suspicious of intruding strangers. In the process, not only did these young activists achieve a heightened sense of self-worth and autonomy, they also learned the skills of movement building and the nuts and bolts of organizing.

Particularly important was the problem of getting people, long passive, to act on their own behalf. SDS women began by encouraging ghetto women to come together to talk about their problems. This sharing of experiences, they believed, would lead these women to recognize not only that their problems were common but that solutions required changes in the system. In the process of organizing, the organizers also learned. They began to understand the meaning of oppression and the valor required of those who fought it. They found new role models, Evans suggests, in extraordinary southern black women whose courage seemed never to waiver in the face of violence and in those welfare mothers of the North who confronted welfare bureaucrat and slum lord after years of passivity.

But if being in the movement brought a new understanding of equality, it also brought new problems. Men who were committed to equality for one group were not necessarily committed to equality for another group. Women in SNCC, as in SDS, found themselves frequently relegated to domestic chores and treated as sex objects, denied most leadership positions, and refused a key voice in the formulation of policy. Moreover, the sexual freedom that had been theirs as part of the cultural revolution taking place in the 1960s soon began to feel more like sexual exploitation as they saw their role in the movement spelled out in the draft resister's slogan: "Girls Say Yes to Guys

Who Say No." Efforts to change the situation were firmly rebuffed. When SNCC leader Stokely Carmichael joked that the only "position for women in SNCC is prone," he encapsulated views which, while not his own, reflected all too accurately the feelings of males in the New Left as well as many in SNCC.

By 1967 the tensions had become so intense that white women left the movement to organize on behalf of their own "liberation." Black women stayed, resolving to work for change from within and give voice to their own priorities.

The women who left did not leave empty-handed. As radicals, they were impatient with liberalism, critical of capitalism, and profoundly suspicious of authority. Accustomed to challenging prevailing ideas and practices, they had acquired a language of protest, an organizing tactic, and a deep-seated conviction that the personal was political. How that legacy would shape this burgeoning new feminist movement became evident as small women's liberation groups began springing up spontaneously in major cities and university communities across the nation.

## Consciousness-Raising

Initially, at least, the two branches of mainstream feminism seemed almost to be two different movements, so unlike were they in structure and style. Linked only by newsletters, notices in underground newspapers, and networks of friends, women's liberation groups rejected both traditional organizational structure and leadership. Unlike NOW and the other women's rights groups associated with liberal feminism, they had no central headquarters, no elected officers, no bylaws. There was no legislative agenda and little of the activism that transformed the more politically astute women's rights leaders into skilled lobbyists and tacticians. Instead this younger generation of feminists, organizing new groups wherever they found themselves, concentrated on a kind of personal politics rooted in movement days. Looking back on male-dominated meetings in which, however informal the gathering, a few highly verbal, aggressive men invariably controlled debate and dictated strategy and left less articulate and assertive women effectively excluded, they recalled the technique they had used in organizing the poor. They remembered how they had encouraged those women to talk among themselves until the personal became political, that is, until problems which, at first glance, seemed to be personal were finally understood to be social in cause—rooted in society rather than in the individual—and political in solution. Applying this same process in their own informal "rap groups," women's liberationists developed the technique of "consciousness-raising." Adopted by women's rights groups such as local chapters of NOW, consciousness-raising sessions became one of the most important innovations of mainstream feminism.

The immediate task of the consciousness-raising session was to bring together in a caring, supportive, noncompetitive setting women accustomed to relating most intimately not with other women but with men—husbands, lovers, "friends." As these women talked among themselves, exchanging confidences, reassessing old options, and mentally exploring new ones, a sense of shared problems began to emerge. The women themselves gradually gained greater understanding of how profoundly their lives had been shaped by the constraints of culture. Personal experience with those constraints merged with intellectual awareness of women's inferior status and the factors that made it so. By the same token, new understanding of problems generated new determination to resolve them. Anger, aggression, and frustration formerly turned inward in unconscious self-hatred began to be directed outward, becoming transformed into new energy directed toward constructive goals. If society and culture had defined who women were through their unconscious internalization of tradition, they could reverse the process, and, by redefining themselves, redefine society and culture. Or, to put it another way, if woman was a *social construct*—the product not so much of biology, but of what people in a particular society and culture believed to be the implications of biology—then women themselves would re-create the construct. At work was a process of discovery so radicalizing that the individuals undergoing it ultimately emerged in a very real sense as different people. Now feminists, these were women with a different understanding of reality—a new "consciousness," a new sense of "sisterhood," and a new commitment to change.

Consciousness-raising was an invigorating and sometimes frightening experience. As one young woman wrote, "This whole movement is the most exhilarating thing of my life. The last eight months have been a personal revolution. Nonetheless, I recognize there is dynamite in this and I'm scared shitless." "Scared" or not, such women could no longer be contained. Veterans of one rap group fanned out, creating others, often with arresting names such as Cell 16, the Furies, Redstockings, or simply Radical Women. For the feminist movement, this mushrooming of groups meant increased numbers and added momentum. For some of the women involved, it meant confronting and articulating theoretically as well as personally what "oppression," "sexism," and "liberation" really meant: in short, developing a feminist ideology.

# Stonewall and the Gay Liberation Movement

Margaret Cruikshank

In the 1950s homosexuality was viewed as a deviant illness or moral failing. Most gay men and lesbians remained "closeted" about their sexuality for fear of losing their jobs and social standing. Only a small number of them joined the "homophile" organizations formed after World War II. The 1960s and early 1970s marked a turning point in how gay men and lesbians became more open and assertive about their sexual identity. Margaret Cruikshank argues that the emergence of a "gay liberation" movement at this juncture was in part a product of other social movements and trends of the 1960s, including the antiwar movement, the civil rights movement, and the counterculture. The June 1969 incident at Stonewall Inn in Greenwich Village, New York, in which gays, drag queens, and lesbians battled with police following a raid on the gay bar, sparked a new phase in the movement for social and political acceptance of gays and lesbians. Cruikshank is the author of *The Gay and Lesbian Liberation Movement*, from which the following is excerpted.

Gay liberation emerged in the 1970s for several reasons, including pervasive police harassment in the 1950s and 1960s and weakening taboos against frank discussion of

Excerpted from *The Gay and Lesbian Liberation Movement*, by Margaret Cruikshank. Copyright ©1992 by Routledge, Chapman & Hall, Inc. Reproduced by permission of Taylor & Francis/Routledge, Inc.

homosexuality. Other main causes are (1) social changes in the 1960s and the example of 1960s' protest movements and (2) groundwork laid by the early homosexual rights movement. . . .

## The Anti-War Movement and the Hippies

By the late 1960s, the people who would come out in the next decade were either radicalized or deeply influenced by the anti-war movement. Its anti-authoritarian spirit was very significant for homosexuals, especially the young, who questioned the traditional labels applied to them such as sick and sinful. In the 1950s homosexuals felt the heavy weight of medical prejudice, police harassment and church condemnation, but were not able to challenge these authorities with the same confidence that they later felt. Just as the military, the government, and the churches that supported the war in Viet Nam were discredited in the eyes of many, medical figures too lost their aura of infallibility. In 1970, lesbians and gay men disrupted a session on aversion therapy (to discourage homosexuality) at a meeting of the American Psychiatric Association. Neither the homophiles of the 1950s nor the militant homosexual organizers of the early 1960s could have done that because they had no context for rowdy, noisy demonstrations. The anti-war movement provided that context.

At the same time, the hippies symbolized a new spirit of sexual freedom which influenced a great many people who did not actually become hippies. Many kinds of nonconformity flourished in the late sixties, creating a climate in which sexual deviance could be mentioned. Male hippies rebelled against the macho look which symbolized aggression and war. Their inferior status led many women to rethink traditional sex roles and to emphasize sexual pleasure. Since sexual experimentation was encouraged, people who were gay discovered that sooner than they might have in the 1950s. [Writer Henry David] Thoreau's phrase about marching to a different drummer, very popular in the sixties, inspired those who felt different in their sexuality.

Homosexuals could call themselves "gay," that is, assume a political identity, however, only because of the example of other movements, especially civil rights. Without the sixties' protest movements, gay and lesbian liberation would not have emerged in the 1970s. In the early 1960s only a few homosexuals, such as Washington DC activist Frank Kameny, saw the parallel between themselves and Blacks which was obvious to many by the end of the decade.

The sixties' protest movements, especially civil rights and later the women's movement, showed that seemingly entrenched ideas that once seemed absolute—the necessity of war, for example, the inferiority of Blacks or the inferiority of women—could be unmasked as prejudices of a ruling elite rather than as verifiable accounts of reality. The model for mass demonstrations came from the civil rights movement and the anti-war movement, as did the sense of having a righteous cause.

## Gays Active in Protest Movements

Sexual preference alone could not have produced the moral fervor of the gay activists, however; it was the sense of being persecuted for what was normal that drove them to organize. Sustained protest did not begin until large numbers of homosexuals began to see that the prejudices against them were neither natural nor inevitable but the markers of a particular culture. In addition, the civil rights movement, the anti-war movement, and by 1969 the women's movement attracted large numbers of homosexuals. Nearly always closeted, they nevertheless quietly made contact with other homosexuals in these mass movements. A few knew that respected figures such as writer James Baldwin, civil rights leader Bayard Rustin, and pacifist leader Barbara Deming were homosexual. Paul Goodman, admired by the young for his book *Growing Up Absurd*, later joked that FBI films of anti-war demonstrations must have had many shots of him groping another man. When homosexuals active in these causes began organizing under the name "gay," they had an exhilarating sense of creating a movement of their own, as important as the civil rights movement and the women's movement. In a way it was more difficult because homosexuals were more despised than either Blacks or women. Many heterosexual Americans who supported equal rights for Blacks and for women were not prepared to see homosexuals as their equals. And many homosexuals before 1970 did not regard themselves as victims of oppression. Slowly, by analogy to Blacks and women, they began to see themselves in this light and to feel anger at unjust treatment. But before it could be born the movement required a critical mass of people willing first to come out of the closet and second to identify with everyone else who had come out.

Both gay liberation and women's liberation emerged as powerful forces at the end of the 1960s. Both had Victorian roots. Both focused on the right of sexual self-determination and both claimed equality for people long thought to be inferior. The feminist agenda had obvious parallels in the aims of gay liberation: an end to social control of sexuality, institutionalized prejudice, and sexism. Like gay activists, feminists wanted recognition of new relationships. . . .

## The Homophile Movement

In 1950, . . . a small band of southern California men founded the Mattachine Society, taking the name from medieval masked singers, to indicate that homosexuals were an unknown people. As Marxists, Harry Hay and other founders of Mattachine believed that prejudice against them was not a problem individuals could solve because it was deeply ingrained in American institutions. Gradually they came to view homosexuals as an oppressed minority, made up of people who for the most part did not place this interpretation on their private lives. Their goal therefore was to popularize the idea of a homosexual minority, to develop group consciousness. Their discussions allowed participants to feel their self-worth for the first time. Hay resigned from the Communist Party so that it would not be associated with homosexuals at a time when Senator

Joseph McCarthy was attacking both groups. A split developed in Mattachine between the founders, who envisioned a separate homosexual culture, and members who thought this strategy would only increase hostility to them and who preferred to integrate into mainstream society because they felt no different from heterosexuals except in their sexual lives. This latter view prevailed, with the result that a philosophy of individualism replaced that of collective, militant action. . . .

Members of Mattachine and the pioneer lesbian group Daughters of Bilitis (DOB) . . . described themselves as "the homophile movement," literally "love of same." This was a more positive, broader term than "homosexual," suggesting a philosophy or attitude as much as a sexual practice. De-emphasizing sex was strategic because it was sex acts that called down opprobrium on homosexuals.

In the 1960s the movement grew slowly. By then, gay subcultures were thriving in the United States, and heterosexuals began to be aware of their existence. A few books, mostly negative, were published on the subject of homosexuality. Lawyers began to argue for repeal of sodomy laws. As the topic of homosexuality began to lose some of its shock value, homophiles could be more assertive; but the change had a negative consequence as well because the medical view that homosexuality is a mental illness could be more widely disseminated. In 1965, for the first time, small numbers of militant homophiles picketed and paraded for their rights. [Historian John] D'Emilio notes that on the same day in May that 20,000 anti-war protesters gathered at the Washington Monument, seven men and three women marched for homosexual rights in front of the White House. Targets of other demonstrations were the Pentagon, the State Department, and Independence Hall in Philadelphia July Fourth. Del Martin and Phyllis Lyon, two founders of DOB, recall that, on New Year's Day 1965, a costume ball was held in San Francisco to benefit the newly formed Council on Religion and the Homosexual. Police obstructed the entrance with a paddy wagon, flooded the entrance with lights, and took photos of everyone who entered the hall. Five hundred lesbians and gay men, accompanied by many ministers and their wives, defied police by entering. Several people, including lawyers, were arrested. The next day, seven ministers held a press conference to denounce the police, and the ACLU [American Civil Liberties Union] persuaded the judge to dismiss charges. The importance of this incident is that homosexuals were no longer isolated and cowed into submission. A coalition of homosexuals and progressive heterosexuals vigorously protested gross injustices that would previously have been known only to the victims.

In August 1966, movement groups created the North American Conference of Homophile Organizations, which established a legal fund, sponsored protests against discrimination by the federal government, and encouraged new groups to form. New York Mattachine passed out literature in Greenwich Village and sent many members to appear on radio and television shows and to speak to hundreds of non-gay groups. In 1967, the ACLU reversed its earlier position by saying that consensual sex acts between adults were protected by the constitutional right to privacy. Despite many other signs of progress, a daunting problem remained: most homosexuals had not taken the step of joining the homophile movement. From 1950 to 1969, the membership of all the groups totalled only about 5,000.

## Stonewall

Stonewall was the shot heard round the homosexual world. On that day, patrons of the Stonewall Inn, a Greenwich Village bar popular with Puerto Rican drag queens and lesbians, responded to a police raid by throwing beer cans and bottles because they were angry at police surveillance of their private gathering places. In the ensuing riot, which lasted two nights, a crowd of 2,000 battled 400 policemen. Before, the stigma attached to homosexuality and the resulting fear of exposure had kept homosexuals in line. Stonewall was a symbolic end to victim status. Homosexuals had acquiesced to police brutality; gay people fought back. It was fitting that a new phase of the old struggle for acceptance of homosexuals had its start in a bar, for bars held a central place in gay culture: often they were the only places where people could be open. The first visit to a gay bar was often an initiation rite for a person coming to terms with his or her sexuality or for those who accepted their orientation but had never met another homosexual. Also, bars drew people from different races and classes.

## Gay Liberation

After Stonewall, "gay power" graffiti began to appear in Greenwich Village. The Gay Liberation Front (GLF), a New Left group, and the Gay Activist Alliance (GAA) were formed, and similar groups quickly sprang up in other parts of the country. GLF stood for coalitions with other progressive groups, while the GAA, which took a single-issue stance, became more influential in the movement. Gay liberation could not be subsumed by the left, in the view of long-time activist Barbara Gittings, because of its "sheer chaotic nature." In addition, gay liberation tends to promote a high degree of individualism because sexual identity politics rises directly from private experiences that lead to feelings of being different from others. Nevertheless, Marxism exerted a strong influence on the movement: inspired by revolutionary rhetoric, activists no longer feared being known as homosexuals. Through the lens of Marxism the homophile goal of tolerance for homosexuals could be seen as inadequate; sexual freedom required structural change, not just changes in laws. . . .

Now a cliché, the phrase "the personal is the political" made a great impact on homosexuals who heard it for the first time in the 1970s. Declaring their most private feelings was a radical political act. It called on everyone, not just the sexual minority, to rethink their most basic assumptions about love, sex, marriage, the family, and the legitimate role of the state in controlling private life. It rejected centuries of religious teaching and decades of medical hypothesizing. It said that sexual self-determination was a fundamental human right. Homosexuals could not be driven back into the closet because they had left in large numbers. Coming out made gay liberation possible.

# Chronology

## 1960

**February 1**—Four black college students attempt to integrate a Woolworth's lunch counter in Greensboro, North Carolina. The Student Nonviolent Coordinating Committee (SNCC) is founded shortly thereafter to coordinate the growing sit-in movement.

**May 1**—U-2 spy plane pilot Francis Gary Powers is shot down over the Soviet Union in an incident that worsens U.S.-Soviet tensions.

**May 9**—The birth control pill is approved for use in the United States.

**September 26**—John F. Kennedy and Richard M. Nixon engage in the nation's first televised presidential campaign debate.

## 1961

**January 3**—The United States breaks diplomatic ties with Cuba.

**January 20**—John F. Kennedy is sworn in as president.

**March 1**—President Kennedy establishes the Peace Corps.

**April 17**—Cuban exiles armed and trained by the Central Intelligence Agency (CIA) are quickly captured when they invade Cuba at the Bay of Pigs.

**May 5**—Three weeks after Soviet cosmonaut Yuri Gagarin becomes the first human in space, Alan Shepard becomes the first American in space.

**May 25**—Kennedy calls on the United States to place an American on the moon by the end of the decade.

**August 13**—East Germany begins construction of the Berlin Wall.

**December 11**—Kennedy sends four hundred combat troops to South Vietnam.

## 1962

Two influential books raise social issues; *The Other America* by Michael Harrington examines poverty, while *Silent Spring* by Rachel Carson raises environmental awareness.

**June 11–15**—At Port Huron, Michigan, Students for a Democratic Society (SDS) holds its first national convention.

**October 1**—James Meredith is the first black to enroll in the University of Mississippi; three thousand federal troops are deployed there to keep order.

**October 22**—President Kennedy tells the American public that the Soviet Union has constructed nuclear missile installations in Cuba and the United States will blockade Soviet ships heading to Cuba. After a tense few days, Soviet leader Nikita Khrushchev agrees to dismantle Soviet missiles in Cuba.

**December 31**—The number of U.S. military personnel in South Vietnam reaches eleven thousand.

## 1963

**April**—Martin Luther King Jr. leads civil rights demonstrations in Birmingham, Alabama.

**August 5**—The United States, Soviet Union, and Great Britain sign a nuclear test ban treaty.

**August 28**—The March on Washington draws 250,000 civil rights activists to the nation's capital; Martin Luther King Jr. gives his "I Have a Dream" speech.

**September–December**—Students at the University of California at Berkeley protest after university administrators try to limit political activities on campus; the so-called "Free Speech Movement" is curtailed by 796 arrests made on December 3.

**September 7**—Four black girls are killed in a church bombing in Birmingham.

**November 22**—President Kennedy is shot and killed in Dallas, Texas; Vice President Lyndon B. Johnson is sworn in as president; the person arrested for Kennedy's murder, Lee Harvey Oswald, is shot and killed on live television by Jack Ruby two days later.

## 1964

**January 8**—President Johnson declares an "unconditional war on poverty in America."

**February**—The Beatles begin their first tour of the United States.

**June 23**—Three civil rights workers are reported missing in Mississippi; FBI agents find their bodies six weeks later.

**July 2**—President Johnson signs the landmark Civil Rights Act of 1964, prohibiting race and sex discrimination in employment and public accommodations.

**August 7**—Congress passes the Gulf of Tonkin Resolution authorizing the president to take military action against North Vietnam.

**August 11**—Congress passes Johnson's War on Poverty bill.

**September 27**—The Warren Commission issues its report that concludes that Lee Harvey Oswald acted alone in killing President Kennedy.

**November 3**—Johnson overwhelmingly defeats Barry Goldwater in the presidential election.

## 1965
**February 7**—Johnson orders bombing raids on North Vietnam.

**February 21**—Black leader Malcolm X is assassinated in Harlem.

**April 17**—The first major demonstration against the Vietnam War draws more than twenty thousand to Washington, D.C.

**July 25**—Acclaimed folk singer Bob Dylan performs with a rock band at the Newport Folk Festival.

**July 30**—Johnson signs the Medicare bill into law, establishing a program of national health insurance for the elderly.

**August 6**—Johnson signs the Voting Rights Act, outlawing literacy tests and empowering the Justice Department to supervise federal elections in seven southern states.

**August 11–16**—Riots in the black ghetto of Watts in Los Angeles leave thirty-five dead and $200 million in property damages.

**November 27**—Novelist Ken Kesey and his "Merry Pranksters" distributed LSD at a gathering in the first "acid test."

## 1966
**January**—Automatic student deferments from the draft are abolished.

**March**—César Chavez wins a labor contract for migrant farm workers.

**June**—"Black Power" becomes a popular if controversial slogan of young black activists during a civil rights march in Mississippi.

**July**—Urban riots strike Chicago, Brooklyn, and Cleveland.

**October**—The National Organization for Women (NOW) is founded.

## 1967
**January 14**—A gathering, or "be-in," in San Francisco draws national attention to the hippie scene.

**June 16–18**—The Monterey Pop Festival popularizes countercultural rock music and marks the beginning of the "Summer of Love."

**July**—Riots in Detroit and Newark leave sixty-nine dead.

**October 21**—National Stop the Draft Week climaxes with a March on the Pentagon by fifty thousand protesters.

**November 9**—The first issue of *Rolling Stone* is published; the magazine covers the new music scene and provides political commentary.

## 1968
**January 30**—The Tet Offensive begins as North Vietnamese and Vietcong troops temporarily overwhelm many U.S.-held positions in South Vietnam.

**March 16**—U.S. troops kill between two and six hundred civilians, most of them women, infants, and the elderly, in the Vietnamese village of My Lai. The incident is covered up until more than a year later.

**March 31**—President Johnson announces he will not seek reelection.

**April 4**—Martin Luther King Jr. is assassinated in Memphis, Tennessee; riots erupt in 125 cities.

**April 23–30**—Student radicals at Columbia University take over campus buildings.

**June 5**—Robert F. Kennedy, senator and presidential candidate, is assassinated shortly after winning the California primary.

**August 25–28**—Local police beat on antiwar demonstrators outside the Democratic National Convention in Chicago.

**September 7**—Feminists protest the Miss America Pageant in Atlantic City.

**November 5**—Richard M. Nixon narrowly defeats Vice President Hubert H. Humphrey in the presidential election; independent candidate George C. Wallace finishes third.

## 1969

**January**—U.S. troop strength in Vietnam reaches its peak of 543,000.

**March**—America begins a secret bombing campaign in Cambodia.

**June 18–23**—SDS holds its last national convention before breaking into factions.

**June 27–29**—A riot outside the Stonewall Inn in New York City signals the beginning of a militant gay liberation movement.

**July 20**—Americans Neil Armstrong and Edwin Aldrin land on the moon.

**August 15–17**—A half million people attend the Woodstock Music Festival in upstate New York.

**October 15**—National Vietnam Moratorium organizes demonstrations and work stoppages nationwide.

**November 3**—President Nixon appeals to America's "silent majority" to support his plan for gradual American withdrawal from Vietnam.

# For Further Reading

## General

Alexander Bloom and Wini Breines, eds., *"Takin' It to the Streets": A Sixties Reader*. New York: Oxford University Press, 1995.

Peter Collier and David Horowitz, *Destructive Generation: Second Thoughts About the Sixties*. New York: Summit Books, 1989.

David DeLeon, ed., *Leaders from the 1960s: A Biographical Sourcebook of American Activism*. Westport, CT: Greenwood Press, 1994.

Morris Dickstein, *Gates of Eden: American Culture in the Sixties*. New York: Basic Books, 1977.

Tim Healey, *Picture History of the 20th Century—The Sixties*. London: Franklin Watts, 1988.

Gerald Howard, ed., *The Sixties: Art, Politics, and Media of Our Most Explosive Decade*. New York: Paragon House, 1991.

John Javna, *60s!* New York: St. Martin's Press, 1988.

Stephen Macedo, ed., *Reassessing the Sixties: Debating the Political and Cultural Legacy*. New York: W.W. Norton, 1997.

Jon Margolis, *The Last Innocent Year: America in 1964: The Beginning of the "Sixties."* New York: William Morrow, 1999.

Douglas T. Miller, *On Our Own: Americans in the Sixties*. Lexington, MA: D.C. Heath, 1996.

Edward P. Morgan, *The 60's Experience: Hard Lessons About Modern America*. Philadelphia: Temple University Press, 1991.

David R. Pichaske, *A Generation in Motion: Popular Music and Culture in the Sixties*. New York: Schirmer Books, 1979.

David Steigerwald, *The Sixties and the End of Modern America*. New York: St. Martin's Press, 1995.

Jules Witcover, *The Year the Dream Died: Revisiting 1968 in America*. New York: Warner Books, 1997.

Harris Wofford, *Of Kennedys and Kings: Making Sense of the Sixties*. Pittsburgh: University of Pittsburgh Press, 1980.

David Wright, *America in the 20th Century 1960–1969*. New York: Marshall Cavendish, 1995.

## Camelot and the Great Society

John A. Andrew, *Lyndon Johnson and the Great Society*. Chicago: I.R. Dee, 1998.

James N. Giglio, *The Presidency of John F. Kennedy*. Lawrence: University Press of Kansas, 1991.

Myron Magnet, *The Dream and the Nightmare: The Sixties' Legacy to the Underclass*. New York: William Morrow, 1993.

Allen J. Matusow, *The Unraveling of America: A History of Liberalism in the 1960s*. New York: Harper and Row, 1984.

Thomas C. Reeves, *A Question of Character: John F. Kennedy in Image and Reality*. New York: Free Press, 1990.

Irwin Unger, *The Best of Intentions: The Triumphs and Failures of the Great Society Under Kennedy, Johnson, and Nixon*. New York: Doubleday, 1996.

## Cold War

Michael R. Beschloss, *The Crisis Years: Kennedy and Khrushchev, 1960–1963*. New York: HarperCollins, 1993.

Diane B. Kunz, ed., *The Diplomacy of a Crucial Decade: American Foreign Relations During the 1960s*. New York: Columbia University Press, 1994.

Earnest R. May and Philip D. Zelikow, eds., *The Kennedy Tapes: Inside the White House During the Cuban Missile Crisis*. Cambridge, MA: Belknap Press of Harvard University Press, 1997.

William F. Melberg, *Moon Missions: Mankind's First Voyages to Another World*. Plymouth, MI: Plymouth Press, 1997.

Thomas Paterson, ed., *Kennedy's Quest for Victory: American Foreign Policy, 1961–1963*. New York: Oxford University Press, 1989.

## Vietnam

James Kirkpatrick Davis, *Assault from the Left: The FBI and the Sixties Antiwar Movement*. Westport, CT: Praeger, 1997.

Charles Debenedetti and Charles Chatfield, *An American Ordeal: The Antiwar Movement of the Vietnam War*. Syracuse, NY: Syracuse University Press, 1990.

Marvin E. Gettleman et al., eds., *Vietnam and America: A Documented History*. New York: Grove Press, 1985.

Patrick J. Hearden, ed., *Vietnam: Four American Perspectives*. West Lafayette, IN: Purdue University Press, 1990.

George C. Herring, *America's Longest War: The United States and Vietnam, 1950–1975*. 3rd ed. New York: McGraw-Hill, 1996.

Guenter Lewy, *America in Vietnam*. New York: Oxford University Press, 1978.

James Olson and Randy Roberts, *Where the Domino Fell: America and Vietnam, 1945–1990*. New York: St. Martin's Press, 1991.

**Youth Revolt**

Terry H. Anderson, *The Movement and the Sixties*. New York: Oxford University Press, 1995.

Todd Gitlin, *The Sixties: Years of Hope, Days of Rage*. New York: Bantam Books, 1987.

A.E. Hotchner, *Blown Away: The Rolling Stones and the Death of the Sixties*. New York: Simon & Schuster, 1990.

Martin A. Lee and Bruce Shlain, *Acid Dreams: The Complete Social History of LSD: The CIA, The Sixties, and Beyond*. 2nd ed. New York: Grove Weidenfeld, 1992.

Philip Norman, *Shout! The Beatles in Their Generation*. New York: Simon & Schuster, 1981.

Irwin Unger, *The Movement: A History of the American New Left 1959–1972*. New York: Harper & Row, 1974.

Peter O. Whitmer, *Aquarius Revisited: Seven Who Created the Sixties Counterculture that Changed America: William Burroughs, Allen Ginsberg, Ken Kesey, Timothy Leary, Norman Mailer, Tom Robbins, Hunter S. Thompson*. New York: Macmillan, 1987.

**Minority Protest**

Rhoda Lois Blumberg, *Civil Rights: The 1960s Freedom Struggle*. Rev. ed. New York: Twayne, 1991.

Clayborne Carson, *In Struggle: SNCC and the Black Awakening of the 1960s*. Cambridge, MA: Harvard University Press, 1981.

J. Craig Jenkins, *The Politics of Insurgency: The Farm Worker Movement and the Politics of the 1960s*. New York: Columbia University Press, 1985.

Alvin M. Josephy Jr., ed., *Red Power: The American Indians Fight for Freedom*. Lincoln: University of Nebraska Press, 1985.

Carlos Muñoz Jr., *Youth, Identity, Power: The Chicano Movement*. New York: Verso, 1989.

Steven B. Oates, *Let the Trumpet Sound: A Life of Martin Luther King Jr.* New York: HarperPerennial, 1994.

Hugh Pearson, *The Shadow of the Panther: Huey Newton and the Price of Black Power in America*. Reading, MA: Addison-Wesley, 1994.

Harvard Sitkoff, *The Struggle for Black Equality 1954–1992*. Rev. ed. New York: Hill and Wang, 1993.

## Sex and Gender Revolutions

Barry Adam, *The Rise of a Gay and Lesbian Movement*. Boston: Twayne, 1987.

Elaine Brown, *A Taste of Power: A Black Woman's Story*. New York: Anchor Books, 1994.

Flora Davis, *Moving the Mountain: The Women's Movement in America Since 1960*. New York: Simon & Schuster, 1992.

Martin B. Duberman, *Stonewall*. New York: Dutton, 1993.

Alice Echols, *Daring to Be Bad: Radical Feminism in America, 1967–1975*. Minneapolis: University of Minnesota Press, 1989.

Sara Evans, *Personal Politics: The Roots of Women's Liberation in the Civil Rights Movement and the New Left*. New York: Knopf, 1979.

Betty Friedan, *The Feminine Mystique*. New York: Dell, 1963.

# Index